LIZZIE BORDEN: RESURRECTIONS

LIZZIE BORDEN: RESURRECTIONS

A history of the people surrounding the Borden case
before, during, and after the trial

SHERRY CHAPMAN

Photos by Stephen Chapman

Fall River, MA

PearTree Press
P.O. Box 9585
Fall River, MA 02720
peartree-press.com

All rights reserved. No part of this book may be used or reproduced in any manner whatsoever scanned, or distributed in any printed or electronic form without written permission from the publisher, except in the case of brief quotations embodied in critical articles and reviews.

For information, write us at PearTree Press, P.O. Box 9585, Fall River, MA 02720.

LIBRARY OF CONGRESS CONTROL NUMBER: **2014911473**

ISBN-10: 0-9819043-9-4
ISBN-13: 978-0-9819043-9-9

Printed in the United States of America on acid-free paper.

Book design by Stefani Koorey

Copyright © 2014 by Sherry Chapman

Printed in the United States of America

CONTENTS

Introduction	xv
Part One — The Victims	3
Part Two — Law and Order	
Melvin Ohio Adams	35
John William Coughlin	41
George Ferguson	43
John Fleet	47
Philip Harrington	51
Marshal Rufus B. Hilliard	57
Josiah Hunt	63
Joseph Hyde	67
Andrew J. Jennings	71
Hosea Morrill Knowlton	77
William H. Medley	87
John Minnehan	95
Arthur Sherman Phillips	97
George Potter	101
Hannah B. Reagan	105
George Dexter Robinson	109
Mary U. Russell	115
Part Three — Men of Medicine	
Dr. Seabury Warren Bowen	119
Dr. William Andrew Dolan	125
Dr. Benjamin J. Handy	129
Dr. John Quincy Adams Toutellot	133

Part Four — They Thickened the Plot
    Eli Bence   137
    William S. Borden   141
    Joseph Wilmarth Carpenter   143
    Marianne Chagnon   147
    Addie B. Cheetham   149
    John Crowe   151
    Ellen Eagan   155
    Henry J. Hawthorne Jr.   157
    James Johnston   159
    Joseph Lemay   161
    Hyman Lubinsky   163
    Hannah B. Gifford   165
    John C. Milne   167
    Lucie Collet Normand   169
    John Crompton Newton   171

Part Five — Friends
    Generva Almy   175
    William M. Almy   177
    David Anthony Jr.   179
    Cook Borden   183
    Phoebe V. Bowen   185
    Elizabeth Hitchcock Brayton   187
    Mary Brigham   189
    Alice Lydia Buck   191
    Reverend Edwin Augustus Buck   193
    Adelaide Buffinton Churchill   199
    Hiram & Lurana Harrington   203
    Anna Covell Holmes   207
    Charles Jarvis Holmes   209
    Mary Anna Holmes   211
    Mary Louisa Holmes   215
    Grace Hartley Howe   217
    Louis McHenry Howe   221
    Lucy S. Macomber   225
    Franklin Harrison Miller   227
    Southard Harrison Miller   231
    Alice M. Russell   235

    Ellen "Nellie" Shove   239
    Adelaide B. Whipp   241
    Lizzie's Pets   243

Part Six — The Hired Help
    Matilda Anderson   249
    Gertrude M. Callow   251
    Charles C. Cook   253
    Winifred F. French   257
    Catherine Mary McFarland   259
    Helen Smith   261
    Bridget Sullivan   263
    Ernest Alden Terry   267
    Vida Turner   269
    Theodore D.W. Wood   271

Part Seven — All in the Family
    Abraham Bowen Borden/Wives and Daughters   277
    Alice Esther Borden   279
    Sarah Anthony Borden   281
    George B. Fish   283
    Priscilla S. Fish   285
    Oliver Gray Family   287
    John Vinnicum Morse   289
    Abbie Borden Potter   293
    Sarah Gray Whitehead   295

Part Eight — 'The Girls"   301

Part Nine — P.S.
    Edmund Lester Pearson   329
    Edwin H. Porter   333
    Julian Ralph   339

Acknowledgments   343

LIZZIE BORDEN: RESURRECTIONS

INTRODUCTION

Sigh! Is there really a need for another Lizzie Borden book? Yes!, I say. And most assuredly, this will not be the last one. There are still things to be discovered, unearthed, and stories to be told. Non-fiction and fiction, there is room for all. Luckily, the public at large, myself included, seem to not be able to get enough of the subject.

It helps that the murderer was never found—unsolved crimes are the most interesting cases to explore. Endless, fascinating discussions go on to this day of possibilities of all angles of Lizzie, from the crime, the time period, and the persons involved around this historical event. There is no wrong answer, since there is no answer—yet. Oh, I still hold out the hope that maybe some day, somehow, when we least expect it, we will hear somebody say, "Smile! The Borden murders are solved!"

Would everyone be smiling? I've read so often that people in the Liz Biz don't want the murders solved because there would die their cash cow. I don't think so. I think should the case be solved in our lifetimes, it would be welcome news to all.

I think I've read a book on who the author thought the murderer was that named every character known to have been close to the Borden case, along with some that weren't.

This book makes no guesses. I have my own personal guess, which I do not approach even slightly here.

This book, *Lizzie Borden: Resurrections*, I chose to write because of something someone said. During a trip to New England, with my had-to stop in Fall River, I was walking along in a cemetery and I commented that, "I wish someone would write a book and put all the Lizzie characters' grave photos in it." And my husband said, "Why don't you?" Yes. Why didn't I?

Thus followed a journey I did not expect to ever take. I loved reading Lizzie books but had no desire to write one. But since that day, I never looked at a cemetery the same way again. I was always searching, thinking, note taking, reading. The more I thought about it seriously, the more interested I became.

Up to that time (around 2001) and to this day, I did write on Lizzie Borden. In 1998, I was comfortably watching a documentary on her, salivating when Michael Martins, curator of the Fall River Historical Society, appeared, talking so professionally but beautifully in an accent pleasing to the ear. (Okay. I had a celebrity crush on Michael Martins. Okay. I still do.)

Our daughter, Marla, in her last months of high school, came in the living room with slight hesitation. "Mom? I just wrote a Lizzie Borden joke. It's dumb. But do you wanna hear it?" Did I?? "Yes!" I answered with real enthusiasm, happy to hear her creating something she wasn't forced to by a teacher. I muted Michael Martins. I had seen the show many, many times. I did leave his face on, though.

"Okay," she said, clearing her throat. "If Lizzie Borden WAS found guilty, what would her excuse have been?" I had no idea. "It was an axe-ident!" Oh, I laughed. She was surprised. "You liked it?" I said, "It's great! It's really good!" She sat near me, and we talked, I dunno, about creativity and probably stuff like that, when I stopped suddenly.

"Marla! … What if we wrote a bunch of Lizzie Borden jokes and sent them in to the *Lizzie Borden Quarterly*?" And we spent the next hour or so coming up with twenty jokes Some were pretty bad and I told her, "Don't worry. They have an excellent editor, and he'll take out the bad ones."

In a few weeks we got a response in the mail from editor Maynard Bertolet. He enjoyed our jokes and was running them in the next issue! We jumped up and down a few times until something fell off the piano.

As promised, there in the next issue were our jokes. I have learned from experience that Maynard Bertolet was an excellent editor. To my slight embarrassment, he left the 'bad' ones in. He wrote us a very nice letter, encouraging us to send him more.

I got an idea for another humorous piece at Lizzie's expense, but Marla wasn't interested in writing with me. I was disappointed but you can hand a pen to a writer but you can't make them ink.

I sent more in; I got a phone call from Mr. Bertolet. I ended up writing several humor pieces, and he dubbed me their Resident Humorist. I found some new and different snippets for some serious articles and those were published as well. Then one sad day came the news that publication of the *LBQ* was folding after ten years of publishing.

It was not long before I got a call from Dr. Stefani Koorey, then in Florida, asking me if she started a new Lizzie magazine, would I write for her as their Resident Humorist? I had known Stefani for a while Online, liked her, and said yes. Fast forward to 2014—she has just published the 30th issue of her magnificent publication *The Hatchet: A Journal of Lizzie Borden & Victorian Studies*.

She asked if I would do a column called "Dear Abby," where I composed incoming letters for advice and answered them as Abby Borden might. I got the photo of my face put in place of Abby's, and I had Abby's hair and dress stuck on me too (creativity by Harry Widdows). At the last minute, I called her with an idea I wanted to try called "Bridget's Kitchen" where I'd write in the voice of the Borden servant on the goings-on in the household and give a real old-time Irish recipe. I got emails telling me how much people enjoyed both features, and I was surprised to hear that a lot of people, when receiving their issues, turned first to those. Now and then I would write a historical article and other humor articles for the beloved *Hatchet*.

So I'm happily busy working for the new magazine, but at the same time I'm preparing my notes so I could make a trip to Fall River for researching and have all my source material already known to me. When I got out there, I would already know the names of the newspapers certain obituaries were and the page and column. I knew which cemetery many of the Borden characters' graves were, and I contacted each one asking if the office could please give me the location of the grave. Everybody helped me! It was wonderful.

In the spring of 2003, I went with my husband, Steve, and our son, Stevie, a 5th grader, to Fall River ready for picture and note taking. Being Easter vacation for our son, the school gave him ten days off for a family vacation.

We drove, and it wasn't until we were a day and a half away from home when my husband asked me if I had my notes with me.

I said of course. I can't do anything without them.

He asked me what I had put them in to travel, and I said a zippered bag with lighthouses on it. Why would he ask that?

"You packed it, didn't you?" I could feel my blood pressure beginning to rise.

"I—I don't know," he said hesitatingly, probably afraid of my reaction if he didn't. It was too late. I was already having a reaction.

"Oh, no, no, no! My God, no! I can't work without those notes! I had everything arranged. Oh, I'll have to cancel Michael Martins! Geez! We might as well turn around right now." I wasn't mad at him. Well, this was the shock of initial bad news. I probably would have been if my notes had been left behind by him. Were they?

"Uh, what should we do?" I love it. Somebody is at fault for doing something monumental, and they ask the victim what they should do.

"I know," I said. "Pull into the next rest area and we'll check the trunk."

"I'll tell you, if it IS with us, it's way up in the trunk where it's dark. Um. Um…. I didn't see it the last time we stopped."

Well, keep talkin', Mister Man. "You have something in the back seat there you can use."

"That's Rebello's book. It's not my notes."

A rest area came up blessedly fast. We ran to the trunk, and he opened it. Didn't see the bag on first look. Nor on second. We started removing things out of the trunk and setting them on the asphalt. It started to rain. That was nice. We had quite a bit of stuff stacked on the pavement when I saw it. It was there, along with many months of work, ready for the trip to Fall River. Suddenly all was well with the entire world.

When we got back into the car, we were both so thankful. (I'm still not sure why Steve was so thankful. Maybe he likes me or something. You cannot tell with engineers. Those jokes you read about them? They are true.) We were exchanging sentences of gratitude, then he asked, "What would you have done if we hadn't found it?"

That was an easy one. "I would have had to go home. I'd have nothing to work with. I couldn't go into the Historical Society without any notes."

"Ah, you have that big book with you."

"Rebello's book?"

"Yeah."

"It's useless to me without my notes. I had everything in order in different files. I worked months doing that alone."

"Well," he said. "I guess you'd just have to resurrect it all."

"WHAT?! No, that would be –", and I stopped in my seat. And that's how my title was born.

The day after our arrival, I was to be in the archive room which was in the basement of the Fall River Historical Society. I had a hard time falling asleep the night before, knowing I would be meeting Michael Martins. I thought of canceling the appointment, I was so nervous. I had seen him in person before, but I never had occasion to talk to him. I took as many pills as I could safely, and when I fell asleep I dreamed of him. And, no, I choose not to share that.

Still nervous in the morning, I thought I'd take things in "baby steps," like in the movie *What About Bob?* That really works, by the way. We arrived at the museum promptly on time, and someone answered the door and told me to go down to the basement. Seconds felt like um, more than seconds, like seconds-and-a-half. Somehow I got down to the basement, family behind me. And there he was. Michael Martins in the flesh, and he was waiting for me! He was twice as cute in person. And he wore blue jeans and a flattering plaid shirt. He stuck out his hand to shake mine and said, "Hi. I'm Michael Mahtins."

I froze. It was 'Lucy Meets a Celebrity.' I don't know how much time went by when he started to give me this look that read, "And what nut do we have here?" 'Say something! Anything!' I told myself. Out blurted, "You got your hair cut!"

He had the natural good grace to smile and said, "Well, yes, I guess I did!" Uhhhhh ... That came out because the last time I saw him on TV his hair was longer. Made no dang sense.

But somehow that broke the ice, and I had a list of questions to ask him, and I was at ease as we talked and I realized that he was a real person, and a nice one with a good sense of humor. My four hour reserved block of time went fast, but I was to return the next day. So my family and I took photos of things in the area that I needed. The following day, it was back to the museum archives where I was not nervous this time and so enjoyed my time there. I felt a little warm, but I didn't remember it being warm in the basement the day before so I said nothing of it.

That afternoon we started working cemeteries. There were several in Fall River that only had two or three Borden characters buried there, and I had brought the instructions leading me right to the graves of them.

It felt like a gorgeous summer day in Fall River. The sun was out, and it was warm. But I felt warmer than just that. I think I realized what it was. I had visited a friend just before my trip out to Massachusetts who had pneumonia. I took her a pot of soup and visited, her trying not to breathe toward me. I think that didn't work. I thought I had probably caught her pneumonia. Well, if I was gonna have pneumonia, or something less, I was gonna get all the research in that I could.

At St. John's Cemetery there were three graves I was looking for: Ellen Eagan, Philip Harrington, and someone else. The main gate was closed, so we all hiked over the wall and jumped down onto the grass. No harm done.

It was difficult to count rows in the cemetery. So the three of us walked the grounds several times. We found none of the graves we sought, even though I had the places of where they were buried. It was about 6 p.m., and we thought we'd better quit and go to dinner. Well, if there was no way into the cemetery, there was no way out. And jumping in we had soft grass to land on. Jumping out there was a cement sidewalk.

My husband and son had long legs, and they made it easily over the spiked fence. I have no legs (to speak of), so it was the stone wall for me. I stacked some big rocks I found scattered nearby, piled them up, and when I stood on them I was able to get myself up on top of the wall in a sitting position ... Now what? My family had gone to the car and drove it to a spot near me, but they couldn't see me. My husband kept honking his horn. Then he was impatiently honking. Then he was blasting it. It made me so mad, I just jumped. Straight down to the sidewalk, about 4 ½ feet below. I landed on my feet and felt no pain. At first. It hit me suddenly and I collapsed.

Now this was a busy road, and the speed limit was 45 mph. There I am, laying on the sidewalk, and nobody cared! Talk about not wanting to become involved ... And to top it off, I started to roll toward that fast traffic. My family wasn't coming. I expected them to. But that infernal horn blasting continued every couple minutes, like my husband did it as a paid job.

Then a very big black pickup truck pulls over and starts to stop for me. The windows were tinted, and I couldn't see who was in it. I thought Boston. And the famous Strangler case ... That got me up. I couldn't straighten my back, and I was making my legs walk. And that's how my husband and son saw me emerging from the corner of that stone wall. I looked like the Hunchback of Notre Dame. Their startled faces were Kodak moments. I was always getting into something. Steve motioned to me to hurry up (!). An angel must have taken me to the car, and I threw myself in and started to tell them what happened. I broke out laughing near the beginning, and finally finished the story with all of us in good humor. I suffered through the night with one leg. In the morning, I went to St. Anne's Hospital, where they x-rayed me and found a broken bone "in an unusual place." And pneumonia. I did have that. So they gave me crutches and prescriptions, and off we went back to the hotel room, where I wasn't to be seen again by outsiders for some days. I slept deeply on the medicines I was on. I remember waking up and seeing Steve reading a novel in a chair, while Stevie was rolling the same two model cars back and forth and over again. It was the sweetest sight I can ever remember. It reminded me of Atticus Finch watching over Jem.

Then the ticks came in. Steve took our little poodle we were traveling with outside and into a tick nest. We knew when I saw a couple crawling on me. Good times.

I had the nerve to go out to Fall River again the following spring. I started out with researching at the museum, which was fun! I got to see some of Lizzie's original stuff. The next day we went to the courthouse at Taunton, Massachusetts, and I got to handle and read all these Borden characters' handwritten legal letters. Now, there are some who think Abby Borden's first name could have also been spelled "Abbie." But on a legal paper that both she and Andrew Borden signed, I saw her legal signature as "Abby." Is it enough proof that she spelled it "Abby"? It never is!

When I finished with my work at the courthouse, I needed the restroom, so my son and I had to walk downstairs for one. My husband said he'd wait on the floor above. We had not walked many steps when suddenly there were no more steps to walk down. I had my head turned toward our son talking and wasn't watching where I was walking, and, well, what happened you can guess and get it right the first time. I fell. Well, I rolled. These were big, wide, very hard marble stairs and there were a lot of them. I rolled all the way to the bottom. Poor Stevie was scared. One of my ankles cracked against a stair, and it was so painful that I stayed down until that initial throbbing went away, so I could see what on me was hurt. I told Stevie to get his Dad. When he did, Steve thought it was a joke. "You're kidding!" he said, and took his time getting to me.

Funny, before with that stone wall incident nobody was interested. Not a soul (well, that person in the big, black truck did stop for me). My ankle was throbbing so that I could hardly speak. I just needed a few minutes. And now people were interested! Is it because it happened indoors? And to ignore me there made people look bad?

Some ladies were eating lunch at a table down there, and one calls to me, "Come on, now. Get up! You don't need to be embarrassed!"

Really? I was sitting there because of embarrassment. I don't know, but it makes no sense to me.

Then a man who looked like Kramer of Seinfield was all worked up. He called down "Somebody need an ambulance??"

"I don't know yet!" Then every few minutes I kept seeing his head appear at the top of the stairs, like a parrot saying that same line again and again.

At last the throbbing stopped and I got up. I was able to walk to the restroom. My ankle hurt, and I thought I felt various bumps and bruises, but nothing was broken.

I wasn't going to use two research vacations laying in bed. I wasn't even going to go to the doctor until my work was completed and then I'd see my own doctor at home.

For the remainder of the trip I walked cemeteries. It was very difficult for me to find the graves I wanted photographed at Oak Grove. Steve got mad at me, saying I didn't have my research prepared right, which was not true. I felt bad because he didn't have more faith in my work. I was tired. My foot hurt. I suddenly lost my anger and was like a deflated balloon. "I quit," I said. And I meant it. Not mad at anybody. "Let's go home."

Steve—I'm not sure what happened to him. He did a turn-around and suddenly it was, "Let me see that paper you have there." I sort of motioned to it with a glance toward my lap. He, with his mechanical engineering abilities had little trouble and started finding each and every grave to be found on my list. That angel was with me again.

We got to work in Providence, RI, a couple of days at their incredible library. I needed original obituaries of the Borden characters. They were on microfilm, filed by newspaper. Steve was getting very tired, and he brought a book with him he thought he would read while I did this part. But every time I worked at the microfilm machine I'd get motion sickness. Surprisingly Stevie wasn't just eating lunch and coming home from school every day. He was a whiz at the microfilm, and still today his elementary school handwriting remains on the backs of many prints of articles from those days.

I took a picture that day of Tilden-Thurber, which was then unbeknown to me soon to be sold and no more Tilden-Thurber. Some guy was just loitering by the building, and he tried very hard to be in the picture, and I have no idea why. He wasn't gonna see the picture. That's okay. Neither was I. I wasn't gonna take a picture of that store that I had only read about for many years and have a forever memory of him in it. I outwaited him, and he eventually got moving.

It was entirely cool to accidentally drive by Brown University. It was like right there, almost in the street. On the days I worked in Providence we liked to get out of there before rush hour. Sometimes we made it. Sometimes we didn't …

I finished up my research at home, which involved calling a lot of people and corresponding with some. The photo of Edmund Pearson's grave was so courteously taken for me by the curator of the museum in that town.

It was finally time to write. I give the story of the murders first, to refresh peoples' memories or to tell it to those who never heard it. Then I tried to put the people into some sort of category that pretty much coincided with the chronology of Lizzie's story.

I know, there is more information on the people in Lizzie's Fall River in the book by Michael Martins and Dennis Binette in their wonderful *Parallel Lives* book (2010, Fall River Historical Society). But I would not touch their meticulous, hard, hard work and the jewels their book contains and just use it for mine, which was finished long before theirs came out.

I had some lengthy setbacks in getting this book to the editor and publisher I chose to publish it, Dr. Stefani Koorey by her PearTree Press. I never considered anyone else.

She was patient with my calamities on this end: Three family deaths; taking care of my elderly mother for one year; losing the first two parts I had put on a Zip Disc—just gone, no reason (I don't have a Zip Disc anymore); and lastly losing nearly all of my finished book because I stored it on a Buslink. I don't have a Buslink anymore, either.

The writing and the research were the easiest—and most enjoyable—parts. The injuries I wish hadn't happened (a year after that stone wall jump doctors were finding a fractured tooth and other injuries, hidden at the time). The traveling we loved as a family. The clam chowdah we loved—different in every restaurant we went in. We voted "Chad's Chowderhouse" at 1160 G.A.R. Hwy. (Rte 6), Somerset, Massachusetts, 02726, the best. (For take-out orders Phone: 672-5505.) We have seen that place when it was very small, to when it doubled in size due to the excellence of its food. The people I met and worked with I so enjoyed and really liked them.

Sherry Chapman
Minnesota, 2014

Part One

The Victims

Andrew and Abby Borden

FALL RIVER, August 4, 1892: *The Boston Advertiser*—An aged man and his aged wife were killed today, their heads chopped to pieces by repeated and fiendish blows with an axe, the murderer and the implement of slaughter both disappeared, and now, 12 hours after the bloody deed, the police and the people are in just as utter ignorance as they were when it was first noised abroad this afternoon.

And so, the mystery of the Borden case would remain, unsolved, for the next 120 years—and counting.

Called by some the most baffling case in history, persons to this day, both professional and amateur students of the gruesome crimes, continue to read and study about the Borden murders, hoping that some little glimmer might catch their eye, that some clue missed by all the others would reveal its solution to them alone and the case stamped *Solved at Last*.

The victims, Andrew J. and Abby D. Borden, were without any obvious enemies. Andrew Jackson Borden was born in Fall River in 1822. For thirty-three years he was in the furniture business with partner William Almy. They called their firm Borden & Almy and were successful as undertakers and furniture makers. He gradually built up his real estate holdings and invested in good stock. Belonging to one of the "lesser" Borden families financially, he climbed his ladder of success himself, every rung of the way.

On Christmas Day, 1845, Andrew married Sarah Anthony Morse Borden. They had three children: Emma, Alice, and Lizzie. Alice died when she was about two years old. When Sarah passed away, Andrew re-married two years later, taking Abby Durfee Gray Borden as his second wife.

Andrew Borden accumulated vast holdings in his lifetime and, if not loved, was respected by fellow businessmen. He owned two farms in Swansea. He owned two- and three-story business buildings at 70, 92, 94, 96, 98, 100 and 102 South Main, and a building on Spring Street he purchased in 1891, referred to as the "Birch property."

Andrew was president of the Union Savings Bank, a director of the B.M.C. Durfee Safe Deposit and Trust Company, a director in the Troy and Merchants mills, and a director of the Globe Street Railway Company. In the works when he was murdered was the A.J. Borden Building, a fabulous, huge brick building at the corner of South Main and Anawan Streets.

He had plans to build another large brick building at the corner of Second and Spring Streets. Musing about it to a reporter of the *Fall River Daily Globe* he said, "I could secure tenants readily for two floors, but it wouldn't be just the thing in my mind to leave a third floor for hall or dancing purposes. Second Street will eventually become an overflow business highway, but it won't be in my time." He was speaking shortly before his murder. The article was printed after his death, in the August 19, 1892, real estate column.[1]

"The Assessor's books show that he was taxed for $173,650 worth of real estate, most of which is situated on South Main Street, in the very centre of the city," a *New York Times* article stated after his murder.

> His latest purchase was the Birch property, for which he paid $23,000 ... He rarely, if ever, owed anybody. Whenever he made a purchase he paid for it in cash or checks, never caring to handle notes of any kind. One of the largest financiers here said this morning that he doubted if a summary of his debts would show more than $1,000 due. His personal estate is variously estimated at between $175,000 and $250,000. Most of it is invested in mill stocks, bank stocks, and Government bonds.[2]

Andrew Borden is most often characterized as a miser, comparable to Ebenezer Scrooge. Andrew Borden was raised a Quaker and, as such, was an unassuming, plain man who did not put much emphasis on frills at home or in his manner of dress. His home at 92 Second Street was a Greek Revival, painted a "dark drab" with darker trim and no gas lighting (kerosene lamps were used). The only running water was in the kitchen and barn. A privy in the barn, a "two-seater" in the cellar, and chamber pots in the bedrooms took care of the family's personal needs as good as any modern conveniences he could have had installed.

The furniture was outdated. And he was rather outdated. Wearing black and donning his long Prince Albert coat winter and summer, it was a common sight to see Andrew Borden walking in Fall River to collect rents owed him and tending to his business, sometimes carrying a basket of eggs from his Swansea farm to sell for a few cents apiece. With all that he had, he gave his daughters Lizzie, 32, Emma, 41, and his wife Abby a grand total of four bucks a week. Each. Out of Abby's allowance came the money for any extras for the house, doilies and such, that Andrew did not deem of necessity.

Information has come to light to combat this one-dimensional view of Mr. Borden—such as when Lizzie ran out of money during her Grand Tour of Europe in 1890, which Andrew financed, it is said he helped her out with additional monies. Lizzie possessed a sealskin cape and ample clothing made by dressmakers, which her four dollars a week probably could not cover. Emma was sent to Wheaton Female Seminary (now Wheaton College) in Norton, Massachusetts, for a year and a half. She lived on campus and studied Algebra, Ancient and Modern History, Moral Philosophy, English Grammar, Piano, and French. Andrew provided well for both of his daughters and assisted his wife's family when they were experiencing financial distress (this later caused a major rift in the relationship between the daughters and their father in the years before the murders).

Mrs. George Brigham, who knew Lizzie intimately, told a newspaper,

> It has been said that Mr. Borden was angry with and did not speak to Lizzie upon her return from Europe. That, too, is a falsehood, distorted out of facts that were as contrary to the statements as could be. On the night Lizzie arrived the family had given her up and Mr. and

Mrs. Borden had gone to bed. Lizzie was very tired and only spoke a few words to Emma that night and retired. The next morning Mr. Borden found her steamer chair in the hall and bounded up stairs three at a time to see and greet her, and Lizzie told me her hand ached all day he pressed it so hard. Going down town, he met a man who said to him: 'Well, I would guess that some one had come home judging from your bright face this morning.'

Mr. Borden was, as they say, not a demonstrative man, but he loved his daughters and showed it at such times when they came back after being away ....[3]

"He was a pattern of the old New England type of industry, thrift and conservatism, and was outspoken in his advocacy of temperance and moral issues … He was what is called close fisted, but square and just in his dealings," as the *Boston Advertiser* of August 4, 1892 printed.[4]

According to the *Fall River Daily Globe*, Andrew Borden

was a man of tall stature, erect as a post, and dressed very plainly, almost to the point of shabbiness. His reputation among his neighbors was that of a severely honest man, who if in debt to any man, would pay the debt to the last farthing, and who, if he occupied a place on the credit side of the ledger, would collect his payment as did Shylock of yore, even to the pound of flesh … He was famous for wearing shocking bad hats, and retained a tie until it was almost thread-bare.[5]

When Andrew Borden's father died, he offered his sister, Lurana Borden Harrington, their father's house for a certain amount of money. Lurana chose to take the money. After the papers were signed and everything supposedly settled, Andrew hung in there for $3 he wanted Lurana to pay for a water tax on the homestead.[6]

According to the *Fall River Herald*, "The family was better off than several families of the Fall River Bordens who live in grand style."[7]

The *Fall River Daily Globe* reported,

Andrew J. Borden was a peculiar man in many respects. While his tall, neatly clothed figure was familiar to all the older citizens, he had few intimates and was reticent to a marked degree. When he started in life his means were extremely limited and he made his money by saving it. The habits of economy and thrift which he formed then clung to him to the last … He lived modestly and continued to count the pennies. … Mr. Borden had the manners of a gentleman of the old school. He was always dignified, but at the same time he was courteous and kindly, and as reported, was scrupulously upright in all his dealings and expected the same fairness in others. He was positive in his views, unbending in will, and at times appeared to lack sympathy. Deceased was domestic in his tastes and although he had considerable leisure time, was rarely to be found where men are accustomed to congregate.[8]

"Chief Hilliard said to me to-day that Mr. Borden was about to make a will," the *New York Herald* printed after the murders. "This statement was made to the Chief by a man whose name he declines to mention. He avers [asserts], however, that the old gentleman had been at work making an inventory of his property during the ten days preceding his murder. Mr. Borden had even departed from his usual reticence about his own private affairs and had told Chief Hilliard's informant that he intended to devise his property 'according to his own ideas.'"[9]

According to daughter, Emma, Andrew did indeed have a will. Uncle John Morse had told her about it, she said. This corresponds with Morse's testimony during the preliminary hearing. Morse said Andrew talked of his will not once, but twice.

> Q. I also meant to have asked you whether at any time you had any talk with Mr. Borden about a will, about his making a will?
> A. He told me that he had a will once.
> Q. Did you ever have any talk about it?
> A. No sir.
> Q. Did he ever say anything to you about a will, or anything that he proposed to do? I do not ask you what yet.
> A. He told me that he had a will.
> Q. Did he ever say anything to you about any proposition as to his purpose to make a will?
> A. No sir.
> Q. Or what he proposed to do by way of a will?
> A. No sir.
> Q. Did he ever tell you anything about any legacies he proposed to give in a will?
> A. No sir.
> Q. Did he ever tell you about any bequests that he had a notion of making?
> A. I think he said something about making--- he did not say how or anything like that.
> (Mr. Jennings.) I would like to have the time fixed.
> Q. Whether he ever did say anything to you about any purpose?
> A. I think sometime he made a remark about a bequest.
> Q. When was that?
> A. I think somewhere within a year.
> Q. Where were you and he at the time?
> A. I think on South Main Street.
> Q. What doing, walking together?
> A. Just walking along.
> Q. What was it he said?
> A. That is all he said.
> Q. What?
> A. Something about some bequests that he would make; he did not say what they were, or anything about it; something about giving something away, bequest to somebody, he did not say who; something about these bequests that he—he did not say anything more about it.
> Q. What did he say?
> A. He did not know but he might make some public bequests; words to that effect.
> Q. Wont you tell me what he said?
> A. He talked like he was going to make some public bequests; just in that way.
> Q. That was sometime within a year?
> A. Yes sir.
> Q. Can you fix the time any better than that?
> A. I could not.
> Q. Did he say anything more specific than that?
> A. No sir.
> Q. Did he say anything about his farm, about giving that away?
> A. We were going over—
> Q. Was that another talk?
> A. Yes sir.
> Q. I will ask you when that was too.
> A. That was some time in May of this year.

Q. What was it he said about that?
A. We were riding over by his place, we got to speaking about the Old Ladies' Home, you know. He says "I would give them some land here, if I thought they would accept of it"; something to that effect.
Q. Nothing about a will then?
A. No sir.
Q. About giving it to them?
A. Yes sir, that is all.[10]

The Reverend W. Walker Jubb of the Central Congregational Church, who was a strong supporter of Lizzie, told a reporter that Mr. Charles J. Holmes, a staunch citizen of Fall River, supporter of Lizzie, and leading deacon of the church of which Andrew Borden was previously a member, "He never attended," Jubb said, "however, out of pique toward Mr. Holmes. Mr. Borden had a piece of property that the corporation desired to buy, but would not accede to Mr. Borden's price. Mr. Holmes voted against paying the price, as he thought it too high, and as a result Mr. Borden never attended the church afterwards."[11]

He did not belong to any of the fraternal organizations of the day and was largely close-mouthed about the doings at home. Except for shortly before his murder, he told someone that there was trouble at home.

Abby Durfee Gray Borden was born on January 28, 1828. She was 37 years old and never before married when she wed Andrew Borden on June 6, 1865. The Reverend Asa Bronson performed the nuptials. His grandson would be Charles C. Cook, financial advisor to Andrew Borden, and then to Andrew's daughters.[12] Durfee was a big name in Fall River, but there is nothing in the records to show what relation, if any, Abby was to the affluent family.[13]

The common tale of Abby Borden goes like this: She was a woman who was resigned to spinsterhood and jumped at the chance when Andrew asked for her hand. She was a fat, friendless, ugly recluse and Andrew really didn't love her. They had no love life at all because all he wanted was a housemaid. She was a mean and nasty old thing and her stepdaughters despised her.

Well, that last part is true. Stepdaughters Lizzie and Emma did despise her. According to one woman quoted at the time, Lizzie was overheard to say that Abby was the kind that "never died."

The rest is conjecture—in fact, probably untrue. She was not all that fat, by today's standards. There are literally tons of women today that weigh two hundred pounds and are still attractive. A photo of Abby taken about three years before her marriage actually shows a nice looking, perhaps plain, woman. Granted, beauty is in the eye of the beholder, but she did not deserve to be called "ugly." The first Mrs. Borden was no great beauty herself, but this opinion has yet to be written about Sarah.

Nor was Abby friendless. Comments after her sudden death revealed what people thought of her:

- Bridget Sullivan, the servant girl at the Borden house for almost three years prior to the killings, said that she wanted to go back to Ireland, but Mrs. Borden told her she would be lonely without her. She said that Mrs. Borden was a very kind mistress and that she was much attached to her. Bridget said she did not have the heart to leave her.[14]

- Mrs. Southard Miller, who lived across the street, said that she had lost in Mrs. Borden the best and most intimate neighbor she had ever met.[15]

- There was Abby's half-sister, Sarah ("Bertie") Whitehead, whom Abby saw as often as she could, mostly Abby traveling to Sarah's. Abby was thirty-six years older than Sarah and the two were very close. Sarah named her daughter after Abby.

- A former teacher of Lizzie's got to know Abby when he lived on Second Street and spoke of her as being "a kindly-hearted, lovable woman, who tried, but ineffectively, to win the love of the stepdaughters."[16]

- Mrs. Phoebe Bowen, daughter of Mrs. Southard Miller, was upset to lose her friend.

- Dr. Seabury Bowen, her husband, testified that he was not only the Borden family doctor but a social friend as well. When Dr. Bowen came to see Andrew the day before the murders because Abby had told him she felt she and Andrew had been poisoned, Andrew was rude and said he would not pay for a house call. The doctor seemed to not catch Andrew's attitude, or would not admit to it, when questioned about this visit in court. But when the doctor left, Mrs. Borden chewed Andrew out and said she was ashamed for him to use Dr. Bowen so. She said, "I told him you were sick and he came over to see you and I think it is a shame you can't treat him decent. He is all the neighbors we have got and I think it is too bad."[17] Abby's behavior, as relayed to Alice Russell by Lizzie, also shows us that she did speak up to her husband if she thought him wrong—no spineless housewife, she.[18]

Abby was not a recluse. She sometimes did the daily marketing, leaving Bridget to complete other duties. Abby was in charge of choosing the meals served at the Borden home, telling Bridget what to fix, as well as giving her all her orders. One has to wonder if Andrew decided the menu at times, trying to stretch out every last morsel of mutton in those hot August days, or if Abby actually wanted it repeatedly warmed over. Abby spent time at the farm in Swansea, often visited her half-sister, Sarah, and had company come to stay from time to time. She was also expecting "company," that was going to stay at least one night, on Monday, August 8. Unfortunately for historians, however, the identity of this person was never determined, nor did anyone come forward to admit that they were the expected houseguest.

It seems that the only persons to say bad things about Abby were Lizzie and Emma. Up until five years before the murders, Lizzie had called Abby "Mother." But in 1885, Andrew bought and deeded to Abby half of the house Sarah Whitehead was living in nearby on Fourth Street, when Jane Gray, Abby's stepmother, was selling her half of the house. Abby was afraid her sister would be out on the street, and Andrew came to the rescue. According to Lizzie's own inquest testimony shortly after the murders, it was this incident that caused her to stop calling her "Mother" and to start calling her "Mrs. Borden." How that must have hurt Abby. Both stepdaughters virtually stopped eating their meals with Abby and Andrew and the tension in the house was uncomfortable, according to several persons who had visited the home. Though much has been written about Lizzie disliking her stepmother, Emma admits that she herself disliked her even more.

At the coroner's inquest, Hiram Harrington, Andrew's brother-in-law, said that "everything was very, very pleasant, uncommonly so for a step-mother" early in the marriage. After Andrew bought the house for Abby, Uncle Hiram testified. Lizzie went from calling Abby 'Mother' to "Mrs. Borden" or "Mrs. B." Lizzie spoke of her "sneeringly" and "unfriendly," sometimes making jokes about the property deal.[19]

In 1890, cousin Anna Howland Borden took the Grand Tour of Europe with Lizzie and other girlfriends. Sharing a cabin with Anna on the way home, Lizzie said she didn't want to go home because Fall River was dull and boring and she disliked her stepmother.[20]

Mrs. Hannah Gifford, garment maker for the three Borden women, testified at the inquest and the trial of what she heard Lizzie say about her stepmother.

> She says 'well she is a mean old thing.' I says 'O, you don't say that Lizzie?' She says 'yes, and we don't have anything to do with her, only what we are obliged to,' she says ... 'We stay up stairs most of the time; we stay in our room most of the time.' I says, 'you do, don't you go to your meals?' 'Yes, we go to our meals, but we don't always eat with the family, with them; sometimes we wait until they are through,' she says.[21]

Abby Borden has been dealt most unfair character blows. But the very worst injuries to her occurred on Thursday, August 4. She would not live to see her company arrive on Monday.

Abby and Andrew Borden were murdered in their home in the light of day on Thursday, August 4, 1892. Both Lizzie and Bridget Sullivan were at home. The weapon, which was never found, was probably a hatchet. Though Abby was the earliest to be butchered, at about 9:30 a.m., it was Andrew's body that was discovered first, a little after 11 a.m.

It was Lizzie who found Andrew's body. She had been outside in the back yard, she said, to get some pears from under the tree. While under the pear tree, "I stood looking around. I looked up at the pigeon house that they have closed up," she said the only time she ever testified, at the inquest.

Animal lover Lizzie, who would leave a large bequest in her Last Will and Testament to the Fall River Animal Rescue League, must have remembered the following scene in horror as she answered District Attorney Hosea Knowlton's questioning at the inquest.

Mr. Knowlton asks Lizzie about any axes there might have been in the house, particularly ones with blood on them:

> A. No sir, he killed some pigeons in the barn last May or June.
> Q. What with?

92 Second Street, 1892 or 1893

A. I don't know, but I thought he wrung their necks.
Q. What made you think so?
A. I think he said so.
Q. Did anything else make you think so?
A. All but three or four had their heads on, that is what made me think so.
Q. Did all of them come into the house?
A. I think so.
Q. Those that came into the house were all headless?
A. Two or three had them on.
Q. Were any with their heads off?
A. Yes sir.
Q. Cut off or twisted off?
A. I don't know which.
Q. How did they look?
A. I don't know, their heads were gone, that is all.
Q. Did you tell anybody they looked as though they were twisted off?
A. I don't remember whether I did or not. The skin I think was very tender, I said why are these heads off? I think I remember of telling somebody that he said they twisted off.
Q. Did they look as if they were cut off?
A. I don't know, I did not look at that particularly.[22]

After spending time in the barn, or not, Lizzie said that she came into the kitchen, went into the dining room, and laid down her hat. She opened the sitting room door, which was not latched. She found her father and rushed to the foot of the stairs. According to her own testimony, she called up two flights to the attic where Bridget was napping, "Go for Dr. Bowen as soon as you can. I think Father is hurt."

The man was creamed—leaning back on the left hand arm of the black horsehair sofa with his head freshly bashed in by eleven hatchet blows, blood fresh and flowing from the wounds. 'But Maggie (as the Borden sisters called Bridget), Lizzie says, you go get Dr. Bowen and see if he can help him. I'm not sure, but I think Father is hurt.'

Bridget's version in her trial testimony makes more sense: "She says, 'Maggie, come down, and she hollered with such a voice that I says, 'What is the matter?' She says, 'Come down quick. Father is dead. Somebody came in and killed him.'"[23]

Lizzie prevented Bridget from going into the sitting room and sent her to fetch Dr. Bowen. When Bridget promptly returned with the news that Bowen was not at home, she was instructed to go get not another doctor or a policeman, but Miss Russell—Miss Alice Russell, who lived a few streets away, and who had, for a time, lived next door to the Bordens. Lizzie and Emma had kept up their friendship with her. It was Alice Russell whom Lizzie visited just the night before, predicting gloom and doom for the household from Father's enemies that, she claimed to Alice, made Lizzie want to sleep with one eye opened for fear 'they' would burn the house over their heads.

Mrs. Adelaide Churchill, who lived next door, and whose kitchen window looked out on the side entrance of the Borden abode, noticed the excitement between Lizzie and Bridget and asked if everything was all right. "Oh, Mrs. Churchill," said Lizzie, "do come over. Some one has killed Father."

When Mrs. Churchill reached the Borden house, Lizzie sent her to get a doctor. Mrs. Churchill knew that the man that worked for her was at the stable nearby, and she stepped over there and called for him. She told him to go get a doctor and she went back to the Borden home. At that time only Lizzie was at the house. Soon Bridget returned and then Dr. Bowen arrived. He was told where the victim lay.

"He came out shortly and made some exclamation," according to Mrs. Churchill's trial testimony. "I do not remember what, then he turned to me and said, 'Addie, come in and see Mr. Borden.' I said, 'Oh, no, doctor. I don't want to see him. I saw him this morning. I don't want to see him.'"

Mrs. Churchill had seen Mr. Borden alive and well, outdoors earlier that morning.

Dr. Bowen asked for a sheet. Contrary to some books written on the case, Lizzie Borden never then said, "Better get two."

At Lizzie's trial in June of 1893, Dr. Bowen testified:

A: (Bowen) Then I asked for a sheet to cover up Mr. Borden.
Q: To whom did you address that request?
A: I addressed that to Mrs. Churchill and to Miss Lizzie Borden at the same time. They were both in the same room. And to Miss Russell. There were three there.
Q: What was done in consequence of your request? Describe everything that was done.
A: Bridget Sullivan brought me a sheet.[24]

Bridget and Mrs. Churchill went into Mrs. Borden's room using the back stairs and tended to the doctor's request. "I saw his feet after he was covered with the sheet," Mrs. Churchill said.

Lizzie asked Dr. Bowen to send a telegram to Emma, who was visiting friends in Fairhaven. She asked him to put it as gently as he could because there was an old person there and it would shock her.

Mrs. Churchill testified:

> After Miss Russell came Lizzie said she wished some one would try to find Mrs. Borden for she thought she heard her come in. So Bridget and I started to go find her, went through the dining room out of the sitting room at the head, or where Mr. Borden was sitting or lying, and up into the hall. Bridget was just ahead of me. She led the way, and as I went up stairs I turned my head to the left; and as I got up so that my eyes were on the level with the front hall, I could see across the front hall and across the floor of the spare room. At the far side or the north side of the room I saw something that looked like the form of a person.

The spare, or guest room, door was open according to both Adelaide Churchill and Bridget Sullivan.

Adelaide turned and went back downstairs. Miss Russell said, "Is there another?" She replied, "Yes, she is up there."

"Miss Lizzie said to me that she should have to go to the cemetery, and I said, 'Oh, no, the undertaker will attend to everything for you,'" Mrs. Churchill testified. She also told the courtroom about Lizzie: "I never saw any tears." She went back to her house next door about noon.[25]

When Dr. Bowen returned from sending the telegram to Emma about her father's death, Mrs. Churchill greeted him with, "They have found Mrs. Borden."

"Where?" he asked.

"Upstairs in the front room."

During his trial testimony, he told of his first sighting of Mrs. Borden's body. "She said I had better go up and see. I went directly through the dining room and the corner of the sitting room into the front hall, up the stairs -- front stairs -- and stopped a moment at the door of the front chamber - guest chamber, front bedroom. At that point I looked over the bed and saw the prostrate form of Mrs. Borden."

He stood, he said, directly in the door of the room. "I went around the back of the bed -- that is, the foot of the bed -- and between the form and the bed, and placed my hand on her head. It was a little dark in the room, somewhat dark, not very light. I placed my hand on her head and found there were wounds in the head. Then I placed my -- felt of her pulse - that is, felt of the wrist, and found she was dead."[26]

Dr. Bowen went downstairs, told everyone that Abby was indeed dead, killed, he thought, by the same instrument. "I thought it was fortunate for Lizzie that she was out of the way, or else she would have been killed herself."[27] Before anyone, except Abby's murderer, had touched her, Dr. Bowen found that she lay "directly on her face with her hands under her."[28]

During the same time frame, Marshal Rufus Hilliard, City Marshal of Fall River, received a phone call from reporter John Cunningham about 11:15 a.m., saying that there was "trouble" at the Borden house. He ordered Officer George Allen to see about it. Officer Allen ran from the station to the Borden home (about 400 yards). He saw the body of Andrew Borden. Before he returned to the police station, he deputized Charles Sawyer, a passerby, and told him to allow no one in the rear door except the police. When Allen came back with Officer Mullaly a short time later they then learned of Abby Borden's murder upstairs.[29]

The crime scene was unsecured, except for anyone Charles Sawyer refused admittance to. Medical Examiner William Dolan happened to be driving his buggy down the street and stopped, entered the house, and had his hands on the victims to examine them. The amount of doctors, policemen, and ordinary people that went into the house that day and might have touched the Borden bodies—and most certainly disturbed any evidence—is certainly amazing.

To understand this seeming lack of diligence on the part of the Fall River Police Department one needs to know that in the year 1892 there was no police academy in Fall River. True, many of the policemen were off that day at a clambake at Rocky Point, a popular amusement park in not-too-distant Warwick, Rhode Island. But even if they had been all in Fall River, it probably would have turned out much the same. There was no book of procedures for something like this, no formal training, no yellow crime tape. One of Fall River's policemen had been a longshoreman. So when he was hired as a policeman, they assigned him the wharf district. Makes sense, if you lived in 1892.

Fingerprinting, though invented by that time, was in its infancy and not universally used. If there was any evidence preserved by keeping people out, would they have known what to do with it? It seems that with what the police had to work with, they did pretty much the best they could.

The crimes were also shocking. The Andrew J. Bordens butchered to death in their own home in the daytime—with two others in residence, Lizzie and Bridget. To hear the news was terrible. But to have actually seen the bodies, especially if one knew them in life, was more than some could bear.

Dr. Seabury Bowen, who had lived diagonally across the street from the Bordens for twenty-one years and had practiced medicine in Fall River for twenty-six years, had been the Borden family physician for about twelve years. He knew them both professionally and socially.[30] The doctor acted very surprised and upset. If he had thought rationally at first, he probably would not have offered Adelaide Churchill a peek at Andrew. And he would not have voiced an opinion that Abby ran upstairs when Andrew was being attacked and fainted, dying of fright. Perhaps out of embarrassment, Dr. Bowen later denied this action when asked about it on the stand.

One of the many who walked into the Borden house that morning was Charles Henry Wells. He accompanied the Reverend Augustus Buck to the home. According to the Fall River Historical Society's newsletter, Mr. Wells saw Dr. Dolan measuring the gashes in the head of Andrew Borden with a two-foot rule. "The appearance of his face was like a mass of raw meat. So many blows had been reined upon his head that there was no semblance to a human face. The top and back of his head did not seem to be seriously injured."[31]

Two days later, on August 7, 1892, the *New York Herald* printed the following about Abby Borden's injuries:

The wounds on Mrs. Borden's head offer a wide field for theorizing. First she was struck a straight blow in front of her forehead, delivered either when she was standing or when she reclined upon her back. This was with the edge of the hatchet. The other blows were along the side of the head and dealt with the back of the hatchet. The body lay face downward on the floor six feet from the bed. Yet the servant girl at work on the same floor did not hear it fall. How did it get into that position? That is one of the puzzles for which nobody has suggested an adequate solution. The hemorrhage was very small from both bodies.

Abby suffered three contusions on the front of the face. According to Dr. Dolan, "Two of them over the left eye and one on the bridge of the nose, just over the bridge of the nose." These contusions were bruises on the left side of her face and consistent with injuries she would receive as she fell to the floor.[32] Dr. Dolan was quoted by the *Fall River Herald* as saying that death must have been almost instantaneous to both cases after the first blow.[33]

The right side of her head was crushed in. There was a hole in the right side of the skull an inch and a half by five and one-half inches. There were eighteen wounds on Abby's head. "With the contusions, eighteen," Dr. Dolan testified. With a wound on her back that was a "glancing blow" (where the perpetrator had missed) it brings the total of her wounds to nineteen.[34]

When speaking of the left side of her head, Dolan was asked if it was a clean cut of the hair. He replied, "Some of it was so matted you could not tell. There was one large one on top that was cut as though you had cut it with shears. It was the wound that took out the piece of skull on the left side. It was not glancing, but neat and clean."

Q: As though done with a razor?
A: Yes, sir.[35]

Dr. Dolan testified later at the trial:

Q: I neglected to ask you one question. When I was inquiring about the position of the assailant of Mrs. Borden, you told me, I think, that in your opinion the assailant stood astride of the body and over it. If in that attitude the assailant stood, would there be a general spattering of blood over his body?
A: I don't know whether there would be a general one over the entire body. I think there would be surely some on the lower part of the body.
Q: Didn't the injuries on Mrs. Borden's head bleed a good deal?
A: Very much, yes, sir.
Q: And saturated the carpet and came entirely through it, and formed a large pool of blood?
A: Yes, sir.[36]

On the lower part of the dressing case in the guest room where Abby was found were fifty very large blood spots, quite a lot on the mirror all over the glass, and some spots were also found on the marble top of the dresser. Abby's "rat," her false hair piece, was found on the freshly made bed, and some blood can still be seen on the white bedspread at the Fall River Historical Society to this day.

As if she didn't suffer enough, it is believed that Abby was facing her attacker when the assault began.

When Andrew's body was discovered, blood was still flowing from the wounds. Dr. Dolan describes it at the trial:

A: The blood was of a bright red color and still oozing from the head. At the head it was dripping on the carpet underneath, between the wood work, the head of the sofa and the sofa body. It was not coagulated.
Q: How was the body? Was there any blood underneath the sofa?
A: Yes, sir, on the carpet.
Q: Describe the blood you saw there?
A: The blood had been soaked in that was on the carpet. There was no blood really on top of the carpet.
Q: How large a space was soaked with blood?
A: I should think -- they were in two spots, -- I should judge eight or ten inches in diameter.
Q: Where were those spots?
A: Right under the head of the sofa, that is practically underneath where the head of the sofa joins the body of the sofa.
Q: You say that they were practically soaked into the carpet?
A: Yes, sir.
Q: I was going to ask you, perhaps you have answered already without being asked, as to whether the blood on the body of Mr. Borden or any of the blood flowing from him was coagulated?
A: No, sir, I saw none.[37]

Dr. Dolan also testified at the trial that the upper portion of the assailant would have been spattered with cast off blood from the attack.[38] Mr. Borden had received ten wounds to the head.[39] However, the doctor said later that the murderer would not necessarily be spattered and sprinkled with blood because it would not have spurted in the direction of the assailant.[40]

From the appearance of the crime scene, Dr. Dolan testified that, in his opinion, the assailant "stood close behind the head of the lounge, that is between the parlor door and the head of the lounge."[41]

Neighbor and friend, Dr. Seabury Bowen was shook up by the Borden murders. In retrospect it is somewhat of a wonder that he was able to perform as well as he did that day.

Q: You were then, if you will pardon me for saying so, quite excited?
A: I was.
Q: You were very excited?
A: Yes sir.[42]

As soon as I got at the door, I could see the whole room and saw him. Of course I was prepared for something awful, as I did not hear him, and there was no sound. He lay there still, unrecognizable, his face was cut in such a manner I never should have known who it was.[43]

Q: Will you give further description, doctor, as far as you can, as to the injuries that appeared upon inspection?
A: Upon an inspection I found that his face was very badly cut with apparently a sharp instrument, and there was blood over his face; his face was covered with blood. I felt of his pulse and satisfied myself at once that he was dead, and I took a glance about the room and saw there was nothing disturbed at all.
Q: Any of the furniture or anything else disturbed about the room at all?
A: Not that I noticed.
Q: Will you describe the position on the sofa?

A: He was lying with his face towards the south on his right side apparently at ease, as any one would if they were lying asleep.
Q: Was the face to be recognized by one who knew him?
A: Hardly, I should say.[44]

At the preliminary hearing, Dr. Dolan was asked:
Q: What was the appearance that presented itself to you when you took the sheet off?
A: It was the gastly thing I have ever seen. (sic)

The First Autopsy

At 3:30 p.m. a partial autopsy was performed on both victims at the Borden home. The medical team consisted of Dr. J.Q.A. Tourtellot, Dr. John W. Coughlin, Dr. Albert C. Dedrick, Dr. John H. Leary, Dr. Thomas Gunning, Dr. Anson C. Peckham, Dr. Emmanuel Dutra, Dr. Seabury Bowen, and Dr. William Draper.

Nobody was given an autopsy on the dining room table. Undertaker boards were brought in—held on the ends by two chairs. It was not even a 'first autopsy,' but merely a 'partial' one. There was a concern that the couple had been poisoned. Dr. Draper wanted the stomachs of each body removed. They were placed in jars and sealed, prior to their trip to Harvard University to be tested by Professor Wood. During the stomach removal procedures, Andrew was in the sitting room. Abby was in the dining room.[45]

It has been commonly believed that Andrew's eye ball was hanging out and dangling on his cheek. But such was not so.

From the preliminary hearing, the testimony of Dr. Seabury Bowen:

Q: The eye ball was hanging out itself?
A: It was cut in two, in halves.
Q: And lay on one cheek or the other?
A: No it was not lying on the cheek. It was cut in two, or cut in halves, and remained almost in the natural position.

During the trial, Dr. Dolan also testified about the eye that was cut in half:
A: ... This next wound ran into that {another wound}, came down through the eye, and cut the eye completely in half and cut through the cheek bone, severing it, and ended just below the cheek bone. That wound was four and a half inches long.

"That cut into the skull," Dolan said.[46]

Bridget Sullivan helped get the milk that was in the ice box. That too would be tested.

The Partial Report

Copy of the findings of the inquest as presented to presiding judge Blaisdell:

Bristol ss., to J.C. Blaisdell, Justice of the Second District Court of the County of Bristol.

In conformity with section 9 of chapter 200 of the acts of the year 1877, I return herewith a copy of my record of an autopsy of the body of Mrs. Andrew J. Borden aged 67 years, found lying in Fall River and supposed to have come to death by violence. The said autopsy was made by authority of Mayor Coughlin at 3 o'clock in the afternoon of Thursday, the fourth day of August, A.D., 1892, in the presence of W. T. Learned, residing at Fall River, and J. Q.

A. Tourellot (sic), residing at Fall River, who were required by me to attend the same as witnesses thereof, viz: The body was found lying upon Second Street. Before proceeding with the autopsy I called the attention of the witnesses summoned by me to the appearance and position of the body, and caused them carefully to observe the same. The autopsy then proceeded as follows: On the left side of the head over the ear was a wound two and a half inches long by one and a quarter wide. On the right side of her head was a number of cuts penetrating the brain and so intermingled as to be practically impossible to count, and I further declare it to be my opinion that the said Mrs. A. J. Borden came to her death from shock, the result of blows from an axe or a large hatchet.

Dated at Fall River, in the county of Bristol, this 8th day of August, A.D., 1892.
W. A. Dolan, Medical Examiner.

The other autopsy was in the presence of the witnesses, and was on the body of Andrew J. Borden. It states: "The autopsy then proceeded as follows: The left side of the face and head was cut and smashed in by no less than 12 distinct blows of an axe or large hatchet." In other respects it does not differ from the above copy of the report of the autopsy on Mrs. Borden.[47]

The Full Autopsy

Commonly referred to as The Second Autopsy, the document originally was put on paper as one extensive paragraph—an arduous read to be sure. This transcription includes paragraph breaks for ease of reading.

Fall River, Mass., August 11th, 1892

Record of Autopsy held at Oak Grove Cemetery on body of Andrew J. Borden.

Autopsy performed by W. A. Dolan, Medical Examiner, assisted by Dr. F. W. Draper. Witnesses F. W. Draper of Boston and John W. Leary of Fall River. Clerk D. E. Cone of Fall River. Time of Autopsy 11:15 am, August 11, 1892, one week after death.

Body that of a man well nourished. Age seventy years. 5 feet 11 inches in height. No stiffness of death on account of decomposition, which was far advanced. Inguinal hernia on right side. Abdomen had already been opened. Artificial teeth in upper jaw. There were no marks of violence on body, but on left side of head and face there were numerous incised wounds and one contused wound penetrating into the brain.

The wounds beginning at the nose and to the left were as follows:
1. Incised wound 4 inches long beginning at lower border of left nasal bone and reaching to lower edge of lower jaw, cutting through nose, upper lip, lower lip, and slightly into bone of upper and lower jaw.

2. Began at internal angle of eye and extended to one and 3/8 inches of lower edge of jaw, beginning 4 and 1/2 inches in length, cutting through the tissues and into the bone.

3. Began at lower border of lower eye lid cutting through the tissues and into the cheek bone, 2 inches long and one and 3/8 inches deep.

4. Began two inches above upper eye lid 1/2 inch external to wound No. 3, thence downward

and outward through middle of left eyebrow through the eye ball cutting it completely in halves, and excising a piece of the skull one and 1/2 inches in length by 1/2 inch in width. Length of wound 4 and 1/2 inches.

5. Began on level of same wound superficial scalp wound downward and outward 2 inches long.

6. Parallel with this 1/4 inch long, downward and outward.

7. Began 1/2 inch below No. 5, 3 inches in length downward and outward, penetrating cavity of skull.

8. Began directly above No. 7 and one inch in length downward and outward.

9. Directly posterior to No. 8 beginning at ear and extending 4 inches long, 2 inches in width, crushing bone and carrying bone into brain. Also crushing from without in.

10. Directly behind this and above it, and running downwards backward 2 inches long superficially.

The general direction of all these wounds is parallel to each other.

HEAD. Right half of top of skull removed. Brain found to be completely decomposed; and in fluid condition.

CHEST. Chest and abdomen opened by one incision extending from neck to pubis. Right lung glued to ribs in front. Left lung normal.

HEART normal.

ABDOMEN. Spleen normal, kidney normal, liver and bladder normal. Stomach and portion of liver had been removed. Lower part of large bowel filled with solid formed feces. Feces also in lower part of small bowel.
William A. Dolan, Medical Examiner.

D. E. Cone, Clerk[48]

An additional wound (#11) was discovered by Dr. Dolan and its location was written in the marginalia of the original autopsy report as follows: *On top of skull was a transverse fracture 4 and 1/2 inches in length*. This description was handwritten at the end of the details for wound #7.

Fall River, Mass., August 11, 1892

Record of Autopsy on body of Abby D. Borden, aged 64 years. Thursday August 11, 1892, at 12:35 P.M. One week after death.

The Autopsy was performed by W. A. Dolan, Medical Examiner, assisted by Dr. F. W. Draper, and witnessed by F. W. Draper of Boston, and J. H. Leary of Fall River. Clerk of Autopsy D. E. Cone of Fall River.

Body that of a female, very well nourished and very fleshy 64 years of age. 5 feet, 3 inches in height. No stiffness of death, owing to decomposition, which was far advanced. Abdomen had already been opened. Artificial teeth in upper jaw. No marks of violence on front of body. On back of body was

FIRST AN INCISED WOUND 2 AND 1/2 INCHES IN LENGTH, AND 2 AND 1/2 INCHES IN DEPTH. The lower angle of the wound was over the spine and four inches below the junction of neck with body, and extending thence upward and outward to the left. On the forehead and bridge of nose were three contused wounds. Those on the forehead being oval, lengthwise with body.

SECOND The contusion on bridge of nose was one inch in length by one half in width.

THIRD On the forehead one was one inch above left eyebrow, one and 1/4 inches long by 3/8 inch in width, and the other one and 1/4 inches above eyebrow, and one and 1/2 inches long by 1/4 inch wide. On the head there were 18 distinct wounds, incising and crushing, and all but four were on the right side. Counting from left to right with the face downwards, the wounds were as follows:

1. Was a glancing scalp wound two inches in length by one and 1/2 inches in width, situated 3 inches above left ear hole, cut from above downwards and did not penetrate the skull.

2. Was exactly on top of the skull one inch long penetrating into but not through the skull.

3. Was parallel to No. 2, one and 1/2 inches long, and penetrating through the skull.

4. Was 2 and 1/4 inches long above occipital protuberance and one and 1/2 inches long.

5. Was parallel to No. 4 and one and 1/2 inches long.

6. Was just above and parallel to No. 5, and one and 1/4 inches long. On top of skull was a traverse fracture two inches in length, a continuation of a penetrating wound.

7. Was two inches long and two inches behind ear hold crushing and carrying bone into brain.

All the wounds of the head following No. 7 though incised crushed through into the brain.

8. Was 2 and 1/2 inches long

9. Was 2 and 3/4 inches long

10. Was one and 3/4 inches long

11. Was 1/2 inches long

12. Was 2 and 1/4 inches long

13. Was one and 3/4 inches long

14. Was two and 1/2 inches long

15. Reached from middle line of head towards the ear 5 inches long

16. Was one inch long

17. Was 1/2 inch long

18. Was 3 and 1/2 inches long

These wounds on the right side were parallel, the direction being mostly from in front backwards.

HEAD. There was a hole in right side of skull 4 and 1/2 to 5 and 1/4 inches, through which the brain evacuated in fluid condition being entirely decomposed.

CHEST. The chest and abdomen was opened by one incision from chin to pubis.

LUNGS bound down behind but normal.

HEART normal.

ABDOMEN, Stomach and part of bowel had been removed. Spleen, pancreas, kidneys, liver, bladder and intestines were normal. Womb was the seat of a small fibroid tumor on anterior surface. Fallopian tubes and ovaries normal. Lower bowel empty. Upper portion of small bowel containing undigested food.

W. A. Dolan, Medical Examiner
D. E. Cone, Clerk[49]

The Skulls

After the second autopsy, the heads of the Bordens were removed at Oak Grove Cemetery. It was August 11, 1892 the same day as the autopsy in the tomb, one week after death and five days after the funeral, the same day that Lizzie Borden was arrested.[50]
Dr. Dolan is asked about the skull of Andrew Borden during the trial:

Q: And removed the flesh from the bone?
A: Yes, sir.
Q: And you have it in your possession?
A: Yes, sir.
Q: What is the process of removing the flesh from the bone? I will ask you this question. Perhaps my friends will know the reason I ask it in the form I do just now. What is the process of removing the flesh from the bone? Does it in any way affect the integrity of the bone?
A: No, sir.
Q: What is the thickness of the skull at the point where those four wounds went through the brain?
A: About one sixteenth of an inch.

The cast of Andrew Borden's skull was placed on its side on the rail in front of the stenographer's table, and Dr. Dolan described in detail the wounds that Mr. Borden received.

The Bloody Clothing

On the day Andrew Borden died, he wore black trousers, a black vest, a cardigan/woolen jacket and a pair of Congress shoes. Though Lizzie testified at the inquest that she took off Andrew's footwear, it is clear that either she did not or the shoes were put back on Andrew's body for the infamous death scene photograph.[51]

On his person were a watch and a pocket book, where Dr. Dolan found some money amounting to $81.65. The denominations were: four $10 bills; five $5 bills; one $2 bill; eleven $1 dollar bills, two 50-cent pieces; three quarters, six dimes, five nickels, and five pennies.

His watch was in his upper vest pocket.[52]

Undertaker Winward had also given Dr. Dolan a ring of keys and some chewing tobacco, supposedly from Andrew's pockets, yet it was known that Mr. Borden did not use the product.[53]

When Dr. Dolan saw Abby Borden's body, he said, "I noticed that it was bloody -- the back of her clothing; that is the upper part of it; her waist ... I found a handkerchief, an old silk handkerchief ... [It was] loose ... It seemed to be an old silk handkerchief, in some places shredded from wear ... I did not see that it was cut."

It was dark colored and Dr. Dolan saw that there was blood on it. When asked how near her head was the handkerchief, he replied, "It was quite near. The hands were in there between the head and the handkerchief."[54]

John Morse, the brother of Andrew's first wife Sarah and uncle to Lizzie and Emma, had spent the night in the Borden guest room the night before, Wednesday, August 3. He seemed concerned about getting the clothing buried fast.

The *Fall River Herald* states:

John V. Morse has been interested in the search. He wanted to hire somebody to bury the bloody clothes. Towards the close of the afternoon Morse grew irritable, and had quite an altercation with David P. Keefe, who hired a man to bury the blood-stained clothes and pieces of the skull for him. Keefe charged $5 for the work, and Morse pronounced it robbery. Keefe said he wouldn't do the job for $100, though under some circumstances he allowed that he might be glad to do it for nothing. Morse finally paid $3.[55]

Albert E. Chase tells what his part was in the disposal of the victims' clothing the day after the murders.

Fall River, Mass. August 5, 1892. The following articles and wearing apparel were this afternoon taken from a washtub in the cellar wash room of the Borden House by orders of the City Marshal and Medical Examiner, and were buried under my direction in the yard back of the barn.

1 sofa pillow and tidy, one large piece of Brussels carpet, one roll of cotton batting, one sheet and several pieces of cotton cloth, three towels, one napkin, one chemise, one dress, one pair drawers, one skirt, two aprons, one hair braid and several pieces of hair from Mrs.

Borden's head from five to eight inches long, one neck tie, one truss, one piece of black silk braid or watch guard.

I also found mixed in with the hair of Mrs. Borden a piece of bone, which from its nature I took to be a piece of Mrs. Borden's skull, it was cut so smooth, that I thought it might be of use in determining what kind of instrument was used, as the bone and hair both had the appearance of being cut with a very sharp instrument, I gave this piece of bone to Dr. Dolan. About the middle of the next week Dr. Dolan ordered all the articles dug up. After taking out pieces of clothing and of the carpet, they were ordered buried again. This time they were all put in a box.[56]

Alderman John Beattie went to police headquarters and gave his story of the bloody clothing, which supported Chase's.

On the day they buried the blood-stained clothes, I noticed that they were about to bury a piece of the skull which had been cut away from the head of one of the victims by the axe of the murderer. I told Officer Chase to preserve it. He wrapped it up in a piece of paper and is carrying it around with him. The appearance of that portion of its surface which was cleanly cut by the axe might give some clue as to the exact nature of the weapon in regard to the smoothness of its blade or the cleanness of the blade.[57]

After the inquest had begun the *Fall River Herald* reported:

Medical Examiner Dolan went to the Borden house in the afternoon and had the clothing worn by the victims of the murder dug up and spread on the grass for examination. There were certain parts that he wanted for further investigation, and he carried them away with him and had the remnants buried behind the barn.[58]

The press reported that Dr. Wood "was closeted with Dr. Dolan for awhile. The bits of clothing and other souvenirs taken from the pile buried behind the Borden barn were turned over to him for further examination. Just what he did here is not known."[59]

Q. There was of course clothing which was found on the bodies of both Mr. and Mrs. Borden, that clothing has not been talked about at all; but I believe it was at one time put in the earth back of the barn?
A. Yes Sir.
Q. That is to say, the clothing was buried without any envelope or box that first time?
A. I was not there, but I understand that to be so.
Q. Then it was taken up, and examined and buried again?
A. Yes Sir, put into a box.
Q. When it was buried again, it was put into a wooden box?
A. Yes Sir.
Q. It was taken up two or three times?
A. Twice I think.
Q. What has become of that clothing?
A. It is down stairs.
Q. In the marshal's office?
A. Yes Sir.
Q. Is all the clothing that was found on the bodies of each there?
A. Yes Sir.[60]

The Funerals

The funeral will take place to-morrow at 11 o'clock and will be strictly private. The services will be conducted by City Missionary Buck, who is a close friend of the family, and the interment will take place at Oak Grove Cemetery. At the present time both bodies are lying in the dining room, the windows of which the servant girl was washing shortly before the tragedy became known.[61]

The bodies of the murdered couple were buried today. As early as 9 o'clock the house was surrounded by a great crowd of curiosity seekers. Reporters, artists, photographers, and policemen were active among them. Mr. Morse came from the house and talked freely with a group of reporters. He said it was a terrible thing to be suspected and shadowed as he has been, but he courts the fullest investigation and is anxious and willing to do all that he can to trace the perpetrators of the great crime. He said that Miss Lizzie Borden's health was in about the same condition as it was last Thursday afternoon. She did not mingle with the family to any great extent. When Mr. Fish of Hartford, a nephew of her stepmother appeared she gave him a very cool reception. About 11 o'clock preparations were commenced for the funerals. People numbering between 3,000 and 4,000 assembled in front of the house and about twenty policemen maintained a clear passageway.[62]

Second Street from Borden and Spring Street was packed with at least 2,500 people in the immediate vicinity. Officers Richard Hurley, Daniel Golden, Albert Chace, Mark Shay, Joseph Hyde, George Ferguson, Michael Reagan, Bernard Welsh, Patrick Doherty, Philip Harrington, and John Devine were kept busy in keeping back the crowds. Marshal Hilliard and Assistant Marshal Fleet were on the scene and held a consultation as to the best line of action should any demonstrations take place.[63]

The coffins were made of cedar with three silver handles on each side. Inscribed on the top of one was "Andrew Borden, Died Aug. 4, 1892, Aged 70 Years." Abby's coffin only gave her name and age.[64] Both were covered in black broadcloth. The bodies were laid out in the dining room and the coffins were open.[65] The heads were placed toward the east. Upon Andrew Borden's lay a wreath of ivy. A bouquet of white roses, ferns and pea blossoms tied with a white satin ribbon adorned his wife's. Both were placed in the sitting room.[66]

Andrew Borden was not 70 years old. He was born in Fall River on September 12, 1822, which would make him 69 at the time of his death.[67]

Lizzie was not in mourning. She wore a black lace dress with bead trimmings, "which fitted her rounded and shapely body faultlessly. She wore a bonnet of dark material, relieved by small, high flowers and was not in mourning."[68]

The funeral was very private. Some who attended were: Abby's stepmother, Mrs. Oliver Gray, and Gray's daughter; Hiram Harrington, Andrew's brother-in-law; George Whitehead and his wife, half-sister of Abby; Abby's sister and her husband J. L. Fish; Mr. Fish's son and wife; Miss Mary Ann Borden; Charles Borden of Westport, Massachusetts; William S. Wilcox and his sister, Mrs. Cluny and Mrs. Macomber, cousins of Andrew Borden; daughters of Mr. Wilcox, Mrs. John Durfee and Mrs. Strickland; Dr. Seabury Bowen and wife Phoebe; Southard Miller and son Franklin; Adelaide Churchill and her sister, Mrs. Thomas Cheetham; and Mrs. Rescomb Case, Mrs. James D. Burt.

There were no singing and no remarks. A simple service was performed by Reverend Dr. Adams of the First Congregational Church and City Missionary Buck. "There were no

The Borden monument at Oak Grove Cemetery, Fall River, Massachusetts.

flowers in the room. The funeral ceremony consisted of a reading from the Scriptures and the recitation of a series of prayers."[69]

At the end of the services, the coffins were brought out to the two waiting hearses. There were eleven hacks also standing at the curb in anticipation of the trip to Oak Grove Cemetery. Emma and Lizzie were the principal mourners. Lizzie came out of the house first, leaning upon the arm of undertaker James Winward.[70] "Her nerves were completely unstrung, as was shown by the trembling of her body and the manner in which she bore down on her supporter. When she reached her carriage she fell back exhausted on the cushions."[71]

The pallbearers for Andrew Borden were: John H. Boone, businessman; Andrew J. Borden, treasurer of Merchant Manufacturing Company; Jerome Cook Borden, cousin to Andrew; Richard A. Borden, well known businessman of Fall River; George W. Dean, businessman; Abraham Gifford Hart, treasurer of Union Savings Bank; and James M. Osborn.

Pallbearers for Abby Borden were: Frank L. Almy; John H. Boone, businessman; Henry S. Buffinton, businessman; Simeon B. Chase, treasurer of King Philip Mills; James C. Eddy, president of Jesse Eddy Mfg.; and Henry J. Wells, treasurer of Fall River Spool & Bobbin Company.[72]

"The funeral procession traveled north on Second Street to Borden Street on to South Main Street by the Andrew J. Borden Building. It continued north to Cherry Street, to Rock Street and east on Prospect Street and to the main gate at Oak Grove Cemetery."[73] As the procession made its way along North Main Street many associates of Andrew Borden were seen to raise their hats.[74]

They arrived at Oak Grove Cemetery about 12:20 p.m. There were several hundred people standing about, kept back by policemen led by Sergeant John Brocklehurst. During the ceremonies, everyone stayed in their carriages except for John Morse, the clergy, pall bearers, and those undertaker's assistants necessary at this time. All stood in a vacant lot opposite during the brief service. After Reverend Buck read "I am the resurrection and the life" and other passages for burial, Dr. Adams delivered a prayer. Everyone paused for about five minutes. An elderly woman was about to kneel before the graves when she was moved away by a policeman. Going off in tears, she was identified as a prior employee of the Bordens. The tops of the graves were covered with fir branches. The sides were lined with thin cloth.[75]

After the carriages left, the bodies were not buried. They were put in a receiving tomb, under official orders to await a second, complete autopsy, where the heads would be removed and the skulls de-fleshed and cleaned. The bodies would be buried after the August 11th autopsy. The skulls would be buried after the trial.[76]

You Can't Take it With You

Had Lizzie been convicted of the murder of her father and step-mother, she could not have inherited her father's estate.[77] The *New York Times* in 1893 claimed that had Andrew Borden died first, the daughters would have no claim at all to any of Andrew's estate.[78] In Leonard Rebello's masterful reference work on the case, titled *Lizzie Borden, Past and Present*, he states that, "If Andrew Borden was killed first, Abby Borden's heirs would have been entitled to one-third of the estate. Emma and Lizzie would have received two-thirds of their father's estate."[79]

The day after the murders, Emma and Lizzie signed a probate court document stating that they were the sole heirs of Andrew Borden and he left no widow. Emma was appointed administratrix of Andrew's estate in probate court a month after the murders, with a bond of $50,000 and sureties from Franklin L. Almy, Joseph A Bowen of Fall River, and S. Stevens of Swansea, Massachusetts.[80]

Abby Borden's Estate

Real Estate: One undivided half of house and land at 45 Fourth Street. Fall River, Massachusetts.	$2,000.00
Personal Estate:	
Deposit in Fall River Savings Bank	$1,522.66
Deposit Fall River Union Savings Bank	$103.39
Cash on Hand	$90.00
	$1,716.05

The Probate Court ruled that Abby's estate would be divided between two parties: her sister, Priscilla S. Fish of Hartford, Connecticut, and Sarah B. "Bertie" Whitehead, her beloved half-sister in Fall River.

Abby Borden's $1,716.05 estate value was divided between the two, each receiving $788.84 on November 2, 1894. Abby's heirs also received Emma and Lizzie's half interest of 45 Fourth Street, bank deposits of $4,000, and personal belongings on August 13, 1893. Emma and Lizzie still owned half of the Fourth Street property, but they later sold this half interest to Sarah Whitehead for $1.00 after Lizzie's acquittal.[81]

Andrew Borden's Estate

Real Estate	$8,190.00
Personal Estate	$13,408.04
	$21,598.04

Real Estate

Durfee land on Bay Street	$1,200.00
Lot east side of East Main	$1,100.00
Lot west side of East Main	$2,000.00
Undivided third of land on Bay Street	$3,850.00
Butler & Globe Streets	$40.00
	$8,190.00

Personal

10 shares Chace Mills stock	$1,000.00
Dividends on deposit Fall River Five Cents Savings Bank	$175.00
	$1,800.00
Deposit Pocasset National	$129.36
Deposit Union Savings Bank	$1,106.87
Deposit Citizens Savings	$1,800.00
Deposit Citizens Savings	$1,436.84
Deposit Citizens Savings	$1,307.14
Deposit Citizens Savings	$1,241.10
Fall River Savings	$1,757.48
Fall River Savings	$268.93
Fall River Savings	$1,384.00
	$1.32
	$13,408.04

This does not represent Andrew's total wealth by a long shot. This is the only account there is of Andrew's estate, taken from a handwritten Probate Court record.

On August 5, 1892, the *Fall River Daily Globe* estimated Andrew Borden's worth as:

Real Estate:	$173,650.00 - $173,650.00
Personal Estate:	$175,000.00 - $250,000.00
Total Worth:	$348,650.00 - $423.650.00[82]

The Borden Monument

The Borden monument that today towers over the graves of the entire family was not installed until 1895. The Borden family plot is located in the north section of the cemetery. As partners in life, Andrew Borden is buried in half of the same plot that William Almy and family rest. So many people are interested in seeing the Borden graves that there are white arrows painted on the roadway in the cemetery to lead you there.

The monument is about ten feet high and tastefully done in Westerly granite. Its base is four by five feet. The south side bears the inscription "A.J. Borden." The north side reads, "Andrew Jackson Borden, 1822 - 1892. His Wife, Sarah Anthony Borden, 1823 - 1863. His Wife, Abby Durfee Borden, 1828 - 1892." The side facing west lists the three children of Andrew and Sarah Borden.

It was built by the Smith Granite Company, and their workmen placed it under the supervision of Superintendent Jonathan P. Morill. Emma and Lizzie were at the cemetery while the men were at work. Some spectators hung around as well. Lizzie and Emma left their carriage to take a closer look at the work. Lizzie glanced at the monument and swiftly re-entered the carriage. Emma had some criticisms and gave directions to the workmen, returned to her sister in the waiting carriage and departed.[83]

It was not until 2009 that the real answer to this question was answered by Dr. Stefani

Simple headstones of Andrew and Abby Borden.

Koorey. Due to the huge size of the burial books, it was discovered that Abby's mother was never moved to Oak Grove at all. The handwritten lines of the entries were close and easy to confuse, and confuse the original founder of this "re-burial" did as well as subsequent clerks who were questioned. Sarah (Sawyer) Gray still lays, undisturbed, where she has been since her death in 1860: the Old North Burial Ground in Fall River.[84]

NOTES

1. Kenneth M. Champlin, "Some Other Bordens," *The Lizzie Borden Quarterly* III.3 (July 1996): 15.
2. David Kent, ed., *Lizzie Borden Sourcebook* (Boston: Branden Publishing Co., 1992), 13.
3. The *Fall River Herald*, n.d., in Kent, *Lizzie Borden Sourcebook*, 136.
4. The *Boston Advertiser*, n.d., in Kent *Lizzie Borden Sourcebook*, 5.
5. *Fall River Daily Globe*, 6 August 1892, in Leonard Rebello, *Lizzie Borden, Past & Present* (Fall River, MA: Al-Zach Press, 1999), 25.
6. *Fall River Daily Globe*, 6 August 1892, in Rebello, *Lizzie Borden, Past & Present*, 26.
7. *Fall River Herald*, n.d., in Kent, *Lizzie Borden Sourcebook*, 115.
8. *Fall River Daily Globe,* 5 August 1892, in Rebello, *Lizzie Borden, Past & Present*, 25.
9. The *New York Herald*, 13 August 1892, in Kent, *Lizzie Borden Sourcebook,* 111.
10. Harry Widdows, Stefani Koorey, Kat Koorey, eds., *The Preliminary Hearing in the Lizzie Borden Case, New Edition* (Orlando, FL: PearTree Press, 2005), 263, 264.
11. The *Fall River Herald*, n.d., in Kent, *Lizzie Borden Sourcebook*, 100.
12. Rebello, *Lizzie Borden, Past & Present*, 22.
13. Ibid., 23.
14. *Fall River Herald*, n.d., in Kent, *Lizzie Borden Sourcebook*, 41, 42.
15. Ibid.,10.
16. William L. Pavao Jr., "Abby Durfee Borden: Portrait of a Stepmother," *Lizzie Borden Quarterly* IX.1 (January 2002).
17. Sherry Chapman, "Dear Abby?" *Lizzie Borden Quarterly* IX.2 (April 2002): 7.
18. Michael Martins and Dennis Binette, eds., *The Knowlton Papers* (Fall River, MA: Fall River Historical Society, 1994), 227-229.
19. *Inquest upon the deaths of Andrew J. Borden and Abby D. Borden, August 9 - 11, 1892* (Orlando, FL: PearTree Press, 2005), 134.
20. Paul Dennis Hoffman, *Yesterday in Old Fall River: A Lizzie Borden Companion* (Durham, NC: Carolina Academic Press, 2000), 32.
21. *Inquest*, 158.
22. Ibid., 82.
23. Harry Widdows, Stefani Koorey, Kat Koorey, eds., *The Trial of Lizzie Andrew Borden, 1893* (Orlando, FL: PearTree Press, 2001), 286.

24. Ibid., 304.
25. Ibid., 342-376.
26. Ibid., 307, 308.
27. Ibid., 309.
28. Ibid., 309.
29. Hoffman, *Yesterday in Old Fall River*, 7.
30. *Trial*, 296, 297
31. *Fall River Historical Society Newsletter* 14.3 (June 2003).
32. *Trial*, 896.
33. Kent, *Lizzie Borden Sourceboook*, 8.
34. *Trial*, 924
35. Ibid., 953.
36. Ibid., 974.
37. Ibid., 861.
38. Ibid., 977.
39. Ibid., 924.
40. Ibid., 947, 948.
41. Ibid., 946.
42. *Preliminary Hearing*, 413.
43. *Inquest*, 117.
44. *Trial*, 301.
45. Rebello, *Lizzie Borden, Past & Present*, 99.
46. *Trial*, 890.
47. *Evening Standard* (n.d.).
48. *Preliminary Hearing*, 201, 202.
49. Ibid., 199-200.
50. *Trial*, 977, 978.
51. Ibid., 864.
52. Ibid., 864, 865.
53. *Preliminary Hearing*, 194.
54. *Trial*, testimony of Dr. Wm. Dolan.
55. Kent, *Lizzie Borden Sourcebook*, 28.
56. *The Witness Statements for the Lizzie Borden Murder Case, August 4 - October 6, 1892* (Orlando, FL: PearTree Press, 2001), 42.
57. Kent, *Lizzie Borden Sourcebook*, 39.
58. Ibid., 36.
59. Ibid., 42.

60. *Preliminary Hearing*, Testimony of Dr. Wm. Dolan, 189.

61. *New York Times*, 5 August 1892.

62. *New York Times*, 6 August 1892, in Kent, *Lizzie Borden Sourcebook*, 16.

63. *Fall River Evening News*, 6 August 1892, in Rebello, *Lizzie Borden, Past & Present*, 103.

64. *Boston Daily Globe*, 6 August 1892, in Rebello, *Lizzie Borden, Past & Present*, 102.

65. *Fall River Herald*, n.d., in Kent, *Lizzie Borden Sourcebook*, 28.

66. Rebello, *Lizzie Borden, Past & Present*, 103.

67. Rebello, *Lizzie Borden, Past & Present*, 3, 6.

68. *Boston Daily Globe*, 6 August 1892, in Rebello, *Lizzie Borden, Past & Present*, 102.

69. Robert Sullivan, *Goodbye, Lizzie Borden* (NY: Penguin Books, 1974), 38-40.

70. Ibid., 38-40.

71. *New York Times*, 6 August 1892, in Kent, *Lizzie Borden Sourcebook*, 16.

72. Rebello, *Lizzie Borden, Past & Present*, 104.

73. *Boston Daily Globe*, August 6, 1892, in Rebello, *Lizzie Borden, Past & Present*, 102.

74. *New York Times*, 6 August 1892, in Kent, *Lizzie Borden Sourcebook*, 16.

75. Rebello, *Lizzie Borden, Past & Present*, 103, 104.

76. Ibid., 104.

77. *Fall River Evening News*, 30 August 1892, in Rebello, *Lizzie Borden, Past & Present*, 277.

78. *New York Times*, 10 September 1893, in Rebello, *Lizzie Borden, Past & Present*, 277.

79. Rebello, *Lizzie Borden, Past & Present*, 277.

80. Ibid., 277.

81. Ibid., 278.

82. Ibid., 280.

83. Philip T. Silvia Jr., ed., *Victorian Vistas, 1886-1900*. (Fall River, MA: R.E. Smith Printing Co., 1988), 500.

84. Stefani Koorey, "Myth Busting Lizzie Borden," *The Hatchet: A Journal of Lizzie Borden & Victorian Studies* (Fall 2009), 25.

Part Two

Law and Order

Melvin O. Adams

LAWYER ADAMS CROSS-QUESTIONING DR BOWEN—DID YOU NOTE THE TIME THAT YOU SENT THE TELEGRAM?

Melvin O. Adams, *Boston Globe*, June 9, 1893

Melvin Ohio Adams

November 7, 1847 – August 9, 1920

Melvin Ohio Adams was born in the small town of Ashburnham, Massachusetts, on November 7, 1847, at 269 Russell Hill Road. The house still stands today and is privately owned. The fourth generation of Ashburnhams, he was the son of Joseph Adams, the grandson of the original owner of Melvin Adams' birthplace, and Dolly (Winship) Whitney Adams.

Adams attended the public schools in Ashburnham. He graduated from Dartmouth College in 1871, and in the school term of 1871-1872 was sub-master of Fitchburg High School. He also read law with Hon. Edward Avery of Boston and Hon. Amasa Norcross of Fitchburg. He earned his Bachelor of Law from Boston University in 1874 and was admitted to the bar of Suffolk County the same year.

In 1875, Adams married Mary Colony of Fitchburg. His legal residence was his birth town until 1876, though he had practiced law in Boston since 1874. He became the assistant district attorney for the district of Suffolk in 1876, then resigned to devote his time to private practice.

When he was Assistant D.A., the New Bedford *Evening Standard* reported, "the queer but complementary criticism was often passed upon him that he ought not to be retained in the office because his skill and eloquence often procured convictions when the facts were probably in favor of the prisoner."

In 1890 Adams served on Governor John Q. A. Brackett's staff with the rank of colonel.

Adams was a friend of Andrew Jennings, having both studied law at the University of Boston Law School. He had a reputation as an excellent trial lawyer in criminal cases as well as for being "graceful." Jennings was characterized in the papers as "nervous."

It was Andrew Jennings who approached Mr. Adams to join Lizzie Borden's defense team in 1892. When Lizzie was in the Fall River jail, she and her sister had an argument where Lizzie is purported to have said that Emma had given her away. This was overheard by Police Matron Hannah Reagan, who then told reporter Edwin Porter. Although Mrs. Reagan later recanted it, and according to Victoria Lincoln, "As soon as the *Globe* and the *Providence Journal* hit the local stands with the story, Mr. Jennings took the first train to Boston and came back with Melvin O. Adams, a well-known trial lawyer; this was the first outside help engaged by the defense."

Apparently Adams knew Dr. Wood as well. As Borden trial prosecuting attorney Hosea Knowlton writes to Attorney General Pillsbury on September 2, 1892: "If you see Wood give him a little caution about disclosing anything, particularly with reference to the broken hatchet. Some of my Fall River friends have a feeling that Adams and he are too thick. This is partly caused by Wood's frankness in saying that he was a special friend of Adams, and was also his client."

Robert Sullivan in *Goodbye, Lizzie Borden* writes: "Despite his prominence, a study of the official trial transcript indicates to this writer that Robinson was not an experienced trial lawyer when contrasted with his co-counsel Jennings and, more particularly, Adams. ... Cross-examination was conducted by Melvin O. Adams for the defendant. By contrast with Robinson, Adams was an effective cross-examiner."

According to the New Bedford *Evening Standard*, while Marshal Hilliard was being examined,

> Mr. Knowlton and Attorney Adams pulled their chairs together and leaned over on each other's shoulders, engaged in a very confidential whisper while Marshal Hilliard was being examined. Both were shaking with laughter and they belied the deadly hostility which has been frequently displayed during the hearing. Their disputes, in fact, have been the most entertaining exhibitions in court. On such occasions they addressed each other as brothers. Mr. Adams is blandly sarcastic, and Mr. Knowlton cutting and aggressive. No one enjoys these professional bouts more than Judge Blaisdell, unless indeed it be the prisoner.

Both Jennings and Adams had worked for Lizzie almost a full year. Their fee was $15,000 each.

After the verdict of "not guilty" was announced in the Borden trial, the Rochester (NY) *Democrat & Chronicle* reported that when Lizzie saw "the handsome face of Melvin Ohio Adams, the famous Boston lawyer, she reached out a hand toward him, but one was not enough for this hearty friend and he took both."

Adams served as president of the Boston, Revere Beach, and Lynn Railroad and of the General Alumni Association of Dartmouth College. He was also very civic minded of his own home town.

In 1901, a Cemetery Commission was formed to make improvements in the old burying ground on Meetinghouse Hill. Adams donated several hundred dollars to make substantial improvements. He had a giant Celtic cross made and erected in the old cemetery, placing it as near as possible to its old entrance. He had wished to symbolize in some way the unity of life.

Adams had built a much-needed four-room schoolhouse, which was named after his mother, the Dolly Whitney Adams School.

He sold to the town of Ashburnham a piece of land for the construction of a new town hall. He used the $5,000 from this sale to have a Civil War Memorial built. The sculpture is of a standing figure of a uniformed Union soldier marching with his rifle over his proper right shoulder. It is made of bronze with a granite base. The sculptor was Theo Alice Ruggles Kitson (1871 – 1932). Its dedication took place on the same day as the new town hall in 1907. The Civil War Memorial still stands in front of the memorial hall as a reminder of the 213 townsmen who fought for the Union.

Melvin Ohio Adams died on August 9, 1920, at his home in Boston. His obituary in the Boston *Daily Globe* ran on page one the following day.

DEATH COMES TO MELVIN O. ADAMS

Noted Lawyer and Railroad Man
Succumbs to Heart Failure
At His Boston Home

Col. Melvin O. Adams, one of the best known lawyers of Massachusetts, president of the Boston, Revere Beach & Lynn Railroad, and trustee of many estates and corporations, died suddenly last evening at his home, 36 Beacon st.

He was sitting in a chair at a window with his wife, following a very busy day, when he was seized with heart failure and died almost immediately.

Karl Adams, their only son, who is assistant to the corporation counsel of the city of Boston, is at Nantucket with his family, but was notified by wire and will be home today. Pending his arrival no plans for the funeral were made.

Born in Ashburnham in 1850

Melvin O. Adams was born in Ashburnham, Nov 7, 1850, the son of Joseph and Dolly (W.) Whitney Adams. His father was a farmer. The boy attended the schools of Ashburnham and Appleton Academy in New Ipswich, N.H. He entered Dartmouth College in 1867, and graduated in 1871 at the age of 21. Then he taught school at Fitchburg and at the same time carried on law studies with Amasa Norcross, ex-Congressman from that district.

In 1874 he came to Boston and had since made his home here. He continued his law studies at Boston University, graduated in 1875 and was admitted to practice. For ten years, from 1876 to 1886, he was assistant district attorney to Suffolk County, when he retired to become associated with the late Augustus Russ in the practice of law.

In 1904 Mr. Adams was appointed United States district attorney for Massachusetts by President Roosevelt and held that office for two years. In politics he was a Republican and presided over the State convention in 1899. He was candidate for Congress in 1902 in the 10th District, but was unsuccessful.

Rarely in Court of Late

In recent years Col. Adams had rarely appeared in court, but during his active career he was one of the most brilliant members of the Massachusetts bar. He was associated with George D. Robinson in the famous Lizzie Borden murder trial in 1893.

The title of "colonel" came from an appointment on the staff of Gov. Brackett in 1891. Col. Adams was easily the most prominent Dartmouth man in Boston and had contributed liberally to the college. He was one of the founders of the Dartmouth Club of Boston and had always been a leading spirit at all Dartmouth reunions. He had long been a trustee of Dartmouth College. In 1912 Dartmouth gave him the honorary degree of LL.D.

Made Success of Narrow Gage

In 1891 Mr. Adams became president of the Boston, Revere Beach & Lynn Railroad, a property which fills a unique place in Boston's transportation system and which he developed into a very successful road.

But Mr. Adams made the railroad fulfill some other interests. One of his greatest joys was to give employment during the Summer vacation days, when traffic on that road is at its height, to college students working their way through school, and he was especially pleased when he was able to place Dartmouth students.

He also showed warm affection for interests near his heart by naming the ferryboats of the railroad for his native town, Ashburnham, for his alma mater, Dartmouth, and for his island Summer home in Boston Harbor, Brewster.

Many Other Activities

Besides his college interest, Mr. Adams found time for many other activities. For many years he had served as president of the board of trustees of Cushing Academy at Ashburnham. He made numerous gifts to the academy, while to the town he presented a schoolhouse and a park, the latter in memory of his mother.

He was one of the older members of the board of managers of the Farm and Trades School on Thompsons Island and was never weary of recommending the school to his clients when helping to draw their wills.

He was a member of the Union League Club of New York, and of the Union, Unitarian, University, Exchange and Boston Yacht Clubs in this city. On Jan. 20, 1874, he was married to Miss Mary Colony, daughter of George C. and Harriet M. Colony of Fitchburg, who survives him, together with a son, Karl Adams, assistant corporation counsel of Boston.

Sources:

Boston Daily Globe 10 August 1920.

Brown, Arnold R. *Lizzie Borden: The Legend, the Truth, the Final Chapter*. NY: Dell, 1991.

Democrat & Chronicle (Rochester, NY) 21 June 1893.

Lincoln, Victoria. *A Private Disgrace: Lizzie Borden by Daylight*. NY: International Polygonics, Ltd., 1967.

Martins, Michael and Dennis Binette, eds. *The Commonwealth of Massachusetts vs. Lizzie A. Borden, The Knowlton Papers*. Fall River, MA: The Fall River Historical Society, 1994.

New Bedford Evening Standard 27 August 1892.

New Bedford Evening Standard 1 September 1892.

Rebello, Leonard. *Lizzie Borden, Past & Present*. Fall River, MA: Al-Zach Press, 1999.

Snow, Edward Rowe. *Boston Bay Mysteries*. NY: Dodd, Mead & Company, 1977.

Sullivan, Robert. *Goodbye Lizzie Borden*. Brattleboro, VT: Stephen Greene Press, 1974.

Above: Adams' birthplace, Ashburnham, Massachusetts.
Below: Grave stone of Melvin O. Adams.
Photographs courtesy of Joseph F. vonDeck of Ashburnham, Massachusetts.

Joe Howard and Mayor Coughlin, *Boston Globe*, June 12, 1893

John William Coughlin

June 9, 1861 – December 3, 1920

John Coughlin was born in Fall River. He was the son of William and Abbie (Maley) Coughlin. He studied law for a year in the office of Coffee & Dubuque. Working for the Providence Steam and Gas Pipe Company, he traveled a great deal while in their employ and became interested in workers' rights. Eighteen months later found him working in the drug store of Dr. John Chagnon, where an interest in medicine was sparked. He was, for a time, conductor on a trolley car. In the office of Dr. C. C. Terry he studied medicine. Coughlin then attended the College of Physicians and Surgeons in Baltimore, Maryland, in 1883, where he graduated at the top of his class. For this he was given the Cathel prize, a gold medal, and was the first northern man to win it. In 1885 he came back to Fall River to practice medicine. He belonged to the Fall River and Massachusetts Medical Societies and the Ancient Order of Foresters.

Though he did not prevail in earlier mayoral elections, he was voted into office for four one year terms, from 1891-1894. He was thirty-two, the same age as Lizzie Borden, when the murders took place.

Mayor Coughlin and Marshal Hilliard visited the Borden girls at their Second Street home on the evening of the funerals at about 7:45 p.m. on Saturday, August 6, 1892. They told them that those in the house should not go outside due to the crowds possibly becoming violent. Lizzie asked if someone in the house was suspected. Mayor Coughlin informed her, "Well, Miss Borden, I regret to answer, but I must answer – yes, you are suspected."

By telling Lizzie she was a suspect at this early date ended up becoming a victory for Lizzie's defense. George Robinson argued successfully at the trial that her inquest testimony, given without legal representation, should be excluded under those circumstances, and the court agreed. Should the court have heard her many conflicting statements in that testimony, she may not have won her acquittal.

Coughlin testified at the trial and was paid by Bristol County $80 (or $10 per day) for expenses.

During WWI he served on the Frothingham Committee that looked after the soldiers of Fall River. Mr. Coughlin remained politically active for the rest of his life.

Doctor Coughlin's office was also his home at 121 North Main Street, which was later renumbered to 399. He had many contacts as well as ties to the White House. During a visit to Fall River, Woodrow Wilson stayed at his home.

John Coughlin never married. He died at the age of 60 and was survived by his mother.

President Wilson sent a telegram to Mrs. Coughlin upon the Doctor's death: "Dr. Coughlin was a true and valued friend of mine, and I always believed, a most serviceable public servant. We shall miss him."

He is buried at Oak Grove Cemetery in Fall River. On his grave monument, there is carved: "The Day Breaketh The Shadows Disappear."

Sources:

Caplain, Neilson. "Lizbits." *The Lizzie Borden Quarterly* VI.3 (July 1999).

Hoffman, Paul Dennis. *Yesterday in Old Fall River*. Durham, NC: Carolina Academic Press, 2000.

Martins, Michael and Dennis Binette, eds. *The Commonwealth of Massachusetts vs. Lizzie A. Borden, The Knowlton Papers*. Fall River, MA: The Fall River Historical Society, 1994.

Rebello, Leonard. *Lizzie Borden, Past & Present*. Fall River, MA: Al-Zach Press, 1999.

Siliva, Philip T. Jr. *Victorian Vistas: Fall River, 1886-1900*. Fall River, MA: R.E. Smith Printing Co., 1988.

John W. Coughlin grave at Oak Grove Cemetery, Fall River, Massachusetts.

George Ferguson

January 3, 1852 – July 9, 1912

George Ferguson was a policeman in Fall River at the time of the Borden murders. He was assigned to watch the Borden house on August 4, 1892.

Ferguson was standing on the steps of the front entry at the time Joseph Hyde observed Lizzie Borden and Alice Russell making their visit to the cellar on the night of the murders.

During the funeral of Andrew and Abby Borden, which was held at their home at 92 Second Street, he helped keep the crowds back. It was estimated that some 2,500 people were gathered near the Borden house that morning.

George Ferguson was born in 1854 in Ireland. He was the son of William and Eliza Arbuckle Ferguson. He enlisted in the Fourth U.S. Cavalry, Company M, on November 24, 1871, for five years. He was discharged from service at Camp Robinson, Nebraska.

Ferguson was a member of the regular army for three years and worked in the mills until he was appointed policeman in Fall River on April 7, 1884. He started actual duty on April 10, 1884. He was suspended on September 8, 1886, for fifteen days without pay by order of Mayor William Green for blowing peas at the Salvation Army. Ferguson was appointed driver of the night patrol wagon on March 29, 1896. On February 10, 1902, he was appointed day patrolman. His badge number was #10; revolver #47, Smith & Wesson.

Ferguson lived at 1237 Globe Street in Fall River. He died on July 9, 1912, from pernicious anemia (Bright's disease).

George Ferguson is buried at Oak Grove Cemetery in Fall River.

Sources:

Hoffman, Paul Dennis. *Yesterday in Old Fall River*. Durham, NC: Carolina Academic Press, 2000.

Rebello, Leonard. *Lizzie Borden, Past & Present*. Fall River, MA: Al-Zach Press, 1999.

Widdows, Harry, Stefani Koorey, Kat Koorey, eds. *The Trial of Lizzie Andrew Borden*, Book Two. Orlando, FL: PearTree Press, 2005.

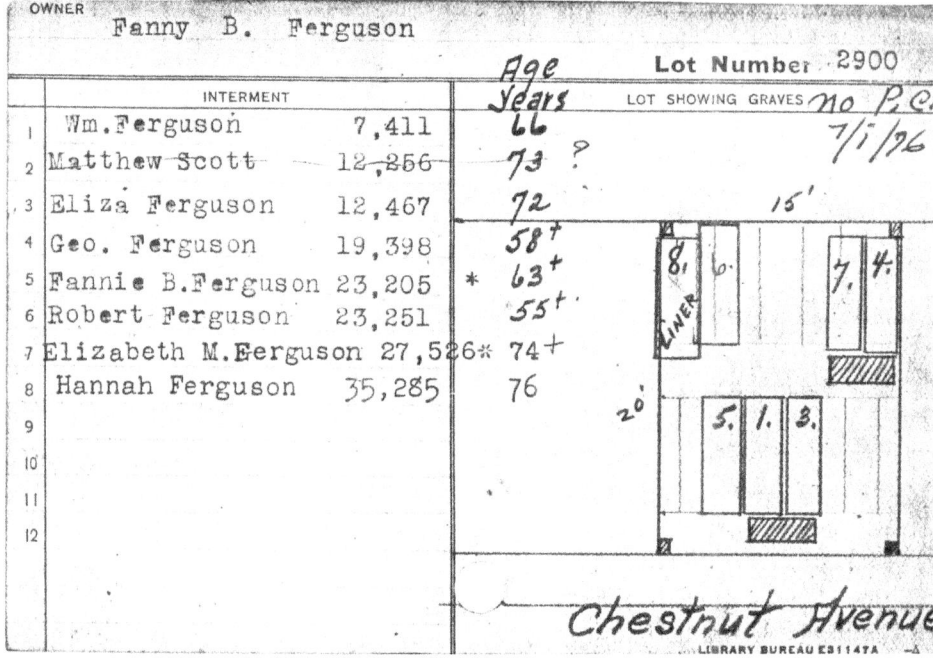

Above: Burial card rear view.
Below: Rear view of Ferguson grave stone.

George Ferguson grave at Oak Grove Cemetery, Fall River, Massachusetts.

ASSISTANT MARSHAL FLEET.

John Fleet

March 29, 1848 – May 10, 1916

Born in Lancashire, England, John Fleet was the son of Richard and Charlotte (Brown) Fleet. He came to America as a youth and worked at the American Linen Company in Fall River, Massachusetts. In 1864, he enlisted in the U.S. Navy as a landsman and served seventeen months. He returned to Fall River after the Civil War and worked for the Fall River Boiler Company. He was a house decorator and painter for a time as well. In 1877, he was appointed to the police department starting as a patrolman. In 1883, he became a sergeant. In 1886, he was assistant city marshal and held this position at the time of the Borden murders.

Fleet caused quite a stir during the trial of Lizzie Borden. He is said to be the only witness to engage defense lead counsel George Robinson in combat. Mr. Fleet was protective of Fall River's police force, and it seems his memory did not often favor the defendant. Mr. Robinson's skillful questioning revealed Fleet as a hostile witness.

On the fifth day of the trial, Officer Michael Mullaly testified that Fleet had taken out the broken handle of the suspected murder weapon, the 'handleless hatchet,' from a box. Mullaly saw him also put the handle back in the box.

Fleet had previously testified that there was no handle at all in the box—just the head.

Fleet was immediately recalled to the stand, with Governor Robinson ordering Mullaly to stay just where he was until Fleet was found. Unaware of Mullaly's testimony, Fleet took the stand again with Robinson asking the questions.

> A: I found a hatchet head, the handle broken off, together with some other tools in there and the iron that was inside there. I don't know just what it was.
> Q: You did not find the handle, the broken piece, not at all?
> A: No sir.
> Q: You did not see it, did you?
> A: No sir.

Spectators stirred and jurors exchanged looks as they heard John Fleet lie under oath.

This testimony was extremely important because to the defense, if there was not a handle to the hatchet the head alone could not be considered a lethal weapon for a woman of little strength. The police wanted to have it believed that the handle had been broken off and disposed of—perhaps stained with blood that could not be washed off. The piece of the handle nearest the striking of the victims' blows would have staining on it. So no, Mr.

Robinson, I never saw any handle at all.

Confusion was caused by further testimonies of Medley and Captain Dennis Desmond when they were each asked what happened to the hatchet head. Both men separately testified that they were the one that wrapped the hatchet head in paper to go to Marshal Hilliard. Both men separately demonstrated how they each wrapped the head in paper, at the request of George Robinson—and Robinson furnished the paper.

Robinson's point—that the police can and do make mistakes, whether unintentionally or not so—was well taken by the uncertain jurors.

After serving as city marshal in 1909, John Fleet retired from the police force in 1915. At 12:10 a.m. on the morning of May 10, 1916, Mr. Fleet died suddenly in his home of heart failure.

Fleet was married to Lydia Wallace of Fall River (October 31, 1850 – March 25, 1926) and was survived by her and their five children.

LAST RITES FOR MARSHAL FLEET

LARGELY ATTENDED FUNERAL SERVICES OF FORMER HEAD OF POLICE FORCE

The funeral of Former Marshal John Fleet of the Fall River police department was held this afternoon from his residence, No. 85 Park street. Services were conducted at the home at 1:30 by Rev. Albert B. Parker, rector of St. John's Episcopal church, for immediate relatives of the family and friends. The body was then taken to St. John's church, of which deceased was a member for many years, and Rev. Mr. Parker conducted services according to the Episcopal rites. The church was crowded with relatives, friends, associates and representative citizens from all walks of life. Marshal Medley, Deputy Chief Feeney, Captain Frederick Barker, Captain John Carr, Captain Patrick Connors and Captain Dennis Desmond, and a number of other members of the police department were present. The services were simple and impressive. The musical program was rendered by a quartet, comprising: Mr. and Mrs. Melville W. Fisher, Mrs. Martha Farwell McCann and Henry H. Fish. The selections rendered were "Lead, Kindly Light," "Nearer, My God, To Thee," and "Heart Be Still."

Following the church services, interment took place in Oak Grove cemetery. At the grave, the Grand Army ritual was carried out by the members of Post 46, G.A.R. The bearers were representatives of various fraternal organizations and Fall River Police Association as follows: Lieutenant Hugh Bogan, Fall River Police Association; John S. B. Clarke, Knights of Pythias, Charles Clarke, Mount Hope Lodge of Masons, Charles Blackway, Mount Hope Lodge of Odd Fellows: John Miniken, Post 46, G.A.R. and William Gardney, vestryman of St. John's Episcopal church. There were delegations present from Richard Borden Post 46, G.A.R., Massachusetts Police Association, Mount Hope Lodge of Masons, Mount Hope Lodge of Odd Fellows, Fall River Police Association and Puritan Lodge, Knights of Pythias.

An unusually large number of beautiful floral tributes were placed upon the casket, which was draped with an American flag. Among the set pieces were wreaths marked: "Grandpa," "Brothers and Sisters," "Father," "Husband," a Masonic emblem from Mount Hope Lodge of Masons; a pillow, Mount Hope Lodge of Odd Fellows; a wreath from the Woman's Relief Corps: gladiolas from the vestrymen of St. John's Episcopal Church; a set piece, "Comrade," from John Miniken. Mr. Miniken and the late Mr. Fleet both enlisted in the same regiment in the Civil War on the same day; a star from the N.E.O.P. No. 99; "Brother," from the Puritan Lodge, Knights of Pythias. The tribute from the Massachusetts Police Association was a huge replica of a police badge and was of lilies, roses and galyx leaves. The Fall River Police Association sent three handsome floral tributes, one a wreath on a pedestal; another a huge floral arch; and the third, a basket of snap dragons. The room in which the casket lay was filled with hundreds of tributes from personal friends of the former marshal.

Sources:

Fall River Evening News 10 May 1916.

Fall River Evening News 13 May 1916.

Kent, David. *Forty Whacks*. Emmaus, PA: Yankee Books, 1992.

Martins, Michael and Dennis Binette, eds. *The Commonwealth of Massachusetts vs. Lizzie A. Borden, The Knowlton Papers*. Fall River, MA: The Fall River Historical Society, 1994.

Rebello, Leonard. *Lizzie Borden, Past & Present*. Fall River, MA: Al-Zach Press, 1999.

John Fleet grave at Oak Grove Cemetery, Fall River, Massachusetts.

Philip Harrington, from Edwin Porter, *Fall River Tragedy*, 1893.

Philip Harrington

April 17, 1859 – October 28, 1893

Philip Harrington was a native of Fall River. His mother was Mary (McCue) Harrington and his father James P., who owned a grocery store. He attended St. Lawrence College in Canton, New York, for two years and had to drop out and go to work due to financial problems with his father's store. He held a variety of jobs: a Western Union messenger boy, clerk/salesman, painting and wallpapering, and for three years was an apprentice cabinet maker at Borden & Almy.

He was appointed to the Fall River police force in 1883. In February of 1893, Mr. Harrington was made captain.

Harrington testified at Lizzie Borden's preliminary hearing and at her trial. Though he was present at the inquest, he did not testify.

At the time of the Borden murders, he had been with the police force for ten years. Though he had known Andrew Borden for twenty to twenty-five years, when he arrived in the Borden sitting room and pulled the sheet back to see him, he could not recognize him. At the trial, he said of it:

> Q: Did you notice anything with reference to the condition of that blood? If you did tell us.
> A: Yes, sir. There was some of it very dark as though it was from the veins, and there was more of it very bright, of an artery hue.
> Q: At that time can you tell us anything with reference to its thickness; did you observe anything?
> A: Yes, sir; it was quite fresh, and as I stood there, or just as I got there and took this sheet, there was a small drop trickled down the side of the face.

Harrington also testified of Dr. Bowen having some scraps of paper in his hand and, when asked what they were, Bowen said, "Oh, I guess it is nothing." The doctor was putting the pieces together to try to see what it was and on the upper left hand corner Harrington spotted the word "Emma," written in pencil just like the rest of the pieces were.

Asked by Harrington again what was on it, Bowen said, "Oh, I think it is nothing. It is something, I think, about my daughter going through somewhere." And Dr. Bowen proceeded to take the lid from the kitchen stove and throw the pieces of paper in.

As he did so, Harrington saw that there was paper, about twelve inches long and two inches around, that was already burned enough to be useless in retracting.

Mr. Harrington, at the trial, described Andrew Borden's shoe as a high laced shoe. Even when presented with the photo by the defense, which clearly showed the dead man wore

Congress boots, Harrington stuck to his testimony: "My impression was laced boots."

He gave a very detailed description of the wrapper Lizzie had worn the afternoon of the murders:

> It was a house wrap, a striped house wrap, with a pink and light stripe alternating; the pink the most prominent color. On the light ground stripe was a diamond figure formed by narrow stripes, some of which ran diagonally or bias to the stripe and others parallel with it. ... the sides were tailor fitting, or fitted to the form. The front from the waist to the neck was loose and in folds. The collar was standing, plaited on the sides and closely shirred in front. On either side, directly over the hips, was caught a narrow bright red ribbon, perhaps three-fourths of an inch or an inch in width. This was brought around front, tied in a bow, and allowed to drop, with the ends hanging a little below the bow. It was cut in semi-train or bell skirt, which the ladies were wearing that season.

Philip Harrington married Miss Kate Connell of Fall River on October 11, 1893. This was his second, and last, marriage.

CAPT. HARRINGTON DEAD
Sad Ending of a Wedding Trip

Captain Philip Harrington died at the residence of Councilman Michael A. McCormick, in Newport, at 9 o'clock this morning. The death did not come unexpectedly, for since the captain was so suddenly taken ill on his wedding day little hope has been held out that he could recover.

The peculiarly sad circumstances attending Captain Harrington's illness and death are already well known, and cannot but demand the sympathy of the entire community. Wednesday morning, Oct. 11, less than three weeks ago, Miss Kate Connell, daughter of Mr. John Connell ticket collector for the Old Colony Steamboat Co., became his wife. The marriage ceremony was performed by Rev. Father Daley, of Woburn, assisted by Rev. Christopher Hughes, at St. Mary's church. The marriage was an event in fashionable Catholic circles, and was largely attended by friends of the couple. Councilman McCormick was one of the ushers, and in the afternoon the bridal couple accompanied him to Newport to his home there. They intended to take the boat for New York that night, but Captain Harrington was not able to leave the house where he went to be a guest with his bride for only a few hours. For some time before his marriage he had not been feeling very well, but he would not give up his duties and rest, and on the day of the wedding he did not appear to be feeling worse than usual. In the afternoon, after he had arrived in Newport, he was stricken with inflammation of the bowels, which was complicated with other troubles. Once during his illness he showed slight signs of recovery, but these were followed by a relapse which resulted in his death this morning. Mrs. Harrington attended her husband constantly until she became prostrated from exhaustion and grief. She is still prostrated at Newport.

Captain Harrington was 34 years of age in April last. He was born in this city and was appointed to the police force on March 2d, 1883, going on duty March 5th. As an officer he was well liked by his associates and by the people with whom he had dealings. On the 10th of February this year he was appointed as a police captain and shortly afterwards went on duty at the central station, first as a night officer, and afterwards as a day officer. He was captain of the central station at the time of his marriage.

His marriage with Miss Connell was his second marriage, he having been married once before since his appointment to the police force. He leaves besides his young widow, a sister, with whom he formerly made his home, and a brother, Charles, who is now traveling somewhere in Europe. His parents have been dead for a number of years, and a brother died not very long ago.

Captain Harrington's death is the fourth in the department since the first of January. The others were Steward Elisha Martin, Officer John Minnehan and Officer Patrick J. Kohoe. Captain Philip McMahon, who was succeeded by Captain Harrington, died two years ago this month.

The body is to be brought to this city this afternoon and the funeral will take place on Tuesday from the residence of Mr. Connell, on Whipple Street.

CAPT. PHIL. HARRINGTON
Funeral Service and Interment at St. John's Cemetery

The funeral of Capt. Philip Harrington, this morning, was very largely attended. The whole of the police force except the [___] required for duty turned out before 9 o'clock and marched to Mr. John Connell's residence, 25 Whipple street. There were 76 men in line. Assistant Brocklehurst, Milton, Devine and Fahey. Inspectors Feeney, Medley, Wordell and Mahoney attended the service at St. Mary's church. Capt. Doherty was one of the honorary bearers; Capt. Desmond, who has taken Capt. Harrington's place at the central station, attended the services at the church; Inspector Perron was one of the active bearers, Lieut. Edson was another. Lieut. Hinckley is ill, and has been confined to his home for several months. The remains were escorted from the house to the church by the department, and the chief mourners were driven to the church, there being no services at the house.

A solemn high mass of requiem was celebrated at St. Mary's church. Father Daley, of Waltham, who four short weeks ago united Captain Harrington and his bride in marriage, was the celebrant. He was a classmate of the captain years ago in college. Father O'Keefe was deacon; Father Sheedy, sub-deacon; Father Cornelius Kelly, of Woonsocket, master of ceremonies. Father Hughes delivered the sermon and with him inside the channel rail, besides those officiating, were Fathers McCabe, Quirk, of Taunton, Cooke, Hanley and Flynn. The altar was draped. Seats at the right of the center aisle were reserved for members of the department. The ushers sat in the first two rows at the right and left of the aisle. On the right, on epistle side, back of the ushers, sat the family. On the left, or gospel side, behind the bearers, sat Mayor Coughlin, Marshal Hilliard and Judge John J. McDonough and Clerk Augustus B. Leonard, of the district court. The church was filled, and there must have been over 8,000 people inside, while another thousand waited in the street.

As the cortege entered the church just before 10 o'clock, Organist Brodkorb played Handel's "Dead March" from "Saul". The Gregorian requiem mass was sung by the choir, and at the close of the services the organist played Beethoven's "Dead March." During the service a quartet consisting of Miss Mary Murphy, Mrs. P. J. Lunney, Mr. Peter McManns and Officer John J. Desmond, sang, "Rest, Spirit, Rest."

In his sermon Father Hughes said this world was not the house of happiness. It was the place of trials, temptations, troubles and vexations. Happiness was not in riches, pleasures or honors. Solomon had found the world a vanity of vanities. No one could be happy who was not a friend of God. The uncertainty of life was emphasized. Death did not come alone to old men and women, but to the young. It came like a thief in the night when least expected. He was a good man whose remains were lying before them. He was ready for a higher life. When death came it found him standing ready with his light burning. He was a man full of faith. Under the brass buttons of his uniform beat a heart filled with the most true sentiments, a heart unsullied by any improper motive. Those who knew him could hardly suspect the noble character of the man. He made no display of his sentiments, but they were there just the same. He performed his duty to the church, and as far as possible set a good example to the men about him.

He was sorry to say that there were many men in the city not like Phil Harrington. An important lesson was taught by the service to-day. If they wanted to die such a death as Captain Harrington died, they must live such a life as he lived. He taught a lesson by his life, and he taught a lesson by his death. In closing, Father Hughes called for the prayers of the many friends of the deceased present, for the soul of Philip Harrington.

After the close of the services, the casket was opened and the people present filed by to secure a last look at the familiar face. The officers present passed first by the casket.

The official bearers were Lieut. F.E. Edson, Inspector A. Perron, Officers John Linnehan, M. Reagan, 2d, B. Welch and Mark Shay.

The honorary bearers were Mr. James D. O'Neil, city editor of the Globe, Councilman M. F. McCormick, of Newport; Mr. M. H. Connelly, Mr. John E. Sullivan, Ald. C. C. Murphy, Capt. P. H. Doherty.

The ushers were James T. Cummings, Esq., Mr. Michael McManus, Mr. John Desmond and Mr. Martin F. W. French.

The floral offerings were very rich and beautiful. They were taken to John's cemetery (sic), where the interment took place, in the patrol wagon and a two-horse dray in which Inspectors Medley and Wordell road (sic). The department gave a magnificent (sic) piece in the form of "gates ajar," composed of roses and chrysanthemums. A white dove hovered over the gates and another was perched on the steps. On the arch appeared the name by which the popular officer has been best known since his promotion, "Capt. Phil."

An anchor also came from the department. A beautiful pillow bore the simple word "Husband," the more touching that the title had been given to be borne so very short a time, and then only in sickness ending in death. Mayor Coughlin sent a wreath and sickle. A large closed book was prominent, and there were a dozen more pieces and bouquets.
There were 60 carriages in line in the march to the cemetery.

During the time since Saturday that the remains have been lying at Mr. Connell's house between 5,000 and 6,000 persons have called to view them.

Philip Harrington is buried at St. John's Cemetery in Fall River. He is buried in Plat 3, Row 10, Grave 20, "new lot." Though numerous attempts were made personally to find his grave, I can only conclude that his headstone is not there. The cemetery is located on the corner of Valentine and St. Mary's Street. It is maintained by the Roman Catholic Diocese of Fall River.

Sources:

Fall River Evening News 28 October 1893.

Fall River Evening News 31 October 1893.

Furtado, Mrs., office clerk of Catholic Cemeteries, Fall River, MA. Personal correspondence, 24 July 2003.

Martins, Michael and Dennis Binette, eds. *The Commonwealth of Massachusetts vs. Lizzie A. Borden, The Knowlton Papers*. Fall River, MA: The Fall River Historical Society, 1994.

Rebello, Leonard. *Lizzie Borden, Past & Present*. Fall River, MA: Al-Zach Press, 1999.

Widdows, Harry, Stefani Koorey, Kat Koorey, eds. *The Preliminary Hearing in the Lizzie Borden Case, New Edition*. Orlando, FL: PearTree Press, 2005.

Widdows, Harry, Stefani Koorey, Kat Koorey, eds. *The Trial of Lizzie Andrew Borden*, Book Two. Orlando, FL: PearTree Press, 2005.

Officer Harrington, *Boston Globe*, August 31, 1892

Sherry Chapman

Marshal Rufus Bartlett Hilliard

May 5, 1850 – December 30, 1912

At 11:15 a.m. on Thursday, August 4, 1892, Marshal Rufus Hilliard received a telephone call from reporter John Cunningham. He said that there was "trouble at the Borden house," and Hilliard sent Officer George A. Allen to investigate.

Marshal Hilliard was today's equivalent of Chief of Police. He and Mayor John Coughlin told Lizzie Borden that she was suspected of the murders of her father and stepmother.

Hilliard testified at the Grand Jury hearing about the daylight robbery in the Borden house the previous summer. While Andrew and Abby were in Swansea at the farm, several of Abby Borden's possessions—and none of Andrew's—were taken, among them tickets for free horse car rides. When people started using the tickets who were not entitled to them, the police asked them where they procured them. They said that Lizzie Borden had given them away. Lizzie had not owned any of these before the daylight robbery. Hilliard spoke to Andrew Borden about the matter. It appears that both were convinced that Lizzie was the thief and Andrew decided to stop the investigation of the crime.

Mr. Hilliard was 62 years old at the time of his death in 1912. The following obituary from the Monday, December 30, 1912, edition of the *Fall River Evening News* gives a good rendition of not only his early life, but his life after the Borden murders as well:

DEATH COMES AFTER A LONG ILLNESS

FORMER CITY MARSHAL RUFUS B. HILLIARD PASSES AWAY AT HIS HOME

Was Connected with the Police Force For 20 Years, for Nearly a Quarter Of a Century at its Head—Handled Notable Murder Cases

Former City Marshal Rufus Bartlett Hilliard passed away at his home, 101 Hanover Street, at about 5:30 o'clock this morning, following an illness which necessitated his retirement from the Fall River police force on June 15, 1909, and which had kept him confined to his home for the greater part of the year prior to his retirement. His death was not unexpected to members of his family, who were warned that his condition was critical about a week ago. He had been particularly low at different times during his illness, and only his magnificent constitution enabled him to combat his fatal illness for so long a time. His death will be sincerely mourned, not only by the immediate members of his family, but by an extremely wide circle of friends, many of whom he had befriended in times of need.

Regrets at his death were publicly expressed by Judge Edward F. Hanify in the second district court at the opening of this morning's court session, when Assistant Marshall William H. Medley made the announcement of the former marshal's demise, in behalf of the Fall River Police department. Marshal Medley's announcement was as follows:

"Upon behalf of the police department of Fall River I regret to announce the death of Former City Marshal Rufus B. Hilliard, who was so long prosecuting officer of this court."

It was then that Judge Hanify tendered the following tribute to Marshal Hilliard, with everyone in the court room standing with bowed heads.

"We all regret to learn of the death of Rufus B. Hilliard, who so long and faithfully served the police department of the city of Fall River. It was always been said of him that he would do a kind act whenever in his power, and I believe that when he goes before his Maker he will receive the benediction, well done, good and faithful servant."

It was on June 15, 1909, after having served the city of Fall River as a police officer most faithfully and continuously since May 15, 1879, and for 23 years of that period as head of the police department, that Marshal Hilliard was retired upon half pay. He had been ill for the greater part of the 14 months prior to the date of his retirement, and he had suffered many attacks of illness prior to that, due primarily to an injury sustained while upon police duty, and it was because of that that he was accorded a pension of half pay, amounting to $950 yearly.

He was appointed a night patrolman on May 15, 1879, and commenced duty on May 21. In 1880 he was transferred to day duty, but was allowed to resume night duty at his own request the following year. On February 2, 1882, he was appointed sergeant of the eastern police station, and in the month of March of the following year he was advanced to the position of assistant city marshal. He was appointed city marshal to succeed Marshal Josiah A. Hunt on March 29, 1886.

Taking charge of the police department when the population of the city was less than 40,000 and the police force comprised less than 50 men, he saw both grow rapidly until, at the time of his retirement, he had nearly 150 men under his command, and the city had become the third largest in the commonwealth. During those years he had the privilege of having some of the most intricate problems to handle in the way of murders, strikes, no-license years, and nearly every sort of crime, and though there was occasional criticism, never once was there a concerted movement to remove him from office. He probably became best known because of his connection with the investigation of the Borden murders in 1892. It was in the following year that he was instrumental in bringing to justice the murderer of Bertha Manchester. He was again very much in evidence during the big strike of 1904, and showed the valuable experience obtained during the labor troubles of 1879, when he first joined the force.

Of large physique, powerful in muscle and quick in action, Mr. Hilliard also was cool under the most trying circumstances and showed good judgement, and it was those points that figured in his rapid advance from patrolman to marshal, and served him in good stead in dealing with hundreds of cases of a diversified nature. He was once complimented by a judge of the superior court as being the best posted city marshal in the state, and another time when complimented on his manner of prosecuting cases in the superior court, he showed one of his noticeable characteristics by giving all the credit to one of his assistants in his office. It was he who established a law library at police headquarters, which has been found of valuable assistance to the entire force.

Sociably Marshal Hilliard was a man who, once met, would never be forgotten, and because of that pleasing, kindly disposition, he was a man whose company was highly prized. He enjoyed fraternal life and was a member of numerous fraternal organizations during his earlier life and retained membership in several of the orders at the time of his death.

Marshal Hilliard was the youngest of the 10 children of David and Elizabeth (Wilson) Hilliard and was born at Pembroke, Maine, on May 5, 1849.* At the death of his mother, when he was but two years of age, he was taken to the home of his grandparents in Pennsylvania. When still a small boy his grandparents died, and he was taken to the home of one of his sisters in Newburyport, and later lived with another relative in Newcastle, N.H. It was when living in Newcastle, and but 15 years of age, that he enlisted in the regular army, in 1865, passing the recruiting officers because of being unusually large for his age. At the expiration of his term or enlistment he went to live with one of his sisters in Lowell, where he took up mechanical engineering, and became so proficient under the Harleys that soon after the latter came to this city they secured him the position of engineer at the local Print Works. That was on September 17, 1874, and he held that position until he joined the police department in 1879.

Marshal Hilliard was married in June, 1888, to Miss Nellie S. Clark, daughter of Mrs. Helen J. Clark, who survives him, together with a son, Dana S. Hilliard. The latter is a graduate of the B.M.C. Durfee high school and is now learning the mill business at the Chace mills.

The deceased was a 32d degree Mason, a member of the Narragansett Lodge of Masons, Metacomet Encampment and Mount Hope lodges of Odd Fellows, of Star Lodge, K. of P., and of the Army and Navy Veterans club of Boston. He was also a past grand chancellor of the Knights of Pythias in Massachusetts.

The funeral services will be held on Thursday afternoon [January 2, 1913].

*Although the obituary above gives the year of Hilliard's birth as 1849, his tombstone reads 1850. In addition, Leonard Rebello's *Lizzie Borden Past & Present* states, "The latter [1850] is correct, as it agrees with Marshal Hilliard's age at the time of his death, 62 years, 7 months and 25 days."

Sources:

Hoffman, Paul Dennis. *Yesterday in Old Fall River*. Durham, NC: Carolina Academic Press, 2000.

Martins, Michael and Dennis Binette, eds. *The Commonwealth of Massachusetts vs. Lizzie A. Borden, The Knowlton Papers*. Fall River, MA: The Fall River Historical Society, 1994.

Rebello, Leonard. *Lizzie Borden, Past & Present*. Fall River, MA: Al-Zach Press, 1999.

Rufus Hilliard grave at Oak Grove Cemetery, Fall River, Massachusetts.

Rufus Hilliard

Josiah Hunt, *Boston Globe*, June 4, 1893

Josiah Hunt

1845 – October 25, 1898

Josiah Hunt was the jail keeper (or 'keeper') of the jail and Bristol County House of Correction in New Bedford during the Lizzie Borden trial. After the murders, Bridget Sullivan stayed with her cousin, Patrick Harrington, at 95 Division Street, then worked for the Hunts as a general housekeeper at their home on Court Street in New Bedford. She was still working there during the trial.

Prior to his position as keeper, Mr. Hunt was city marshal of Fall River. In 1886, his successor as city marshal of Fall River was Rufus B. Hilliard.

Born in Fall River in 1845, his parents were Zebadee and Lydia H. (Young) of Fall River. Josiah Hunt married Julia (Reynolds) Hunt, also of Fall River. They had five children.

Josiah Hunt started his police career in 1875, when he was appointed to the police force as a patrolman. That March, he went on the night watch. In 1876, he was put on the day force. He was made captain in 1879, assistant marshal in 1881, and marshal in 1882. He was appointed as keeper of the jail and master of the House of Correction in New Bedford, Massachusetts, by Sheriff Andrew R. Wright of New Bedford, beginning those duties on April 1, 1886.

On August 8, 1892, the *Fall River Herald* printed Josiah Hunt's opinion of the Borden murders:

DEAD BEFORE THE BUTCHERY

A New Bedford Man's Theory of the Small Flow of Blood

Josiah A. Hunt, keeper of the house of correction, who has had an extensive experience as an officer of the law in this city, in speaking of the tragedy advanced a theory which has thus far escaped the notice of the police, or, if it has not, they are putting the public on the wrong scent.

Said Mr. Hunt: 'It is my opinion that both Mr. Borden and his wife were dead before the murderers struck a blow, probably poisoned by the use of prussic acid, which would cause instant death. The use of a hatchet was simply to mislead those finding the bodies. I believe this to be the real state of the case, for if they had been alive when the first blow was struck, the action of the heart would have been sufficient to have caused the blood to spatter more freely than is shown from the accounts furnished by the papers. There was altogether too much of a butchery for so little spattering of blood.'

On October 26, 1898 on page 7 the *Fall River Daily Herald* ran this story, much to the surprise of its readers:

Master of House of Correction Stricken with Apoplexy

Josiah A. Hunt, keeper of the jail and master of the House of Correction in New Bedford, died very suddenly of apoplexy at his home on Court Street in that city about 10 o'clock last night.

Mr. Hunt has been in his usual robust health up to yesterday morning, when, upon rising, he complained of being unwell. During the day he was forced to take to his bed, although feeling at the time that he was troubled with nothing more than a slight indisposition, and consequently no alarm was felt. About 10 o'clock in the evening he was seized with the attack which resulted fatally, the cause of death being assigned as apoplexy.

Mr. Hunt was born in Fall River 53 years ago. He served this city for 11 years on the police force, receiving his appointment in 1875, and in March of that year first went on duty on the night watch. On June 6, 1876, he was transferred to the day force, and in 1878 was appointed sergeant. In 1879 he was appointed captain, in 1881 elected assistant marshal, and in 1882 marshal, his steady and rapid advancement being due to merit. While he was city marshal of Fall River he had charge of a number of important cases, which he handled with skill and discretion.

In 1886 Marshal Hunt was appointed by Sheriff Wright as keeper of the jail and master of the house of correction in New Bedford, in succession to the late Charles D. Burt, and assumed the duties of his office on April 1 of that year, his successor in Fall River being Rufus B. Hilliard, the present city marshal. Mr. Hunt gave excellent satisfaction in his new position, and upon the selection of Sheriff Evans three years ago was retained in office.

Mr. Hunt was a splendid disciplinarian, and had a good understanding of human nature, and the qualities that made him successful as a police officer stood him in good stead in the position he had filled in New Bedford for the last 12 years. He believed that a prison was a punitive and reformatory institution, and his conduct of the jail and House of Correction was based upon that idea. While never needlessly severe upon the inmates, he met the discharge of his duties in the spirit in which those duties were imposed, and was faithful to every trust. A man of scrupulous honesty, conscientious to the smallest details, and of a most genial temperament, his death is a loss to the public service and an occasion of deep regret among a wide circle of friends who held him in the highest regard.

Mr. Hunt was a veteran of the Civil War. He was prominent in Odd Fellowship and served for a number of years as district deputy grand patriarch of the encampment degree for this district. Mr. Hunt was also active in the Royal Areanum and at the time of his death was ruler of Omega council of New Bedford.

Mr. Hunt leaves a widow and five children. Raymond, a member of Battery E. First Heavy artillery; Herman, a student of the Institute of Technology, and three daughters, Misses Julia A., Lydia and Ivah.

According to the *Fall River Daily News*, October 26, 1898, "Sheriff Evans was notified of Mr. Hunt's death soon after it occurred and he went immediately to the jail and will be in charge until the appointment of Mr. Hunt's successor."

Funeral Services

The funeral of Josiah A. Hunt, late keeper of the jail and House of Correction, was held at the residence on Court Street in New Bedford, Friday afternoon at 1 o'clock. There was a very large attendance, which included, besides relatives, Congressman Greene, the County commissioners and other county and city officials, and members of the various organizations of which the deceased was a member. A special car brought many Fall River friends over. The services were conducted by Rev. J. F. Cooper. The floral designs were profuse. The burial will take place in this city today.

Josiah A. Hunt was buried in Oak Grove Cemetery in Fall River. The Reverend J. F. Cooper conducted the services.

Sources:

Fall River Daily Herald 29 October 1898.

Hoffman, Paul Dennis. *Yesterday in Old Fall River*. Durham, NC: Carolina Academic Press, 2000.

Kent, David. *The Lizzie Borden Sourcebook*. Boston: Branden Publishing Co., 1992.

Martins, Michael and Dennis Binette, eds. *The Commonwealth of Massachusetts vs. Lizzie A. Borden, The Knowlton Papers*. Fall River, MA: The Fall River Historical Society, 1994.

Rebello, Leonard. *Lizzie Borden, Past & Present*. Fall River, MA: Al-Zach Press, 1999.

Widdows, Harry, Stefani Koorey, Kat Koorey, eds. *The Trial of Lizzie Andrew Borden*, Book Two. Orlando, FL: PearTree Press, 2005.

Josiah Hunt grave at Oak Grove Cemetery, Fall River, Massachusetts.

Joseph Hyde, *Boston Globe*, June 13, 1893

Joseph Hyde

1847 – 1937

Joseph Hyde was a police officer guarding the outside of the Borden house on the night of August 4, 1892. At about 8:45 p.m., he saw Lizzie and her friend, Alice Russell, make a trip down to the cellar by lamplight.

Hyde says in the *Witness Statements*:

August 8th 9 o'clock in the morning. I spoke to Miss Russell about her and Miss Lizzie being in the cellar on the night of the 4th. Miss Russell said Miss Lizzie had the toilet pail. Miss Russell said she offered to carry the pail. Miss Lizzie says 'you bring the lamp,' and they went into the cellar. I said to Miss Russell, Miss Lizzie came down into the cellar alone after that time. Miss Russell said that could not be. I said, O, yes, she did; it was about ten or fifteen minutes after you and she went up stairs. Miss Russell said that must have been while I was taking my bath.

During Lizzie's trial, lead defense George Robinson chose to extremely downplay this incident in his closing argument.

I do not care to allude to the visit to the cellar; I do not care to allude to her remarkable coolness of demeanor to the officers that afternoon. She is certainly a remarkable woman. Some people may share with me in that dread of going down below the stairs into the somewhat damp and gloomy recesses of the cellar after dark. I should not want to confess myself timid, but there have been times when I did not like to do it. And all the use I propose to make of that incident is to emphasize from it the almost stoical nerve of a woman, who, when her friend, not the daughter nor the stepdaughter of these murdered people, but her friend, -- could not bear to go into the room where those clothes were, should have the nerve to go down there alone, alone, and calmly enter the room for some purpose that I do not (know) what connection it had with this case.

And on to another subject he went.

According to Joseph Hyde's testimony at the trial, Lizzie spent about two minutes in the cellar alone on that second trip.

Hyde was also a second witness to a suspect spotted on the morning of the murders:

But there was a clew which caused no end of comment, both personal and in the press. Information reached the police that Policeman Joseph Hyde had seen a suspicious-looking stranger in the vicinity of Second street on that morning. On the following Tuesday Dr. B.J. Handy, one of the best physicians in the city, made public the fact that he also saw a very strange appearing man on Second street on the morning of the murder, between twenty-five minutes past ten and a quarter to eleven o'clock.

The doctor took some notice of this man, and in the afternoon while in conversation with his wife, he became more and more impressed with the idea that the stranger had some connection with the awful crime.

This theory became a matter of much importance, and Dr. Handy did not at this time know that Policeman Hyde was reported to have seen a similar person.

Joseph Hyde was born in England. He came to Fall River and worked as a laborer. Then, in 1879, he became a patrolman on the Fall River police force, with which he stayed until 1915. Hyde's wife, Mary E. Burke of Fall River, later became the city's first female lawyer. Joseph Hyde died in Fall River during his 90th year. He is buried in Fall River at Oak Grove Cemetery in the Hyde family plot.

Sources:

Hoffman, Paul Dennis. *Yesterday in Old Fall River*. Durham, NC: Carolina Academic Press, 2000.

"The Borden Mystery: A Strange Story that is Partially Confirmed by an Old Sea Captain." *Portsmouth Herald* (New Hampshire) 16 September 1899.

Rebello, Leonard. *Lizzie Borden, Past & Present*. Fall River, MA: Al-Zach Press, 1999.

Widdows, Harry, Stefani Koorey, Kat Koorey, eds. *The Trial of Lizzie Andrew Borden*, Book Two. Orlando, FL: PearTree Press, 2005.

Witness Statements. Orlando, FL: PearTree Press, 2004.

Joseph Hyde grave at Oak Grove Cemetery, Fall River, Massachusetts.

Andrew Jackson Jennings

Andrew J. Jennings

August 2, 1849 – October 19, 1923

Andrew Jackson Jennings had been the Borden's family lawyer for years prior to 1892. At the time of Lizzie Borden's trial in June of 1893, he was 43 years old, soon to be 44 come August. It was he who made the opening statement, which took twenty-eight minutes. With George D. Robinson as lead attorney, Melvin O. Adams, and Arthur Phillips, this 19th century dream team won Lizzie's acquittal.

In appreciation, the Borden sisters named Jennings to the board of directors of the Globe Yarn Mill, where they owned stock. He remained Lizzie's lawyer until the incident of her accused shoplifting took place in Providence at the Tilden-Thurber store in 1897.

Even though there is no evidence that Lizzie Borden was a kleptomaniac, Mr. Jennings' grandson, Edward Jennings, told the *Brockton Sunday Advertiser* in 1992: "Lizzie was a chronic shoplifter. Several years ago after the trial, she was caught shoplifting in Providence [Rhode Island]. My grandfather got her off, then came home and said, 'I will have nothing to do with that woman.'"

A.J. Jennings, a Fall River native, was elected to the Massachusetts State Legislature in 1878 and served two successive terms. He was elected to the Senate in 1882 and served one term. In 1894, he was elected District Attorney for the Southeastern District of Massachusetts, succeeding Hosea Knowlton, and continued to do so until 1898.

Jennings was involved in many public organizations during his lifetime: Trustee at Brown University; president of the Fall River Bar Association and the YMCA, director of not only Globe Yarn Mills but also of the Stanford Spinning Company, Merchants Manufacturing Company, and Union Savings Bank. He belonged to the prestigious Quequechan Club, was a member of the University Club of Providence, R.I., the Republican Club, and the Second Baptist Church (Baptist Temple). He was affiliated with King Philip Lodge, Free and Accepted Masons, was chairman of the standing committee of the church society, and taught Sunday school. He was also an early member of the Fall River Historical Society.

Andrew Jennings possessed the only known copy of the preliminary hearing transcripts, which we still use today. In 1968, the Waring family, his daughter's married name, donated a collection of fascinating exhibits from the trial of Lizzie Borden. Barbara Ashton, author, relates these items in a chapter of the 100th anniversary conference on the Borden Case published in 1993.

Some of these trial exhibits include: Crime scene photos, the famed 'hoodoo hatchet,' tags from forensic specimens, Abby Borden's false hair, bloody handkerchief, pillow shams, and bedspread from the guest room, three scrapbooks full of newspaper clippings, the preliminary trial minutes, blueprints of the Borden house, hair samples of the victims, and notebooks containing Jennings' notes on the case.

Jennings had been retired some years and was enjoying private life when he suffered a slight stroke at his summer home at Westport Harbor. He had been confined to Truesdale Hospital in Fall River for about ten weeks, when he passed away at 2:30 a.m. on the morning of Saturday, October 19, 1923.

At the time of his death, he was director in the Merchants Manufacturing Company, president and director in the Barnard Manufacturing Co., director in the Crystal Spring Dyeing and Bleaching Co., president and director in the Globe Yarn Mills, and director in the Wampanoag Mills and Metacomet Bank.

One of his last public appearances, if not his last, was as president of the day at the annual Memorial Day exercises on May 30 (1923).

Andrew Jennings was survived by his wife, Marion G. Saunders, and their two children, Oliver S. of Pittsburgh, PA, and Marion Jennings Waring of Fall River.

An obituary in a local newspaper of the time printed the following obituary:

FINAL TRIBUTE PAID ANDREW J. JENNINGS

Professional and Business Men Gather at Funeral of Well-Known Lawyer -
Interment at Oak Grove

Funeral services for Andrew J. Jennings, for years a leading member of the Massachusetts bar, were held at 2 this afternoon, at his late home, 421 June Street, and the high place Mr. Jennings had occupied, not only in his home community but throughout the State, was attested in part by the many members of the bar and judiciary as well as business and professional men who joined with the members of the family in a last tribute to him.

The services were conducted by Rev. J. Wallace Chesbro, pastor of the Baptist Temple, of which Mr. Jennings had long been a member. The interment was in the family lot in Oak Grove cemetery. The active bearers were Oliver Jennings, son; Dwight S. Waring, son-in-law; J. Densmore Brown Jr., and Harvey B. Brown, nephews of Mr. Jennings. The following were the honorary bearers: Isreal Brayton, Judge James M. Morton of the U.S. District court, Joseph D. Milne, Charles B. Cook, William H. Jennings, John W. Cummings, James M. Jackson of Brookline, Dr. Charles Nichols, Worcester. Robert W. Bogle, Velena W. Haughwout; H. E. Dodge, secretary of the Y.M.C.A., George H. Waring, William V. Kellen, Boston, Howard E. Wetherell and Judge Henry K. Braley of Brookline.

At the conclusion of the criminal session of the Second District court this morning, court was adjourned for the remainder of the day in respect to the memory of Attorney Andrew Jennings, whose funeral was held this afternoon.

Sources:

Hoffman, Paul Dennis. *Yesterday in Old Fall River*. Durham, NC: Carolina Academic Press, 2000.

Rebello, Leonard. *Lizzie Borden, Past & Present*. Fall River, MA: Al-Zach Press, 1999.

Ryckebusch, Jules R. ed. *Proceedings: Lizzie Borden Conference, Bristol Community Collete, Fall River, MA, August 3-5, 1992.* Portland, ME: King Philip Publishing Company, 1993.

Above: Unknown newspaper, n.d.
Below: Andrew Jennings later in life.

Above: Jennings home in Fall River.
Below: Andrew Jennings grave at Oak Grove Cemetery, Fall River, Massachusetts.

Andrew Jackson Jennings

Hosea Knowlton, *Boston Globe*, June 5, 1893

Hosea Morrill Knowlton

May 20, 1847 - December 18, 1902

Hosea M. Knowlton was born in Durham, Maine, on May 20, 1847. Both parents came from a long line of clergymen, his father the pastor of the New Bedford Universalist Church from 1866-1871. Hosea Knowlton was very active in that church. He served as treasurer and for twenty-eight years was superintendent of the Sunday school.

Knowlton graduated from Tufts College in 1867 as salutorian of his class. He accomplished so many things in his life, which is to a degree admirable considering he did not come from wealth and he died relatively young.

Holding public office for thirty years continuously, he started as City Solicitor of New Bedford then, in 1872, was register in bankruptcy of the First District of Massachusetts until it was abolished in 1878. He was a member of the School Committee for three years. He served in the Massachusetts House of Representatives in 1876 and 1877. In 1878 and 1879, he was in the State Senate.

In 1879, George Marston resigned as district attorney and Hosea Knowlton succeeded him. He served as such until 1894, when he became Attorney General. According to General William Knowlton (ret.) in the April, 1997 issue of the *Lizzie Borden Quarterly*,

> to quote the words of the memorial prepared by the New Bedford Bar at the time of his death: 'In the Borden trial his work was masterly, and his final argument therein has been pronounced one of the strongest portrayals of facts ever heard in an American court of justice; it made him famous throughout the country, and led to his selection as Attorney General.

Remaining as Attorney General for eight years, he decided to retire into private practice. He formed an office in Boston with assistant Attorney Generals, and a partnership of Knowlton, Hallowell and Hammond, in New Bedford.

Hosea and Sylvia Bassett Almy were married in New Bedford in 1873. They had four sons and three daughters, ranging from the ages of 9 to 27 at the time of his death.

> His last court trial, not long before he was stricken with his fatal illness, he opposed an antagonist of some years before in the Borden case, Andrew J. Jennings of Fall River. This time the tables were reversed, as Mr. Knowlton won for a young woman a $15,000 verdict in a suit for breach of promise of marriage against a city official, both parties being of Fall River, where the case was tried. The loser paid the award.

This was the Kiernan-McDonald case.

The papers followed his illness from almost the moment it occurred. This from the *Boston Daily Globe*, December 7, 1902:

NEW BEDFORD Dec 6—H. M. Knowlton, ex-attorney general of this state, lies tonight critically ill at his Marion home suffering from a stroke of apoplexy.

The whole of his left side is affected, and he has not been able to speak so as to be understood since he fell in his bedroom early this morning.

Mr. Knowlton arose early and saw the sun rise on the water of Marion River just to the east of his pleasant summer home, and made preparations to dress. Mrs. Knowlton had just left the room when she heard a heavy fall and returning found her husband lying beside his bed unconscious.

Dr. A. W. Rice, the local physician, was immediately summoned and did everything in his power for the unfortunate man, and attended him until the arrival of Dr. Charles O. Prescott of New Bedford, the family physician.

Mr. Knowlton remained in a semiconscious condition all day, at times attempting to speak, but being unable to make himself understood. … He went to Marion from Boston last evening, apparently in the best of health and talked with acquaintances about its being his last day in Marion, as the family had made plans to remove to their New Bedford home today.

Being accustomed to ride from the passenger station to his home in the barge that takes train passengers, he got in as usual last evening with the remark to Selectman Andrew, 'Well, Bill, I guess this will be my last ride,' having just told Mr. Andrew that he was going to New Bedford for the winter on Saturday.

Frank Knowlton, a son of the ex-attorney general, stated to a Globe reporter tonight that his father had not been well since early in the fall.

While in New Bedford, trying the Kiernan-McDonald breach of promise case in Fall River, Mr. Knowlton contracted a severe cold which developed into a severe case of grip, and so bad did he become that Dr. Prescott kept him at his new home here for three or four days.

He then went to Marion and remained until he had entirely recovered, as it was supposed, and he has been attending to his duties at his Boston office since then.

Marion people are fond of Mr. Knowlton, and it is a common expression to hear one say, 'Hosea M. Knowlton has a gruff manner, but he's got a great big heart.'

Fell in Late Summer

Some of Mr. Knowlton's acquaintances attribute his recent illness, when it was reported he had kidney trouble, to a fall that he received late in the summer.

Mr. Knowlton was on an electric car, bound to Marion and he spied his wife on an electric, bound in the opposite direction.

Wishing to see her he hailed the other car and not waiting for the car he was on to stop, he jumped off without giving the matter of how fast the car was going sufficient thought, and the result was that he landed on his feet all right, but rolled over and over half a dozen times before he knew what had happened apparently.

Otherwise than receiving a fearful shaking up and some bruises, Mr. Knowlton suffered no apparent ill effect from the accident.

A. E. Perry, a law partner of Mr. Knowlton, in this city, is much concerned about Mr. Knowlton, considering it a serious case.

"Knowlton Still Resting
NEW BEDFORD, Dec. 6, 1902—At 11:30 tonight Dr. Prescott reports that he has just come from the sick chamber and that Mr. Knowlton is still semiconscious and resting quietly."

December 8 headlines from the *Boston Globe*, proclaimed: "Prayers Offered for Hosea M. Knowlton," "Distinguished Patient Rests Easily During Day," "Recognizes Family in Conscious Intervals," and "Robust Physique Gives Hope for Stricken Man."

A physician that saw Knowlton at that time, who was called in by the family doctor, arrived at 2:30 on the afternoon of the 7th. "'There are three courses which the disease may pursue in this case," said Dr. Shattuck to a *Globe* representative after he had left the sick room. "The first is that the patient may recover; the second is that the patient may partially recover the attack of paralysis; the third is that he may not survive the attack. Which course the disease may take, no man can tell.'"

The next day's paper, a "Globe Extra" at 5 o'clock, declared a hopeful: "SLIGHT CHANGE," a possible small positive condition of Knowlton; however there would be no plans to move him from his Marion home to the family winter home in New Bedford "until he shows radical improvement."

The December 10th issue of the *Boston Daily Globe* announced:

HOPE FOR KNOWLTON
His Physician Thinks He Will Recover

That is, if No Inflammatory Action Should Set in

His Temperature and Pulse are Normal

NEW BEDFORD, Dec 9 – The most encouraging report from the bedside of Ex-Atty Gen Knowlton since his attack comes from Dr. Charles D. Prescott, his physician, who tonight made this statement:

'Mr. Knowlton lies in about the same condition. He rouses when spoken to, answers questions intelligently and takes a fair amount of nourishment without trouble. If no inflammatory action sets in I think he will survive this attack. However, he is not out of danger yet.'

Mr. Knowlton has spent a very quiet day, resting easily. His temperature and pulse have regained their normal condition, which is taken as an indication of improvement.

The next day's report was headlined:

KNOWLTON'S CONDITION. Dr. Rice, Who Saw Him at 9 PM, Says He's Doing as Well as Could be Expected.

NEW BEDFORD, Dec. 10 – During the afternoon there was a slight change in the condition of Ex-Atty Gen Knowlton, a rise in temperature occurring.

In the course of a few hours, however, the temperature was reduced to normal condition.

Dr. Rice of Marion, who saw Mr. Knowlton at 9 p.m. said that he was doing as well as could be expected.

The *Boston Daily Globe* of December 12 has him 'Resting Comfortably,' and the same paper's December 14 issue reports Knowlton as 'About the Same.'

But on December 18, the *Boston Daily* ran this story:

SLOWLY FAILING.

End is Near in Case of Hon H. M. Knowlton

Entirely Unconscious at Midnight, His Physician Says.

And at Any Moment He May be Gathered Home.

NEW BEDFORD – Dec 17 – At midnight tonight Dr. Prescott, who is staying at the bedside of Hosea M. Knowlton, said that the patient was slowly failing. Mr. Knowlton is entirely unconscious. The end may come tonight or the time may be prolonged until tomorrow.

Mr. Knowlton's condition recalls a sentiment which he expressed at a hearing which was given on the petition of the New Bedford & Onset street railway company in August, 1900.

The company had petitioned for leave to run through the streets of Marion, and Mr. Knowlton as a summer resident appeared at the hearing. In the course of his address he said: 'I hope that the last sound I hear will be the lapping of the waves on the shore at Marion.'

These words now have a prophetic meaning.

On December 19, the *Boston Daily*'s front page read: "HAD PEACEFUL END. Ex-Atty Gen Hosea M. Knowlton Passes Away. Hosea Knowlton died at 11:03 pm on December 18, 1902. He was 55 years old."

The paper recalled that "his address to the jury in the Borden case is called one of the strongest and most skillful delivered for many years in Massachusetts. ... In his youth he loved music, and about 30 years ago he became the first president of the glee and madrigal society, consisting of a chorus of 60 voices. ... He was the first lawyer in New Bedford to employ a stenographer in his office. He was one of the first to ride a bicycle."

NEW BEDFORD, Dec. 19 – This afternoon the body of Ex-Atty Gen Hosea M. Knowlton was brought from his Marion summer home, where he died, to his residence on Union St. in this city.

The transfer was made on a special electric car of the New Bedford & Onset line, which passes near the Marion home and connects with the Union street railway passing directly by the door of the Knowlton residence.

Knowlton's funeral arrangements were disclosed on Saturday, December 20, in the *Boston Daily Globe*.

All arrangements for the funeral of Ex-Atty Gen Knowlton, which will be held in this city Monday afternoon, have been completed.

The Universalist church, where the funeral is to be held, has one of the smallest auditoriums of any church in the city, and it will be necessary, in order to provide seats, that the attendance shall be confined only to those who receive invitations.

During the noon hour on Monday, however, those who desire will be given an opportunity to look for the last time upon the face of their illustrious townsman. From 11:30 to 12:45 the church will be open to all, and provision will be made for the public to file past the casket. At 12:15 the church will be cleared and only those holding invitations will be permitted to enter…

… Mr. Knowlton's body will be removed to a tomb in Rural cemetery immediately after the services at the church and later will be buried in the Knowlton lot.

In charge of the funeral arrangements was Arthur E. Perry, Knowlton's New Bedford law partner. The funeral would begin on Monday, December 22, at 1:30 p.m.
A "Feeling Tribute from Attorney Gen. Parker" was published on Friday, December 19:

Atty Gen. Herbert Parker, Mr. Knowlton's successor in that office, said:

'In the first moments of sadness at the death of a friend one can speak or think only of the loss he has sustained, and of the pain that comes from the broken ties of affection.

'We cannot yet tell in measured words of those attributes that made him a leading figure in our public life, and a real factor in the jurisprudence of our state.

'The thought of him today is of qualities of the heart that made him loved by all who knew him. Loyal in his devotion to his friends, he gave them without stint his sympathy, his support if need be, and the constant inspiration of a true and kindly nature.

'There are none who are thinking of him today who do not tenderly remember the encouragement his great heart gave them in moments of doubt or depression. He brought happiness to all whom he knew, as he found his own in largest measure in that which he made for others.

'Absolutely frank in his every act and thought, without the least pretence or disguise, he lived among us and was known for what in truth he was – a manly man who loved his fellow man.'

"TRIBUTES TO KNOWLTON" appeared on Sunday, December 21.

Pastor of His Church in New Bedford and Others in Marion Speak Of His Worth

NEW BEDFORD, Dec. 21 – There was a children's Christmas service at the First Universalist church in this city this afternoon and for the first time in 29 years Ex-Atty Gen Hosea M. Knowlton, who was superintendent of the Sunday school and treasurer of the church, was not present.

The minister, Rev. Oliver Howard Perkins, alluded to this fact in his address, and spoke of Mr. Knowlton's relation to the church.

'I think it is for a period of 29 years,' said he, 'that Mr. Knowlton had never been absent from this church at Christmas service on a children's day. This fact alone shows sincerity, especially in such a man as Mr. Knowlton – a man weighted down with the responsibility of public life, and when in spite of all those duties and cares, he came to this place on every Christmas Sunday morning to be with these children it speaks volumes for the worth and integrity of his character.

'Mr. Knowlton was a loyal and conscientious Universalist. He said last winter at a dinner which he attended in Boston, 'I am not a Universalist because my father was one, but because I thoroughly believe in the great teaching of the church.' He was never a man to hide his light under a bushel, and popularity and social prestige never tempted him from the church which was his by choice and reason.

'He always remained a constant Universalist because he believed the principles of the church were one with the advancement of man.

'How we shall miss him in the days to come we cannot realize now. There has never been any enterprise in the church but Mr. Knowlton has been an important factor. He once said, when there was talk of closing the church, 'I can hire a minister for a while, and I'll do it before I see the old church shut up.' He loved the church, and he sacrificed and worked for it.'

It seemed like the entire legal world of Massachusetts attended Hosea Knowlton's funeral on Monday, December 22. The New Bedford Superior Court was closed for the day, as well as law offices there. A host of dignitaries Knowlton had known through his career were in attendance, some sent several representatives of their groups, and many were named honorary pallbearers at the simple service.

For an hour before the service Mr. Knowlton's body lay in state in the church, and hundreds filed past the casket. The front of the church was hidden behind a mass of flowers. On the casket was a wreath of evergreens and violets, the tribute of Kappa chapter of the Theta Delta Chi fraternity, Tufts college, of which Mr. Knowlton was a member.

The Simple Service

The service began with Chopin's funeral march played on the organ by Alden W. Swan. Rev. O. Howard Perkins, pastor of the church, made the opening prayer, and the Unitarian church choir, composed of Misses Spary and Russell and Messrs. Walker and Sprague, then sang 'Lead, Kindly Light'.

The Scriptures were read by Prof. William R. Snipman of Tufts college and after the quartet sang 'How Gentle God's Commands,' Mr. Knowlton's favorite hymn, Rev. Dr. Elmer H. Capen, president of Tufts college, made the prayer.

Dr. Capen alluded to Mr. Knowlton's relationships and responsibilities, his nubile life and many virtues, his consecration to duty and his readiness to help mankind.

He invoked the blessing of God upon the commonwealth, which mourns the loss of one who served her with fidelity so many years; a blessing upon the members of the afflicted family, and lastly upon the institutions with which Mr. Knowlton was associated – particularly the college to which he gave such devoted service, and the church and Sunday school which were so much a part of his life.

After singing of 'Abide With Me,' Rev. Mr. Perkins pronounced the benediction. While the mourners passed the casket the dead march from 'Saul' and Schubert's march were played.
…

The body was placed in a tomb in Rural cemetery.

Knowlton Goes Missing

When I visited Rural Cemetery in New Bedford, the clerk looked up Hosea Knowlton in the sizable metal cabinets that lined an office wall. The cards were not removable, as far as I knew. I was ready to jot down the location of the Knowlton plot, when she broke our silence with an unexpected, "He was removed."

I had read that he was buried there. "What?"

"He was removed."

"Why?"

"It doesn't say."

The date given was in December of 1902. It gave no notation of cremation or any monument being in the cemetery, and said he was moved to Boston. A cemetery in Boston. Well, that ended that. I didn't even have the name of the cemetery. If I had went looking for Knowlton's grave in Boston, I'd still be there.

The cemetery needed this small article I only found recently to find Mr. Knowlton:

CREMATED AT FOREST HILLS

Body of Ex-Atty Gen Hosea M. Knowlton Brought from New Bedford

The remains of Ex-Atty Gen Hosea M. Knowlton were cremated at Forest Hills Saturday morning. The body was brought from New Bedford, arriving at the terminal station shortly after 9 o'clock, and was taken to the crematory.

Mr. Knowlton 's ashes were scattered over the bay at Marion. On a cenotaph in Rural Cemetery his name is inscribed alongside the ashes of his wife, Sylvia, who died in 1937 at the age of 86.

Sources:

Boston Daily Globe 7 December 1902.
Boston Daily Globe 8 December 1902.
Boston Daily Globe 10 December 1902.
Boston Daily Globe 11 December 1902.
Boston Daily Globe 12 December 1902.
Boston Daily Globe 14 December 1902.
Boston Daily Globe 18 December 1902.
Boston Daily Globe 19 December 1902.
Boston Daily Globe 20 December 1902.
Boston Daily Globe 21 December 1902.
Boston Daily Globe 22 December 1902.
Boston Daily Globe 23 December 1902.
Boston Daily Globe 29 December 1902.

Knowlton, General William (ret.). "Hosea Knowlton for the Prosecution." *The Lizzie Borden Quarterly* April 1997.

Noe, Denise. "Portrait of Hosea Knowlton." *The Hatchet: A Journal of Lizzie Borden & Victorian Studies* III.3 (February 2006).

Above: Hosea Knowlton marker at Rural Cemetery, New Bedford, Massachusetts.
Left: Hosea Morrill Knowlton.
Below: Knowlton home, Marion, Massachusetts.

William H. Medley, from Edwin Porter, *Fall River Tragedy*, 1893.

William H. Medley

January 6, 1853 – September 15, 1917

William Medley was born in Oldham, England, the son of Joseph and Hannah (Chambers) Medley. In 1869, his family came to the United States and settled in Lowell, Massachusetts. There he worked in the textile mills. He came to Fall River in 1876 and was employed at the Weetamoe and Granite Mills and was a member of the Mulespinner's Union.

Medley was appointed to the police department on February 2, 1880, as a day steward. In 1881, he was a night steward at the Central Police Station. From 1882-1892, he served as a patrolman. He took part in many facets in the investigation of the Borden murders.

Medley was made inspector with the rank of lieutenant less than a year after the Borden trial. He was appointed assistant city marshal in 1910. When Marshal John Fleet retired, Medley was made city marshal in September of 1915. During that month, the title City Marshal was formally changed to Chief of Police.

Mr. Medley was a member of the Knights of Pythias, St. Paul's Methodist Episcopal Church, the Masonic Fraternity, Star Lodge, Philanthropic Burial Society, and several police associations.

In 1917, Medley, his wife, and daughter were in a serious auto accident on the corner of Locust and Linden Streets in Fall River.

The accident and Medley's condition were featured in the *Fall River Daily Globe*, September 14, 1917:

CHIEF MEDLEY ON DANGEROUS LIST AT HOSPITAL AS ACCIDENT RESULT

Fears Felt That He May Not Recover From His Injuries, Which Were Chiefly About the Head – Skull Was Fractured, Probably by Striking Windshield of His Machine – His Daughter Also Very Seriously Injured While Wife Escapes With Severe Shock – Investigation Being Made as to the Cause of the Accident by the Police Department

Chief of Police William H. Medley this afternoon was in a critical condition at the Union hospital, with a bad fracture of the skull, the result of being pitched from his automobile at the corner of Locust and Linden Streets shortly before 2 o'clock yesterday afternoon, when his car was struck by another machine. Miss Kathleen Medley, daughter of the chief, was resting as comfortably as might be expected. Dr. Ralph W. Jackson, the attending physician, deciding upon an X-ray examination today to determine definitely whether or not Miss Medley has sustained a skull fracture. Mrs. Medley, suffering from a scalp wound and a severe nervous shock, following the collision, is improving steadily.

It is thought that Chief Medley's head came in contact with the windshield before he was thrown to the sidewalk, as his white uniform cap has in it a hole, on the right side, and the operating surgeons removed a foreign substance when they performed the operation on the chief yesterday afternoon, the matter being probably a small portion of the lining of the cap

. . .

Just how the accident happened is not quite clear. Chief Medley, with his wife and daughter were driving down Linden street, on his way to the office at police headquarters. In the Ford touring car, the other machine that figured in the smashup were Joseph O'Hearn, 411 Fourth street, the chauffeur, Frank J. Whalen, connected with the Anawan mills, and owner of the car, and John M. Whittemore, 16_ (169?-author) Washington street, Newton, treasurer of the Anawan mills. Mr. Whittemore was on his way to the Fall River station at the time. Mr. Whalen's car being bound in an easterly direction along Locust street. According to witnesses, Chief Medley's car was almost across Locust street when the touring car struck the door on the left side of his machine. In a moment both cars were heading down Linden street, with both rear wheels of the chief's car off and the body on the ground.

The machine crashed into a telegraph pole to which was attached a letter box, and the latter was demolished, the contents being strewn all about the street. The Whalen car was overturned, and the three occupants, who almost miraculously escaped injury of a serious nature, were obliged to climb out before the car was righted. They suffered nothing more serious than bruises and a shaking up.

Chief Medley and his daughter were both hurled from their seats, but although badly hurt, the chief got to his feet without assistance and asked a bystander who rushed up if he saw his cap anywhere about. Miss Medley apparently went headlong against the telegraph pole and was unconscious on the sidewalk when men attracted to the scene by the sound of the crash rushed up to her side. An automobile coming along stopped and the driver volunteered his services. Patrolman Bartholomew Leary of the Central station, who was also nearby at the time taking his chief and Miss Medley to the Union Hospital. Meantime Capt. Barker and Lieut. Waring of the Central station had been notified to the scene with the patrol wagon. In this Mrs. Medley was also hurried to the hospital, as it was feared she was seriously injured and it was decided not to wait for the ambulance.

Patrolman Young and O'Connor of the auto squad were on the scene in a short time and made a thorough investigation. The operator of the Ford car told the officers the collision was unavoidable and said that both cars seemed to be traveling about the same rate of speed, 15 to 18 miles an hour. The crash, however, was of sufficient force to swing both cars around so that when they brought up both were heading down Linden street.

In a short time Drs. Burns, Curry and McKenna were on the scene and cared for the victims of the accident until they were removed to the hospital. Dr. Burns picked up Mrs. Medley's watch in the street and turned it over to Officer O'Connor. Other property, including money, hurled into the street, was gathered up by others who came along and later turned over to the police. The officers sent out on the case are still investigating.

At 2 o'clock this afternoon it was reported from the Union Hospital that Chief Medley's condition was very serious.

The next day, September 15, 1917, the *Fall River Daily Globe* gave the following report on page one:

CHIEF MEDLEY VERY LOW AT UNION HOSPITAL

Joseph O'Hearn, Chauffeur of Car Which Figured in the Collision Is Arrested on Charge of Speeding

Joseph C. O'Hearn, chauffeur for Frank J. Whalen, whose car figured in the collision in which Chief of Police W. H. Medley, Miss Kathleen Medley and Mrs. Medley were injured early Thursday afternoon, was arraigned before Judge Benjamin Cook, Jr., in the second district court today on a charge of operating an automobile at an unreasonable rate of speed. Through his counsel, R. K. Hawes of Borden, Kenyon and Hawes, the defendant pleaded not guilty and by agreement the case was continued until Sept. 29 for a hearing. Before then Chief Medley's condition will be known definitely, although it is feared he will not survive his injuries.

Chief Medley is still in a very serious condition at the Union Hospital with a bad fracture of the skull. Miss Medley is also seriously ill, but is expected to recover, as is Mrs. Medley, who sustained a scalp wound and a severe shaking up.

Chief of Police William H. Medley is still in a very serious condition at the Union hospital. Advices from the institution this noon revealed that any change from yesterday's bulletin was exceedingly slight, and that on the whole there was no material difference. The patient is unconscious and has been in a state of coma since yesterday.

On September 17, 1917 the *Fall River Daily Globe* published the news of Medley's passing on page one:

CHIEF MEDLEY PASSES AWAY AT THE HOSPITAL

Injuries Sustained in Auto Collision on Thursday Result Fatally – Dead Official Long in Service of the City.

Chief of Police William H. Medley died late Saturday night at the Union hospital, from injuries sustained in a collision between his automobile and a machine owned by Frank J. Whalen, at the corner of Locust and Linden streets shortly before 2 o'clock Thursday afternoon. Joseph C. F. O'Hearn, 411 Fourth street, who was driving Mr. Whalen's car at the time of the collision, was arrested and arraigned on the charge of operating an automobile at an unreasonable rate of speed and later was booked on a charge of manslaughter following the death of Chief Medley. He pleaded not guilty to both charges and will have a hearing on Sept. 29.

Chief Medley was bound down town with his wife and daughter, Miss Kathleen Medley, while the Whalen car was bound west on Locust street, on the way to the Fall River station. The chief's car was thrown against a telegraph pole and he and his daughter were hurled out, Miss Medley being rendered unconscious. The chief picked himself up unassisted and it was thought at first that he had escaped with bad scalp wounds and a shaking up. He lapsed into a comatose state at the hospital and an operation disclosed a serious fracture … Mrs. Medley was not thrown out but is still suffering severely from the shock to her nervous system.

Chief Medley's body was removed to his home on Hood street, and may be viewed late today and tomorrow. Arrangements for the funeral are as yet incomplete, but the services will be held at the family residence tomorrow afternoon and the body will be taken to Lowell Wednesday morning for burial. A delegation of police will be at the Fall River station as the body is taken away and it is expected that a detail of police will meet at Lowell later in the day. Deputy Chief Martin Feeney is now acting chief and is making plans for the police part in the funeral.

Chief Medley was a native of England, where he was born Jan. 6, 1853. He came to this country when very young, however, and for some time worked in the mills.

He was made a member of the police department on Feb. 3, 1880 and appointed day steward. In 1881 he was made night steward at the Central station and in 1882 was appointed a patrolman.

Patrolman Medley was made an inspector with the rank of lieutenant on Feb. 16, 1893, and on Feb. 17, 1908 after seeing much active duty, he was transferred to light duty as lieutenant. He was again assigned on Oct. 27 (year unreadable – author), to temporary duty as an inspector and Nov. 8, 1909, he was designated to take a civil service examination for promotion to assistant city marshal, an office to which he was appointed Jan. 11, 1910.

After the office of city marshal was abolished he was promoted to the chief of police and went into office Sept. 29, 1915, succeeding the late John Fleet as the head of the department.

Chief Medley, as Inspector Medley, working with Inspector Bartholomew Shay, now probation officer in the second district court, worked on many important cases while at headquarters in the old days and made a number of important arrests. Both acquired reputations that made them known in many cities in this part of the country.

Chief Medley was a member of both the local and state police associations and the Association of Police Chiefs of Massachusetts. He was also a member of the Philanthropic Burial Society, Star Lodge, Knights of Pythias, and of the Masonic fraternity.

Another article made the front page in the September 17, 1917 issue of the *Fall River Evening Herald*.

CHIEF MEDLEY TO BE BURIED IN LOWELL

Head of Police Department Did Not Recover Consciousness
Funeral Services to Be Held at Late Home Tuesday Afternoon

Chief of Police William H. Medley died at two minutes before midnight on Saturday night at the Union hospital as a result of a fracture of the skull that he received in an automobile accident at the corner of Locust and Linden streets on Thursday afternoon. Although an operation was performed by Dr. Ralph W. Jackson shortly after the accident Chief Medley continued to fail and did not regain consciousness up to the time of his death. Mrs. Medley and his daughter, Kathleen, who were also injured in the accident continue to improve and at present give every indication of their ultimate recovery.

During slightly more than 37 years spent on the police force Chief Medley distinguished himself as an unusually keen and efficient officer, and during his term as an inspector became favorably know(sic) all over the New England states. His police duties covered an unusually wide range as Chief Medley ran a gamut of police duties that included steward, patrolman, inspector, desk lieutenant, prosecuting officer, assistant city marshal and chief.

Chief of Police William H. Medley was born in England, Jan. 6, 1853 and came to this country Aug. 10, 1869, settling in Lowell, where he worked in the mills. He came to this city July 5, 1876, and pursued the trade of mule spinner in the Weetamoe and Granite Mills.

Appointed to Force in 1880

He was appointed to the police department Feb. 2, 1880, as a day steward at Division 2 station. Later, he was transferred to the Central station as night steward and the year following was appointed a patrolman.

Feb. 10, 1893, he was promoted to inspector, with the rank of lieutenant. From February, until Oct. 27, 1903, he was assigned to desk duty at Division 3, in his capacity as a lieutenant. On that date, he was temporarily transferred to the inspectors' department and Nov. 3, 1909, was designated by the Board of Police to take a civil service examination for the position of assistant city marshal, to which place he was appointed Jan. 21, 1910. He served in that capacity until the death of Marshal John Fleet, when he was made acting city marshal.

The title of city marshal was abolished at a meeting of the Board of Police held Sept. 27, 1915, and changed to chief of police, and at the same time Chief Medley was appointed to the office, his duties as chief of police beginning Sept. ... 1915.

From the time of his boyhood in Oldham, England, the career of Chief Medley was one of exceptional diversity and picturesqueness. He worked in the mills of Lancashire as a boy and he came to this country August 10, 1869 at the age of 16 and worked in the mills of Lowell. Seven years later he came to this city and while employed in the local mills became prominent in the Mulespinner's union. At this time his interest in the labor movement, then at its height was exceptionally keen for a youth of 23 and he became a contributor to "The Labor Standard," a once prosperous union publication of this city.

At the age of 27 his police duties began and in his new field Chief Medley gave early promise of making good. One of the first important cases in which Chief Medley appeared as a witness was the famous Andrew Borden case: several phases of which were investigated by Chief Medley, who subsequently appeared as witness at the trial in New Bedford.

Handled Many Cases

While an inspector, Chief Medley and Probation Officer Bartholomew Shay, then a police inspector, together with Chief Donohue of the Somerset police force investigated the attempt made to dynamite the Brightman street bridge early on Sunday morning April 26, 1903. When a later attempt was made on steel belonging to the Phoenix Construction company of Philadelphia which was engaged in erecting the Brightman street and Somerset railway bridges, Chief Medley worked on the case and later testified against Daniel Davis, alias George O'Donnell, a member of the United Steel Structural Workers of America, where the McNamara brothers and other officials of the organization were tried in Indianapolis.

It was Chief Medley, who as assistant city marshal, had charge of the investigation which finally convicted Antone Retkovitch of the murder of Domke Peremyda (or 'Peremyde' – author). The Peremyda woman was murdered in Jacob Maker's house in Eagan's court on the morning of March 14, 1914. Both Ratkovitch and the woman had been to Fall River for only a short time and when the murder was discovered Retkovitch had disappeared as completely as though the earth had swallowed him. Retkovitch was later taken into custody by Inspector Violette on Salem street, Boston nine days after the murder. Chief Medley was responsible for much of the evidence produced at the two Retkovitch trials by the prosecution.

In addition to his acknowledged reputation as an officious, tactful police officer, Chief Medley was also known as an unusually keen sportsman and was an ardent fight and baseball fan. At one time he was a member of the local Police nine and was a constant (admirerer? – author) of America's national pastime.

Chief Medley was a member of the Fall River and Massachusetts Police Relief associations, the Massachusetts Police Chiefs' association and was also a member of Star lodge, No. 139, Knights of Pythias. He was an attendant at St. Paul's Methodist Episcopal church and after the ___ attended the Union Methodist Episcopal of which his wife and daughter are members.

Funeral services will be conducted at his home on Hood street Tuesday afternoon and Wednesday morning at ___ the body will be taken to Lowell for interment. A delegation of police officers will be at the Fall River station to meet the body and place it on the 8:00 train for Boston.

William Medley is buried at Edson Cemetery on Gorham Street in Lowell, Massachusetts, which is 80 miles north of Fall River. Mr. Medley is buried in Lot 13, Row 30, grave number 7. He was 64 years, 7 months, and 10 days old. He and his wife, Mary E. Medley, have a double gray monument. Mrs. Medley passed away in 1935.

When I visited the cemetery, I could not find any monuments at all in the section I believed to be Lot 13, Row 30. There were, however, a row of headstones that were buried under several inches of grass and hard dirt. My husband and son took a shovel and dug the soil off enough so we could read the name, searching for Medley. We uncovered a lot of them in that row. So, if the staff at Edson Cemetery in Lowell found some 'grave digging' attempts the next morning, it was just us. (It must have looked crazy.)

Interestingly, when those people were buried, there was no cement foundation under the headstones and, in time, they were covered by nature. I learned that these headstones can be raised by one's own expense.

The photos of William Medley's monument were sent to me by the cemetery office department in Lowell.

Sources:

Fall River Daily Globe 14 September 1917.
Fall River Daily Globe 15 September 1917.
Fall River Daily Globe 17 September 1917.
Fall River Evening Herald 17 September 1917.

LIZZIE BORDEN: RESURRECTIONS

Rebello, Leonard. *Lizzie Borden, Past & Present.* Fall River, MA: Al-Zach Press, 1999.

Schaefer, Anne C. Administrative Clerk, Parks, Recreation & Cemeteries Department, Lowell, Massachusetts. Personal phone call and correspondence, 2006-2007.

William H. Medley grave at Edson Cemetery, Lowell Massachusetts.
Photographs courtesy of the City of Lowell Cemetery Division.

St. John's Cemetery, Fall River, Massachusetts.
Photograph courtesy of Mark Amarantes.

John Minnehan

1845 – February 9, 1893

Born in Ireland, then going from Portsmouth, Rhode Island, to Fall River, John Minnehan was part of Tallman, Minnehan & Earle, a grocery business. He then went into the liquor business. Moving to Somerset, Massachusetts, he was a police officer there for four years. Returning once again to reside in Fall River, he was appointed a police officer on November 7, 1889.

John Minnehan lived at 88 Mulberry Street, according to his burial card. According to his Record of Death, he resided at 67 Mulberry Street. He was involved in the first search of the Borden house, and he guarded the property the night of August 4, 1892. He was present when the handless hatchet in the cellar was discovered by Officers Fleet and Medley.

He was also assigned to shadow John Morse during the days immediately following the Borden murders. When Morse just had to go pick up his mail, hundreds, if not a thousand, people followed him. To the public, he was a main suspect.

John Minnehan was not able to testify at the Borden trial. On February 9, 1893, Mr. Minnehan died of pneumonia at 48 years of age. He was buried at St. John's Cemetery in Fall River (Section 18, Lot 390, Grave No. 1).

His wife, Mary, died on August 23, 1908, of acute gastritis. At the time of her death, she resided at 197 Diman Street in Fall River. She was buried on August 26, 1908, at St. John's Cemetery in Fall River.

On October 17, 1932, both John and Mary Minnehan were removed from St. John's Cemetery to an undisclosed location.

Sources:

Burial cards of John, Mary, and son Daniel S. Minnehan. St. John's Cemetery, Fall River, Massachusetts.
Hoffman, Paul Dennis. *Yesterday in Old Fall River*. Durham, NC: Carolina Academic Press, 2000.
Rebello, Leonard. *Lizzie Borden, Past & Present*. Fall River, MA: Al-Zach Press, 1999.

Arthur Sherman Phillips

Arthur Sherman Phillips

January 13, 1866- March 18, 1941

Arthur S. Phillips was the youngest member of Lizzie Borden's defense team. Though he played no active part in the courtroom, he worked behind the scenes, mostly investigating evidence. Only two months before the Borden murders, he had graduated from Boston University Law School. This statement (taken from *Yesterday in Old Fall River* by Paul Dennis Hoffman) leads one to believe he was quite inexperienced. However, he graduated from Williams College in 1887, after attending four years. He then moved to Lowell, and was an assistant bookkeeper for three years at Washington Mills Company, at the same time being in charge of the bookkeeping department in the Lowell Evening School and the Fall River Evening School. Tutoring in mathematics, he started his legal studies with Frederick Fisher. He worked in the office of Morton and Jennings in Fall River in 1890 as a clerk and was admitted to the bar in 1891. He graduated *magna cum laude* from Boston in 1892. No greenhorn he.

Hyman Lubinsky, the Russian ice cream vendor who was making his rounds on the morning of August 4, 1892, told Phillips before the preliminary hearing that he saw a lady on the Borden's property come from the barn to the side of the house. Lubinsky was not called to testify at the preliminary hearing or at the grand jury.

Phillips attempted to interview druggist Eli Bence, who placed Lizzie in a drugstore trying to buy prussic acid shortly before the murders, but Bence refused to speak to him.

Phillips was sure of Lizzie's innocence during his entire lifetime. As Andrew Jennings gave his closing statement at the trial, Mr. Phillips wept openly in court.

Not long after the Borden trial, he opened his own law office with William E. Fuller in the Granite Block of Fall River. He was City Solicitor in 1899, under Mayor Amos M. Jackson. He was a member of the prestigious Quequechan Club and the Fall River and Bristol County Bar Associations. He was counsel for a time for the New England Division of the F. W. Woolworth Company and one of the incorporators and a director and attorney for the Lafayette Cooperative Bank.

Phillips was very active in courtroom cases until a few years before his death, when he only continued his office practice.

An historian, Phillips was working on his *History of Fall River*, written in three volumes. The book was published posthumously by his brother-in-law, Norman Salisbury Easton. It is unclear how much Easton contributed to the final publication.

Phillips was married to Elizabeth (Cheney) Phillips and the couple had three daughters. He had one daughter with his second wife, May (Wiggins) Phillips.

Arthur Phillips died on March 18, 1941, of a heart attack. He died in his apartment that adjoined his law office at 177 Second Street. He had not been in good health for some time, but he continued his law practice until the time of his death. Phillips' home was located at Bristol Ferry, Portsmouth. Private services were held at the Waring Funeral Home, 178 Winter Street. He was buried in the Phillips family plot in East Bridgewater, Massachusetts.

How to Find the Grave of Arthur S. Phillips

Arthur S. Phillips is buried at Central Cemetery in East Bridgewater, Massachusetts. From the center of East Bridgewater, go to Central Street in a southwesterly direction and proceed about 800 feet until you are opposite the Central school building. Directly across you will find a granite post which says "Central" on left and "Cemetery" on right. Enter this drive up hill and proceed as far as you can on this road. Bear right at this point and go easterly to the end of that drive. Then bear left about 40 feet to an intersection, then turn left onto the road and stop. You can then walk across the lot to the Phillips lot, which is enclosed by a granite and iron rail fence.

Sources:

Alexander, Richard. Central Cemetery, East Bridgewater, Massachusetts. Personal correspondence. 3 February 2004.

"Death Takes Lawyer Here." *Fall River Herald News* 18 March 1941.

Duniho, Terence. "Arthur Phillips' Perspective." *Lizzie Borden Quarterly* April 2002.

Hoffman, Paul Dennis. *Yesterday in Old Fall River*. Durham, NC: Carolina Academic Press, 2000.

Rebello, Leonard. *Lizzie Borden, Past & Present*. Fall River, MA: Al-Zach Press, 1999.

Arthur S. Phillips grave at Central Cemetery, East Bridgewater, Massachusetts.

George Potter, *Boston Globe*, June 6, 1893

George Potter

1839 – 1909

George Potter was the first juror selected for the trial of Lizzie Borden in June,1893. He owned a large farm in Westport about twelve miles from New Bedford, where the trial took place. He was a Universalist, a Mason, and had never served as a juror. Potter and his wife, Emma, had no children.

On the day he was questioned as a perspective juror,

> George Potter of Westport walked calmly to the front, was sworn, and answered the usual interrogatives. He had formed an opinion, was not biased, and held no opinion which would preclude him from serving as a juror. Passing the commonwealth, he was also accepted by the defense, and was then sworn in by Clerk Borden as the first juror in the Borden trial. Mr. Potter took his seat in the jury box on the north side of the court room.

According to a reporter's description: "George Potter, of Westport, the first juror who passed muster, is a pleasant featured man, apparently about 40 years of age, and if we can judge by appearances, is a man who will render a verdict strictly in accordance with the evidence." Mr. Potter was about 54 years old.

The jury sat at right, looking toward the judges' bench. About five feet from the jury foreman was the witness box (witnesses had to stand to testify, as they do there to this day). Opposite was Sheriff Wright's seat. From his vantage point he could take in all that went on in the courtroom.

Daily news dispatches were sent out from telegraph offices, located in the stables behind the courthouse.

On June 20, 1893, the jury retired at 3:24 p.m. They returned to the courtroom at 4:32 p.m., after one hour and eight minutes, with an acquittal. When the verdict was read, the jurors broke into cheers.

Augustus Swift, one of the Borden jurors, delivered a sizable unframed photo of the jury to Lizzie Borden. At the time, Lizzie was not at home and the photo was accepted by sister Emma.

George Potter passed away in 1909 around the age of 70. He is buried in Beech Grove Cemetery in Westport.

Sources:

Evening Standard (New Bedford, MA) 5 June 1893.

Rebello, Leonard. *Lizzie Borden, Past & Present*. Fall River, MA: Al-Zach Press, 1999.

Widdows, Harry, Stefani Koorey, Kat Koorey, eds. *The Trial of Lizzie Andrew Borden*, Book One. Orlando, FL: PearTree Press, 2005.

Widdows, Harry, Stefani Koorey, Kat Koorey, eds. *The Trial of Lizzie Andrew Borden*, Book Three. Orlando, FL: PearTree Press, 2005.

George Potter grave at Beech Grove Cemetery, Westport, Massachusetts.

Hannah Reagan, *Boston Globe*, August 31, 1892

Hannah Reagan

1848 - 1924

Hannah Reagan was the first Day Matron of Fall River's Central Police Station. She was appointed in August of 1887, and served until she retired in 1909.

Born in Ireland, she married a stone cutter in Fall River, Quinlan M. Reagan, who became a watchman in later life.

After the coroner's inquest of the Borden murders, Lizzie Borden was kept at the Central Police Station through the arraignment until she was transferred to Taunton Jail in Taunton, Massachusetts. Lizzie again stayed at the jail in Fall River during the preliminary hearing. I have heard two versions of why Lizzie stayed in Matron Reagan's room at the jail. One says there were no female accommodations there; another simply states that the jail had both male and female accommodations. Like most things Lizzie, even in this there is controversy.

Mrs. Reagan is best known for overhearing a startling conversation between the Borden sisters, which took place the day before the preliminary hearing on August 24, 1892:

Lizzie: Emma, you have gave me away, haven't you?

Emma: No, Lizzie, I have not.

Lizzie: You have and I will let you see I won't give in one inch.

Mrs. Reagan supposedly told Edwin Porter, a reporter covering the case who would write *The Fall River Tragedy* in 1893. Reverend Augustus Buck, a staunch Lizzie supporter, asked Mrs. Reagan to sign a paper saying she did not hear that conversation. Marshal Hilliard said whatever Hannah knew she could save for court. And, when witness Reagan was called to the stand, she stuck by her story as true.

At the time the sisters were talking, Matron Reagan heard some loud talk from them. She was just four feet away in a toilet room. She described their physical movements—how Emma at first leaned over Lizzie, then Lizzie turned away from Emma, and the two remained there in silence for almost two hours, when Attorney Andrew Jennings came in.

Several others testified at the trial that Mrs. Reagan was willing to sign the Buck paper—except for Emma, who, not surprisingly, said she didn't remember the conversation.

More amusing was Mrs. Reagan's trial testimony where she told of some fun she and Lizzie had one day at the jail.

We were talking in the afternoon, me and Lizzie Borden, and I says, 'I can tell you one thing you can't do,' and she says, 'Tell me what it is, Mrs. Reagan.' I says, 'Break an egg, Miss Borden,' and she says, 'Break an egg?' I says, 'Yes.' 'Well,' she says, 'I can break an egg.' I says,

'Not the way I would tell you to break it.' She says, 'Well, what way is it, Mrs. Reagan?' So I told her that she couldn't break it the way I wanted her to break it, and I said I would bet her a dollar that she couldn't, and she said she would bet me a quarter, and in the afternoon someone fetched Lizzie an egg, and Miss Emma Borden was sitting down beside her, and I told Miss Emma Borden to get a little ways away, 'because,' I said, 'if she will break the egg the wrong way it will destroy your dress,' and she did get the egg, and she got it in her hands, and she couldn't break it, and she says, 'There,' she says, 'that is the first thing I undertook to do that I never could.'

A quarter. Still Andrew's daughter.

Hannah Reagan died on April 29, 1924, at the age of 76. She is buried in the North Burial Ground in Fall River, Lot Number 202, on Fourth Avenue.

Sources:

Hoffman, Paul Dennis. *Yesterday in Old Fall River*. Durham, NC: Carolina Academic Press, 2000.

Martins, Michael and Dennis Binette, eds. *The Commonwealth of Massachusetts vs. Lizzie A. Borden, The Knowlton Papers*. Fall River, MA: The Fall River Historical Society, 1994.

Rebello, Leonard. *Lizzie Borden, Past & Present*. Fall River, MA: Al-Zach Press, 1999.

Widdows, Harry, Stefani Koorey, Kat Koorey, eds. *The Trial of Lizzie Andrew Borden*, Book Three. Orlando, FL: PearTree Press, 2005.

Hannah Reagan grave at North Burial Ground, Fall River, Massachusetts.

George Dexter Robinson

George Dexter Robinson

January 20, 1834 - February 22, 1896

George D. Robinson was born on January 20, 1834 in Lexington, Massachusetts. His middle name was Washington at first and was later changed to Dexter. He attended Lexington Academy and Hopkins Classical School in Cambridge, Massachusetts. After graduating from Harvard in 1856, he became principal of the Chicopee High School from 1856-1865, and then studied law. He was admitted to the bar in Cambridge in 1866, and practiced in Chicopee, Massachusetts. Robinson was a member of the State House of Representatives in 1874, at the age of forty. In 1876, he was a State senator. He won a Congressional seat (Republican) in 1877, until he resigned to serve as Governor of Massachusetts from 1884-1887. Resuming his law practice in Springfield, Massachusetts, he was hired as lead counsel in the defense of Lizzie Borden's trial for which Miss Borden paid a hefty fee of $25,000 (that's 1892 dollars).

J. Thomas Baldwin of Boston composed a lively piece especially for Robinson, called "Governor Robinson's March." It was played by local bands when he arrived in their town.

Mr. Robinson died on February 22, 1896. He was 62 years old. The following announcement appeared on the front page of the *Syracuse Standard* on Sunday, February 23, 1896:

EX-GOV. ROBINSON DEAD

Passes Peacefully Away in the Midst of his Family

Chicopee, Mass. Feb. 22 – Ex-governor George D. Robinson died this afternoon at 4:30 o'clock. The last signs that he was conscious were observed at about 11 o'clock last night, but since then he lay in a stupor, growing gradually weaker till he died. There were present only the members of the family and the physician, Dr. Prindle, who had remained at his bedside a large part of the last 24 hours. The end was very quiet and peaceful. No arrangements have yet been made for the funeral.
. . .

Governor Robinson's death was very sudden, as he was in the best of health Tuesday, and was stricken with apoplexy (a stroke) as he was on his way home from the courthouse in the afternoon.

Robinson's funeral was written up in the *North Adams Transcript*, North Adams,

Massachusetts, Wednesday afternoon, February 26, 1896:

Ex-Governor's Funeral
Chicopee and Springfield Scenes of Deep Mourning for the Late George D. Robinson

Springfield, Feb. 26 - Hundreds of the most prominent men in the state, including state officials of past and present administrations, members of the bench and bar, delegations from the city government, assembled today at Chicopee to pay the last honors to the memory of ex-Governor George Dexter Robinson. Many mills and stores in Chicopee and Springfield were closed. Flags floated at half mast on every hand in genuine mourning for the great ex-governor. A short prayer service was held at the home of the deceased at 1:30 p.m., only the family and members of the ex-governor's staff being present. Services were then held at the Third Congregational church at 2 o'clock. They were simple, yet impressive. Rev. C.E. Abbott of Chicopee read the scriptures. Eulogies were delivered by Rev. D. Beane of Newburyport and by Rev. E.F. Haywood.

No burial certificate was available for Governor Robinson, per the park superintendent.

George Dexter Robinson, Fairview Cemetery, Chicopee, Massachusetts

How to get there: The town of Chicopee, Massachusetts, is about an hour and a half from Albany, New York. It is two hours north/east from Fall River.

The Fairview Cemetery Commission falls under the jurisdiction of the City of Chicopee Parks and Recreation Department. I chose to write ahead and received a letter from Stanley J. Walczak, the Superintendent, inviting me to stop by their office, located at 687 Front Street, describing it as a brown shack building with a red sign in front. They would, he said, direct me to the cemetery from there if I came Monday – Friday, 8-5 pm.

Arriving one spring morning in the rain, a kind clerk gave me good directions to Fairview Cemetery, which would have been tricky to find on my own. (Okay, impossible.) The clerk and I talked Lizzie for a while, and I felt like such an expert by answering her easy questions of: "Was she found guilty?" "Did they ever find out who did it?" "What happened to her after the trial?" Surprisingly the few persons I talked to in Chicopee did not know who Governor Robinson was and seemed pleased to gain the piece of trivia I came bearing.

The clerk phoned the cemetery and arranged for a worker to meet me there, where I followed his truck to the Robinson monument. I am sure that these courtesies given me saved me a lot of time searching and cursing on my own. I recommend that should you wish to visit the Governor's grave to follow this same route.

Sources:

Jendrysik, Stephen. "Chicopee lawyer George Dexter Robinson aided Lizzie Borden defense." *The Republican*. Masslive.com. 10 April 2013. Web. 16 June 2014.

Memorial of the Harvard college class of 1856: Prepared for the fiftieth anniversary of graduation, June 27, 1906. G.H. Ellis Co., 1906. Web. 16 June 2014.

Payne, Libbie. "Area has Produced its Share of Mass. Governors." *Boston Globe* 15 February 2004.

George Robinson grave, Fairview Cemetery, Chicopee, Massachusetts.

George Dexter Robinson, *Boston Globe*, June 20, 1893

George Dexter Robinson, *Boston Globe*, June 16, 1893

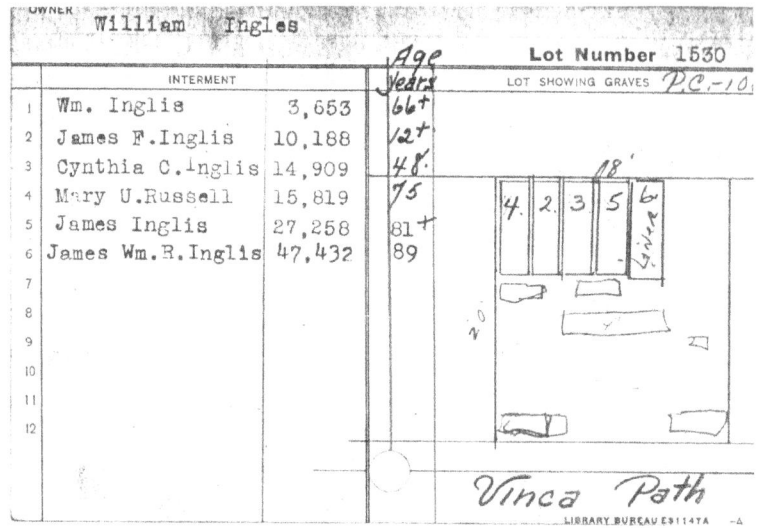

Mary U. Russell grave and burial card at Oak Grove Cemetery, Fall River, Massachusetts.

Mary U. Russell

October 3, 1829 - October 3, 1904

Mary Russell was the first Night Matron at the Central Police Station in Fall River. She took over after Hannah Reagan's daily shift ended. She was born in Danvers, Massachusetts, married in Rhode Island, and moved to Fall River in 1882. She began her matron's position in Fall River on August 1, 1887, where she remained for seventeen years, when she was forced to resign due to illness on October 30, 1902.

Mrs. Russell searched Lizzie Borden after her arrest and led her to her cell. According to the New Bedford *Evening Standard*, August 15, 1892, she was struck by Lizzie's composure and "lack of nervousness." She also thought Lizzie was very determined and bent on having her own way.

Shortly before Lizzie was taken to Taunton Jail she had only one conversation with Mrs. Russell about the crimes.

'So they are going to take me to Taunton, are they?' asked Lizzie.

'I believe they are,' replied Mrs. Russell.

'Well,' continued Lizzie, "they seem to do about as they please with me.'

'They were up to my house and brought me down here – to the inquest twice, and then they brought me here for a rest and I did not know what it all meant. Now they are going to take me to jail. They are having their own way with me now, but I will have mine by and by.'

Mary Russell died in Fall River on October 3, 1904. She was survived by three daughters and two sons. She is buried at Oak Grove Cemetery.

Sources:

Rebello, Leonard. *Lizzie Borden, Past & Present*. Fall River, MA: Al-Zach Press, 1999.

Part Three

Men of Medicine

Dr. Bowen, from Edwin Porter, *Fall River Tragedy*, 1893.

Dr. Seabury Bowen

July 1840 – March 4, 1918

Dr. Seabury Bowen was born in Attleboro, Massachusetts. His parents were Benjamin and Leafa (Clafflin) Bowen. After attending schools in Attleboro, he attended Brown University and graduated with his Bachelor of Arts degree in 1864. After obtaining medical degrees from the University of Michigan and New York City's Bellevue Hospital Medical College, he practiced medicine in Worcester, Massachusetts for one year (1867), taught a year at the Oread Institute of the same city, then came to Fall River.

The doctor was on staff at the Fall River Hospital since its beginning and a trustee for several years at the State Farm (Workhouse) at Bridgewater, Massachusetts. He joined the Bristol South District Medical Society in 1867. He was Fall River's city physician from 1872-1874. He was a member of the Fall River Medical Society and Massachusetts Medical Society. He was vice-president of the Fall River Medical Society in 1894.

Bowen married Phoebe Vincent Miller in 1871. Miss Miller was the daughter of Southard H. and Esther G. Miller. They had one child, a daughter, Florence. As the Millers lived just diagonally across the street from Andrew Borden, he became an instant neighbor. He was also their family physician and friend.

The inquest of the Borden murders states that Dr. Bowen was the first person to arrive at the house. However at the preliminary hearing Bowen testifies, "I have heard all the evidence, and I have no doubt that Mrs. Churchill was there, and Miss Lizzie Borden, those two."

Dr. Bowen arrived secondly. He was the first person to go into the sitting room. He was stunned. He called to Mrs. Churchill to "come see," which she declined to do. He saw Andrew Borden's hacked face, the left eye cut in two. After taking his pulse, Bowen confirmed what anyone who saw Borden would probably think—he was dead.

Dr. Bowen sent a telegram to let Emma Borden, then visiting in Fairhaven, Massachusetts, know of her father's murder and to suggest she return at once, perhaps on the noon train. When Bowen returned from the errand, the body of Mrs. Abby Borden had been discovered in the guest room upstairs. He was very rattled by the scenes he was subjected to that morning, and it took him about a week to lessen his level of high stress.

Officers Harrington and Doherty noted in the *Witness Statements*:

Thursday, August 4, 1892 11:35
At this hour I, with Frank Wixon, entered the Borden house 92 Second street. Dr. Bowen met me at the kitchen door, and said 'I am glad to see you.' I inquired 'what is the trouble?' He

said 'Mr. Borden is dead.' I went into the next room, and there found the remains on a sofa covered with a sheet. In low tones the Doctor told me he was satisfied there was something wrong, for they were all sick the day before. He followed this by saying 'to make matters worse, Mrs. Borden is lying dead up stairs. I suppose she saw the killing of her husband, and run up stairs, and died with fright.'

I requested to see her; and on going up stairs found her lying on the floor, face downward, between the bed and dressing case. Several spots of blood was on the bed, and also a large tuft of hair. On examining the body, I found she was lying in a pool of blood. I informed the Doctor of the fact, and he expressed much surprise. (P.H. Doherty)

About 3 p.m., Bowen took part in a partial (commonly referred to as "first") autopsy in the Borden home. The contents of the stomachs were removed from both victims to be tested for possible poisoning. Samples of milk were taken for the same purpose.

Dr. Bowen testified at the inquest, the preliminary hearing and at the 1893 trial of Lizzie Borden. The night of Lizzie's acquittal, he and Mrs. Bowen attended a party given for her at the home of Charles Holmes.

In November of 1897, the Fall River Medical Society was located in new and larger rooms of the A.J. Borden Building. Dr. Bowen continued to practice medicine in Fall River, in the office in his home, until he died in March of 1918, at the age of 78.

DOCTOR BOWEN DIES IN HIS 78th YEAR

Had Been Resident of this City for Nearly Half Century
Was Lizzie Borden's Physician

Dr. Seabury W. Bowen, a resident of this city since the late sixties, a physician of long practice, died at his residence, 217 Second street, at about midnight, Saturday. Dr. Bowen had reached his 78th year.

For a long time, his health had been precarious; for the last two years it was delicate and during the last 10 days he had been failing so rapidly that it was clear that he could survive but a short time. His mind was clear till almost the end. The affliction which has so long disturbed him was a heart disease. He was attended in his closing sickness by Dr. Arthur I. Connell.

Born in Attleboro

Dr. Bowen was born in Attleboro, the son of Benjamin and Leafa (Claplin – sic) Bowen, residents of the farming section of that town. He was schooled in Attleboro, whence he went to Brown University from which he was graduated in 1864 __ of his graduating class but five or six members now survive. He received his medical degree at Ann Arbor in the University of Michigan, then took a year's practice in Bellevue hospital, New York, and then practiced a year in Worcester with Dr. Clark; he next came to Fall River, and lived here ever afterward engaging steadily in the practice in his profession. While passing through Brown University, he taught a year in Oread Institute, Worcester, in which institution he was always interested, devoting much time to the enterprises and undertaken by it in later years, and being a regular or frequent attendant on its anniversaries.

Married in 1871

In 1871, on Oct. 31, Dr. Bowen was married – to Miss Phoebe V. Miller, daughter of Southard and Esther G. Miller, well-remembered residents of Fall River, and the couple continued to make their home here until Mrs. Bowen's death in 1907. To them was born the daughter, Florence.

The deceased was of very quiet and unassuming manner. He devoted himself sedulously to his profession, and appeared to consider it his duty to adhere to that "one thing", without stretching out to absorb of interest himself deeply in other affairs. His addresses at nurses' graduations indicated how faithfully he followed the course he had set when he left the medical school.

Attended Lizzie Borden

Very little occurred in his career which brought him conspicuously before the community. The only matter which gave him special prominence was the terrible tragedy which resulted in the deaths of Andrew J. and Abby D. Borden, who were murdered in their home on Second street in 1892. Dr. Bowen was a very near neighbor of the Bordens, and was their family physician, he was, accordingly, called to attend Miss Lizzie Andrew Borden, their daughter, when she was under the strain of the discovery on that August morning of the fearful fate which had befallen her parents.

The doctor was one of the first persons to enter the house in which the frightful tragedy had been enacted, and was more intimate at the time, with Miss Borden than any other person. A witness in the case which was brought against her when she was charged with the double murder. During the year which followed Miss Borden's arrest, when she was awaiting trial in Taunton jail, and long afterward his name was among those uppermost in the speech of citizens who discussed the murders, and much space was given to him and his family in the newspaper reports of the trial in New Bedford. The history of the murder mystery will always, however, include his appearance in the case.

Served as City Physician

Dr. Bowen was city physician, here in the early seventies; he was, at his death, a member of the Fall River Medical society; was a member of the Board of Trustees of the Union Hospital at the time of its inception, was long a trustee of the State farm at Bridgewater; was, at his death, a member of the First Baptist church, and was a director of the Laurel Lake mills.

The funeral, which will doubtless be very largely attended, especially by members of the medical and surgical profession will take place at 217 Second street at 3 tomorrow afternoon and the interment in Oak Grove cemetery, Rev. E. C. Herrick will officiate.

DR. S.W. BOWEN

Funeral services for Dr. Seabury W. Bowen were conducted from his late residence, 217 Second Street, this afternoon at 3, and were largely attended. Rev. Everett C. Herrick, assisted by Rev. Clarence F. Gifford, conducted prayer, during which Miss Margaret McLeod and H. Nelson G. Terry sang hymns. Many beautiful floral tributes rested upon the casket. Interment was in Oak Grove cemetery. The bearers were Charles S. Miller, Arthur C. Rounds of Providence, Fred C. Rounds of Attleboro, and Thomas S. Manchester of Bristol.

The house that Dr. Bowen lived in also held his doctor's office. The City Hall records on the house go back to 1883. It had two stories and twenty-two rooms.

In 1883, the house was owned by Florence G. Hathaway, Dr. Bowen's daughter, and Charles S. Miller. Florence Hathaway owned three-fourths of the wooden structure. Charles Miller owned one-fourth. The bills were sent to Dr. Bowen.

In 1936, Nathan Yamms purchased the home. The Rialto Amusement Company, Inc., owned it in 1945. In 1950, the house was bought by Joseph A. Gaboriau of Somerset. In 1953, it was dismantled by the David Laberge Jr. wrecking firm to build a parking lot.

Believed to be over 150 years old, the house was last used as a rooming house for aged people.

Sources:

Fall River Evening Herald 4 March 1918.

Fall River Evening Herald 5 March 1918.

Fall River Herald News 8 August 1953.

Hoffman, Paul Dennis. *Yesterday in Old Fall River*. Durham, NC: Carolina Academic Press, 2000.

Our Country and Its People: A Descriptive and Biographical Record of Bristol County, Massachusetts. Boston History Company, 1899.

Rebello, Leonard. *Lizzie Borden, Past & Present*. Fall River, MA: Al-Zach Press, 1999.

Widdows, Harry, Stefani Koorey, Kat Koorey, eds. *The Preliminary Hearing in the Lizzie Borden Case, New Edition*. Orlando, FL: PearTree Press, 2005.

Widdows, Harry, Stefani Koorey, Kat Koorey, eds. *The Trial of Lizzie Andrew Borden*. Orlando, FL: PearTree Press, 2005.

Witness Statements. Orlando, FL: PearTree Press, 2004.

The Miller/Bowen house diagonally across the street from 92 Second Street.

Dr. Bowen, *Boston Globe*, June 9, 1893

Dr. Bowen grave at Oak Grove Cemetery, Fall River, Massachusetts.

Dr. William Dolan, *Boston Globe*, August 26, 1892

Dr. William Andrew Dolan

July 28, 1854 – October 1, 1922

William Andrew Dolan was the son of Andrew and Jane (McBride) Dolan. He was born on July 28, 1858. His family moved to Fall River when he was very young. In 1879, he graduated from St. Joseph's College in New York. He got his medical degree from The University of Pennsylvania in 1882, practicing medicine in Fall River after graduating. In 1883 Dolan married Nellie B. Hussey, also of Fall River.

Appointed to the medical staff of Fall River Hospital as one of its first physicians, he was a member of the Massachusetts Medical Society and played a chief role in founding the Fall River Medical Society.

In 1892, he was a medical examiner for the Third District Court in Bristol County, Massachusetts. He had only been medical examiner a little over a year (July,1891).

On the morning of August 4, 1892, Doctor Dolan left his office to visit a patient at 86 Fourth Street. Coming back, he noticed some people around the Borden home and asked what had happened. He went into the Borden house, where he saw Andrew, in the sitting room, and then Abby, upstairs.

A partial autopsy was done at about 3:30 p.m. on Andrew in the sitting room and Abby in the dining room, both on undertakers' boards. Despite mutterings of negatives from other doctors there, Dr. Dolan cut out the stomachs of both victims, tied them each at the ends, and sealed them in jars to be sent express to Harvard, where they were to be tested for poison. A sample of milk from both August 3rd and 4th were similarly sent.

The second, or actual, autopsy was performed by Dr. Dolan at the Oak Grove Cemetery. It was held on August 11, 1892, one week after the murders. In 1892, an autopsy cost $30.00. Each view of a body cost $5.00, and $5.00 was given to each assistant.

Andrew Borden's autopsy was held at 11:15 a.m. with Dr. F.W. Draper of Boston, John H. Leary (city physician of Fall River), and Clerk D. E. Cone (physician at 278 South Main Street) of Fall River as assistants.

Abby Borden's autopsy began at 12:38 p.m. with the same assistants and witnesses. It was here that the heads were removed from both and the skulls later cleaned, in Dr. Dolan's kitchen, and made into casts.

Dr. Dolan gave testimony at the preliminary hearing and at the trial of Lizzie Borden. He was in charge of the medical aspect of the Borden murders.

In the June 12, 1893 *Boston Globe*, Dolan was described as a "round-faced fat man," "a bright fellow," and an "excellent arguer." The same newspaper on June 14, 1893, spoke of him as "fat and cheery, good-natured and impassive."

Dolan died at his Fall River home suddenly on October 1, 1922, from heart failure. Survivors were Miss Ellen B.C. Dolan, Miss Mary A. Dolan (daughters and teachers in Fall River), Thomas Dolan, and William A. Dolan (sons). Dr. Dolan's funeral took place at St. Mary's Cathedral. He is buried at St. Patrick's Cemetery in Fall River.

Dr. Dolan is buried in Sec. 3 – 1423, a grave lot of twelve double burials. The site was purchased in 1885, most likely when his father, Andrew Dolan, died. The monument for the Dolan plot is so large, it prevents lots 16 through 19 from being used.

The Graves

1. There are three bodies buried in this plot, including: Andrew Dolan, the doctor's father, was born in Ireland in 1819. He died on December 4, 1885, at the age of 66, and was buried on December 7, 1885.

Mary Dolan, the doctor's daughter, who died at the age of 75 from heart disease on May 20, 1971, and was buried on May 24, 1971. Born in Fall River, she was living at 382 Stetson Street in that city when she died.

2. Jane Dolan, the doctor's mother, died at the age of 62 on July 12, 1893, and was buried on July 14, 1893. At that time, her place of residence was at 220 South Main Street in Fall River.

3. Ellen B.C. Dolan, daughter of the doctor, died on August 5, 1957, and was buried on August 8, 1957. She was 66 years old. At the time of her death, she resided at 384 Stetson Street in Fall River.

4. Unoccupied.

5. Mary B. (nee McMillan) Dolan, the widow of the doctor's son, William A. Dolan, died of acute pulmonary embolism at the age of 75 on March 14, 1970, and was buried on March 17, 1970. At the time of her death, she was living at 382 Stetson Street in Fall River, which is the same address as the doctor's daughter, Mary Dolan, last resided.

6. Francis Augustine Dolan died on January 23, 1898, and was buried on January 28, 1898. Place of residence was 548 South Main Street, Fall River. Probably the doctor's child.

7. William A. Dolan, the son of Dr. Dolan, died at the age of 73 on August 27, 1968. He was buried on September 3, 1968. His last residence was at 1777 So. Eastern 9th Street, Fort Lauderdale, Florida.

8. Dr. William A. Dolan, was born in Shirley, Massachusetts on July 28, 1854. He died on October 1, 1922, of myocarditis and was buried on October 4, 1922. He was 68 years old. His last place of residence was 548 South Main Street in Fall River. He never remarried and was still working up until his sudden death.

9. Unoccupied.

10. Ellen "Nellie" B. Dolan died at the age of 46 on February 3, 1909. She was buried on February 6, 1909. She was the wife of Dr. Dolan. Her last residence was at 458 South Main Street in Fall River.

Sources:

Martins, Michael and Dennis Binette, eds. *The Commonwealth of Massachusetts vs. Lizzie A. Borden, The Knowlton Papers*. Fall River, MA: The Fall River Historical Society, 1994.

Rebello, Leonard. *Lizzie Borden, Past & Present*. Fall River, MA: Al-Zach Press, 1999.

Widdows, Harry, Stefani Koorey, Kat Koorey, eds. *The Preliminary Hearing in the Lizzie Borden Case, New Edition*. Orlando, FL: PearTree Press, 2005.

Dr. Dolan grave at St. Patrick's Cemetery, Fall River, Massachusetts.

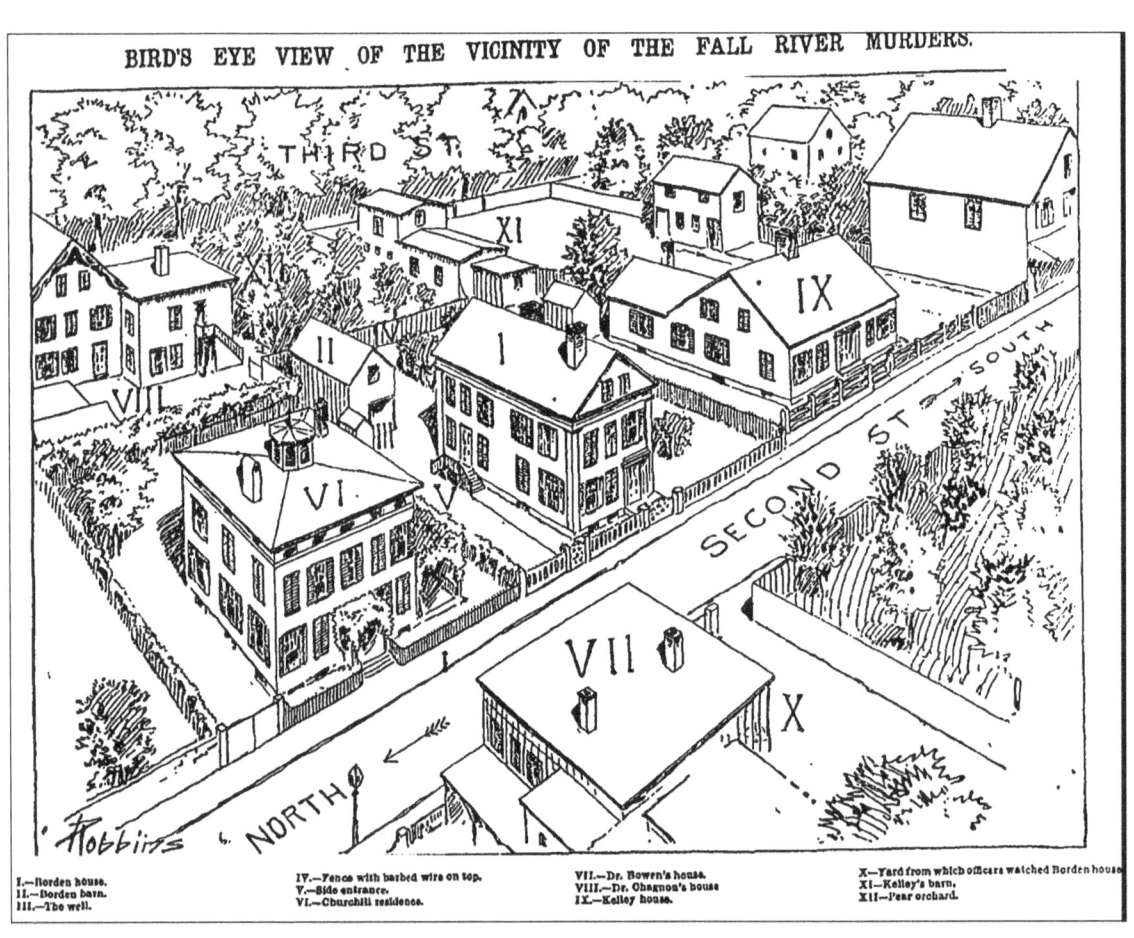

Borden neighborhood, *Boston Globe*, August 11, 1892

Dr. Benjamin J. Handy

1849 – May 14, 1929

Benjamin Jones Handy was born in Marion, Massachusetts. He was the son of Frederick P. Handy and Sarah (Berry) Handy, both of Marion. Dr. Handy was a physician in Fall River. He was an 1872 graduate of Harvard.

Handy married Susan Elizabeth Holmes, who pre-deceased him, as did their two young sons, Benjamin and Frederick.

By the year 1892, he had been practicing medicine in Fall River for eighteen years. Dr. Handy was on Second Street the day of the Borden murders and said he saw a strange looking man near the house. The press dubbed this person "The Wild Eyed Man" or sometimes "Dr. Handy's Wild Eyed Man." Yet, according to Paul Dennis Hoffman in *Yesterday in Old Fall River*, Handy never publicly remarked about "a strangeness in the man's eyes or that they were in any way wild." While many people said they saw strangers near the Borden home, Handy's sighting of the strange man outside the Borden home was accepted as fact by the police because he was a respected and well-known member of Fall River society. Handy testified at both the preliminary hearing and the trial of Lizzie Borden.

On August 3, 1892, the night before the Borden murders, Lizzie visited Miss Alice Russell, claiming she felt someone was going to come and do harm to her father and, possibly, the whole family. She said a curious thing about Dr. Handy that night. Telling Alice how Abby and Andrew were sick, she said that Dr. Bowen came over to the house, after receiving a visit from Abby, to check on Lizzie's father. Apparently Andrew did not treat Bowen kindly.

Alice Russell wrote to Mr. Moody before the trial, telling all she could remember of what Lizzie had said that night.

> After he had gone, Mrs. Borden scolded. She said I am ashamed for you to use Dr. Bowen so. Mr. Borden said 'well I don't want him coming over here Dr. Handy style'. Mrs. B. said he didn't come over here Dr. Handy style. I told him you were sick and he came over to see you and I think it is a shame you can't treat him decent.

What did Andrew mean by his phrase "Dr. Handy style"? It must have been a known one in the household, for Abby knew what he meant. Whatever it was, it was certainly not a compliment.

Dr. Handy owned a cottage in Marion on Buzzard's Bay, where his daughter, Louise, had many of her girlfriends join her and generally vacation. The cottage played an important part in the Borden murders. At the time her father was being murdered, Lizzie claimed to be in the barn looking for sinkers to fish with when she hoped to join several friends at Dr. Handy's cottage on Monday, August 8. The cottage, which looked more the size of a house, appears on an 1855 town map of Marion noted as the residence of F.P. Handy, Dr. Handy's father. In 1903, a map shows it as #69, belonging to B.J. Handy.

A photo of Dr. Handy's cottage was published for the first time in *The Hatchet: A Journal of Lizzie Borden Studies*. The cottage was torn down in 1941. A new home was built on the site for a dentist from New Bedford. The Handy cottage site is at 9 South Street.

Dr. Handy returned to Marion after retiring from his medical practice. He belonged to the Marion Congregational Church. He died in Marion on May 14, 1929, at the age of 81, of arteriosclerosis. Daughter Louise Handy died around 1956, at the Elm Crest Rest Home on North Street in Mattapoisett.

Sources:

Chapman, Sherry. "Dr. Handy's Cottage." *The Hatchet: A Journal of Lizzie Borden Studies* 1.5 (2004).

Hoffman, Paul Dennis. *Yesterday in Old Fall River*. Durham, NC: Carolina Academic Press, 2000.

Martins, Michael and Dennis Binette, eds. *The Commonwealth of Massachusetts vs. Lizzie A. Borden, The Knowlton Papers*. Fall River, MA: The Fall River Historical Society, 1994.

Rebello, Leonard. *Lizzie Borden, Past & Present*. Fall River, MA: Al-Zach Press, 1999.

Dr. Handy's cottage in Marion, Massachusetts.

Dr. Handy's grave at Evergreen Cemetery, Fairhaven, Massachusetts.

Dr. Tourtellot grave at Notre Dame Cemetery in Fall River, Massachusetts.

Dr. John Quincy Adams Tourtellot

1842 – 1892

John Quincy Adams Tourtellot was born in Providence, Rhode Island. He went to Dellevue College and then on to study medicine. He was a doctor for more than twenty years. From 1875 – 1877 he was city physician of Fall River. He was a member of the Fall River School Board for four years, starting in 1881.

The doctor had a large practice, known for acts of kindness and charity, especially his medical work for area benevolent societies. He lived in Fall River with his wife, Ida.

J.Q.A. Tourtellot was a member of the first autopsy team at the Borden house on August 4, 1892.

He is buried in the Notre Dame cemetery in Fall River.

Sources:

Handwritten file from the Fall River Historical Society.

Hoffman, Paul Dennis. *Yesterday in Old Fall River*. Durham, NC: Carolina Academic Press, 2000.

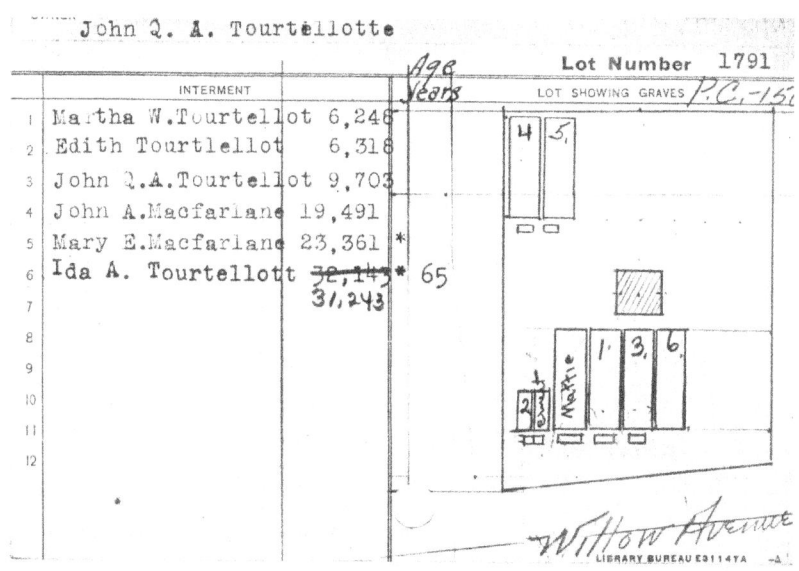

Part Four

They Thickened the Plot

Eli Bence, from Edwin Porter, *Fall River Tragedy*, 1893.

Eli Bence

January 18, 1865 – May 4, 1915

Eli Bence was a druggist at D.R. Smith's in Fall River (near Columbia and South Main Streets) in the summer of 1892. Shortly before the Borden murders, Lizzie was identified by Bence and two others in the store as entering and asking for a most deadly poison, prussic acid. She was told it was available only by prescription and she left the shop.

Bence testified at the inquest and the preliminary hearing. Called to witness at Lizzie Borden's trial, there was much debate concerning the admissibility of his testimony. After a break in the proceedings, nothing more was said and his testimony was excluded, although there is no recorded ruling from the bench in the trial's transcript.

Eli Bence was born in Braintree, Massachusetts, to parents William Bence and Sarah (Hudson) Bence, both from England. He was one of four children. He worked in several drugstores in Fall River. He worked at D.R. Smith's from 1890 – 1895. In 1905, he owned his first store in Pittsfield, Massachusetts.

Bence was married to Sarah J. Mayhurst, of Fall River. His second wife was Annie C. Maxfield, of Fairhaven. They were wed in Fairhaven on April 10, 1904. He had two sons, Roy S. and Maxfield Bence, of Pittsfield as of 1915.

He belonged to many associations in his lifetime: Pittsfield Druggist Association, where he was president; the National Association of Retail Druggists; the Pittsfield Merchants Association; King Phillip Lodge of Masons of Fall River; Berkshire Knights of Templars; Melba Temple of the Mystic Shrine of Springfield, Massachusetts; and the Park Club.

Bence's last address was with his wife and children at 64 Commonwealth Avenue in Pittsfield. He was fatally injured in an automobile accident while driving with his wife, who survived. He died of a cerebral hemorrhage (bleeding inside the brain) and interstitial nephritis (a kidney disorder in which the spaces between the kidney tubules become swollen). He was 50 years old.

Eli Bence is buried in Fairhaven at Riverside Cemetery, which is located at 274 Main Street (Fairhaven).

The land for the cemetery was given by the grandfather of Franklin D. Roosevelt, Warren Delano II. A native of Fairhaven, he lived in New York City and was a leading China trade merchant. As of August 1994, there were 11,824 people buried there. There are a lot of Delanos there, including the mother of FDR. When I was there, I was escorted to the grave of Eli Bence by superintendent Hay B. Reid. Mr. Reid comes from a line of Riverside Cemetery caretakers, his grandfather being personally appointed by FDR's grandfather. His father, Norman Reid, preceded him.

Sources:

Grant, Frederic D. Jr. "The Riverside Cemetery: A Community Resource." n.d. Handwritten file from the Fall River Historical Society.

Hoffman, Paul Dennis. *Yesterday in Old Fall River*. Durham, NC: Carolina Academic Press, 2000.

Rebello, Leonard. *Lizzie Borden, Past & Present*. Fall River, MA: Al-Zach Press, 1999.

Reid, Hay B. Personal conversations. April 2004.

Eli Bence grave in Riverside Cemetery, Fairhaven, Massachusetts.

Eli Bence, *Boston Globe*, August 30, 1892

William Borden

April 20, 1854 – April 17, 1901

William S. Borden was the alleged murderer of the Bordens (and alleged illegitimate son of Andrew Borden) according to Arnold R. Brown in his book *Lizzie Borden: The Legend, the Truth, the Final Chapter*. A source for Mr. Brown's book claimed that Ellen Eagan (the lady who ice cream peddler Hyman Lubinsky might have seen in Andrew Borden's back yard on August 4, 1892) saw William, described him to the police, and was then told to never tell anyone about it.

William was born in Fall River. He married Rebecca Gammons when he was 20. At that time he was working as a peddler and a laborer. He and Rebecca lived with her family from 1872 – 1901, except for him moving twice during that time frame. William spent the year of 1875 in the Taunton Lunatic Asylum. On April 17, 1901, he committed suicide by hanging himself from a tree on New Boston Road in Fall River.

William S. Borden is buried in King Cemetery, which is located at 1300 Middleboro Avenue in East Taunton, Massachusetts. He is buried in an unmarked grave.

Sources:

Brown, Arnold R. *Lizzie Borden: The Legend, the Truth, the Final Chapter*. NY: Dell, 1991.
Fasolo, Debbie, Senior Clerk, City of Taunton, Massachusetts. Correspondence. 16 April 2003.
Rebello, Leonard. *Lizzie Borden, Past & Present*. Fall River, MA: Al-Zach Press, 1999.

Joseph Carpenter grave at Oak Grove Cemetery, Fall River, Massachusetts.

Joseph Wilmarth Carpenter Jr.

September 4, 1855 – October 30, 1899

Joseph Carpenter was born in Fall River to parents Joseph W. Carpenter Sr. and Phoebe A. (Kershaw) Carpenter. There were five children in the family. First working in the produce business of Bruce & Carpenter, Joseph worked as a bookkeeper for Borden & Almy from 1874 – 1878. He married Annie Barney, daughter of Captain George Barney, also of Fall River.

Interestingly, future policeman Philip Harrington also worked for Borden & Almy. Harrington was employed there from about 1874 to about 1877.

Carpenter was fired when it was found he had been embezzling money from his employers since his third day at work.

After the Bordens were murdered, Carpenter became a suspect. Articles such as this one appeared in newspapers:

HERE IS A CLUE

Young Bookkeeper Who Embezzled From Borden & Almy

ROCHESTER, N.Y., Aug. 10—An evening paper published tonight an interview with a resident of this city whose name was not given.

The man said that he formerly lived in Fall River, and knew the family of Andrew Borden well.

Speaking of the theories regarding the murder of Mr. Borden, he said:

'I have my own theories of the murder. A few years ago Borden & Almy employed a young man, 22 years old, as bookkeeper. His wages were $7 a week. Upon this salary he married, and he and his young wife lived extravagantly. He purchased handsome dresses for her, and they cut a big figure for a time. Soon it was found that the young bookkeeper had made alterations in the books, and that, not withstanding his extravagance, he had deposits in two banks amounting to over $1000. He had embezzled the funds of the firm, his speculations having begun three days after he had entered its employ. The bank books were attached by the firm and some of the speculations were thus recovered. I believe a settlement was made by the young man's father and his father-in-law, and he was allowed to go free. A few days ago I saw in the papers that this young man had been arrested in Binghamton for swindling. One of the witnesses at the Borden inquest testified that he saw a young man, a few days before the murder, shake his fist at old man Borden, in front of his house and say: "D—n you, you took my money, and I will get even with you yet." 'Was this the money that the young bookkeeper had deposited in the bank? I think the

Fall River police should investigate this point.'

In 1882, Joseph Carpenter moved with his wife to Holyoke, Massachusetts. His wife, Annie, moved back to Fall River. Carpenter then moved to Albany, New York, and was a drummer (salesman) of inks, pens, and stationery, travelling much of New York State. He was living there in 1892.

It cannot be ignored that there were two persons who said they saw Carpenter in Fall River in early August 1892. Peter Driscoll said that he shaved Carpenter on August 1. A schoolteacher named Dean said he saw Carpenter on August 4, and Carpenter and wife left the city the following day.

Of all the people he could have sent to talk to Joseph Carpenter, Marshal Hilliard asked Officer Philip Harrington, Carpenter's fellow worker from his days at Borden & Almy. Harrington was convinced that Lizzie Borden committed the murders. He went to see Carpenter, but he did not dig too far into Carpenter's claim to innocence.

Carpenter did not have a real alibi. His sales book showed activity on August 3 and August 5, but there was no entry for August 4. Carpenter said he spent nights from July 18 through August 13 in an Albany rooming house. His landlady said yes, he did—as far as she knew. Thus Officer Harrington returned to Fall River, assuring the Marshal of Carpenter's innocence.

Joseph Carpenter died in Worcester, Massachusetts at the age of 44. He was laid to rest at Oak Grove Cemetery in Fall River, Massachusetts.

Note: I had requested his death certificate from the city clerk in Worcester, Massachusetts. I was told there was none on file for him in Worcester.

Sources:

Martins, Michael and Dennis Binette, eds. *The Commonwealth of Massachusetts vs. Lizzie A. Borden, The Knowlton Papers.* Fall River, MA: The Fall River Historical Society, 1994.

Masterton, William. *Lizzie Didn't Do It!* Boston: Branded Publishing Co., 2000.

Rebello, Leonard. *Lizzie Borden, Past & Present.* Fall River, MA: Al-Zach Press, 1999.

"Told to a Friend." *Boston Daily* 20 August 1892.

From Dr. Chagnon's yard (Third Street) showing rear of Borden yard and barn, where Mrs. and Miss Chagnon heard the noise Wednesday evening.

Marianne (Gigault) Phaneuf Chagnon (Mrs. Dr. Chagnon)

Died May 16, 1898

Mrs. Chagnon and her step-daughter, Miss Martha Chagnon, both testified at the preliminary hearing and the trial of Lizzie Borden. The Chagnons lived on Third Street, in back of the Borden home on Second Street.

At about 11 p.m. the night before the murders, they were in the same room of the house and heard noises coming from outdoors. Martha Chagnon, daughter of Dr. Chagnon's first wife, described the noise as like it was pounding on wood, on the fence or a board. She said the noise came from the Borden fence direction. There was a fence between their property and the Bordens. Both testified that the sound lasted about five minutes.

Mrs. Chagnon said there was "space between the noise.".Andrew Jennings asked [trial, page 1341]:

Q: What do you mean by that? Did it cease and begin again?

A: We heard some noise, and after --- we wait, and we heard noise again.

There was a two or three minute pause between the noises.

The Chagnons had a dog house in the corner of their backyard. At the time the noise was heard, their dog ("Well, I think a Newfoundland dog." – Martha Chagnon, *Trial*, 1334) was on the piazza and had no reaction that they knew of to the sounds. Nice try, Mr. Knowlton, but Second Street was a very busy street. Third Street alone had at least an ice house near the Chagnon house. The busy yard of John Crowe, with its working men, must have been heard in the daytime. The dog was probably used to all kinds of sounds. It is quite possible that the dog was pretty sensitized to noises.

Mrs. Chagnon was the second wife of Dr. Chagnon. They were married in 1885, in Biddeford, Maine. Prior to their marriage, she was married to Desire Phaneuf, a merchant in Canada.

In 1898, Mrs. Chagnon was boarding for a short time at La Meterie auxillary of the General hospital of St. Hyacinthe, in the small village of La Providence, near Montreal. Normally a place for retired clergy and a clergy summer resort, the nuns who ran it would take in boarders for a few weeks at a time before the summer season.

Mrs. Chagnon and her family were going to move to the area from Fall River by the winter and she was getting the house ready. She was almost finished with it and had just written to Dr. Chagnon, telling him she would be back in a few days.

A fire broke out in the building she was staying at. The cause of the fire was not known at the time. The entire building was lost, valued at $20,000. Approximately nine lives were lost, at least a dozen injured, and many missing. Mrs. Chagnon died when she jumped out of a third story window and landed on the pavement below.

Mrs. Chagnon was well known in the city in which she lost her life. She had a sister there, Mrs. E. Vadnais. She was survived by a son, Dr. J.S. Phaneuf of Globe Village in Fall River and another son in the Klondike regions, a brother who was an Oblate Father at Lowell, Massachusetts, and a second brother who was a government employee in Ottawa, Canada.

At the time the story first hit the papers, it was surmised that she would be buried in Canada.

Sources:

"Convent Burned." *Lowell Sun* (Massachusetts) 16 May 1898.

Lincoln Evening News (Nebraska) 16 May 1898.

Martins, Michael and Dennis Binette, eds. *The Commonwealth of Massachusetts vs. Lizzie A. Borden, The Knowlton Papers*. Fall River, MA: The Fall River Historical Society, 1994.

Middletown Daily Argus (New York) 17 May 1898.

North Adams Transcript (Massachusetts) 17 May 1898.

Widdows, Harry, Stefani Koorey, Kat Koorey, eds. *The Trial of Lizzie Andrew Borden*. Orlando, FL: PearTree Press, 2005.

Addie B. Cheetham

1864 – 1943

Addie B. Cheetham was born in 1864 to Thomas Cheetham and Estelle Buffinton Cheetham, who was the sister of Adelaide Churchill. Thomas Cheetham was an upholsterer. He died in 1891. Adelaide Churchill's house was next door to the Bordens to the north. Its occupants in August of 1892 were Adelaide Churchill, her mother, her sister, her son, and her niece, as well as a man who did work for them. Mrs. Adelaide Churchill had lived in the house nearly all her life. She had known the Bordens for twenty years and was on "calling terms" with them.

Mrs. Estelle Cheetham and her sister, Adelaide Churchill, were among the few neighbors that were present at the funerals of Abby and Andrew Borden.

Adelaide Churchill's kitchen windows were twenty-eight feet from the Borden's rear screen door. The windows looked over the Borden yard directly opposite.

Addie Cheetham said she was writing a letter while sitting at the kitchen window. She wrote from 10:00 a.m. to about 10:55 a.m. During this critical time of the Borden murders, Miss Cheetham did not see anyone come or go to the Borden house.

There is no official testimony by Addie Cheetham.

Sources:

Rebello, Leonard. *Lizzie Borden, Past & Present*. Fall River, MA: Al-Zach Press, 1999.

Spiering, Frank. *Lizzie*. NY: Pinacle, 1985.

Widdows, Harry, Stefani Koorey, Kat Koorey, eds. *The Trial of Lizzie Andrew Borden*. Orlando, FL: PearTree Press, 2005.

Addie Cheetham grave at Oak Grove Cemetery, Fall River, Massachusetts.

John Crowe grave at Oak Grove Cemetery, Fall River, Massachusetts.

John Crowe

October 17, 1849 – April 30, 1927

John Crowe was born on October 17, 1849, in Scotland. His parents were Robert Crowe and Catherine Bodge, both of Scotland. John Crowe came to Fall River while in his 20s and, except for a few years in Boston, made Fall River his home.

He started working as a mason and soon worked his way up through the ranks of foreman and other positions until he became a contractor. On December 7, 1882, he married Anna Wilder of West Pembroke, Maine. Her parents were Ebid Wilder and Esther Farnsworth, both of West Pembroke, Maine.

John Crowe's yard was of interest when police interviewed persons in the area of the Bordens' house after the murders on August 4, 1892. Several men were working in Crowe's stone yard. Though deputy sheriff Francis H. Wixon entered the yard, none of them saw him. This led to the conclusion that a person could have escaped the Borden house via Crowe's backyard without being seen. The jury of Lizzie Borden's trial in June of 1893 were taken to Crowe's stoneyard as well as other places of interest in the crime.

On June 15, 1893, John Crowe's barn was in the news when some boys were playing on Third Street in front of John Crowe's barn and their ball went on to the roof. Arthur Potter, 14, went up to retrieve it. Instead of coming down with the ball, he found a hatchet and brought that down. It was suspected that it was the hatchet that was used in the Borden murders. Crowe himself did not know of anyone being up on his roof in two years. Crowe's barn roof was not searched by police when they investigated the Borden crimes the previous August.

> The barn is a flat roof structure about 18 feet high. In the rear is an ell, the full width of the main building, but not more than 12 feet high. Still extending to the west and toward the Borden estate is a narrow flat roofed ell, about 9 feet high. A six-foot fence runs diagonally and southeasterly from the north line from the first ell, so that it is very easy to scale the roof.

According to the Associated Press that day: "The handle was weather beaten and the blade covered with rust. Some of the particles of rust being removed a slight coloring of gilt was disclosed, which would either indicate that the hatchet was at one time used as an ornament or was quite new when lost or discarded." There had been gilt found in the wounds of Abby Borden.

Two days later, the *Fall River Daily Herald* reported,

The owner of the Potter-Borden hatchet has in all probability been found. Carl McDonnell, a carpenter employed by William Smith of Second Street, did some work for Dr. Chagnon about the time of the murder or a little later and lost a hatchet of a description similar to this one.

There are so many hatchets of a similar make that it is almost impossible to identify anyone in particular unless marked for that purpose. The axe undoubtedly belongs to McDonnell.

Crowe was president of the John Crow Co., Inc., one of the most prominent contractors in Fall River. He was a member of the Quequechan Club, the First Congregational Church, and the Adams Club affiliated with the church. He was a 32nd degree Mason and widely known in that order.

He was also a member of Massasoit Lodge, A. F. & M. Fall River Royal Arch chapter, Fall River council, Royal and Select Masters, Godfrey de Bouillon - commamndrey, Aleppo Shrine, Massachusetts Consistory, and Fall River Lodge, I.O.O.F., as well as the Fall River Chamber of Commerce.

John Crowe's company erected buildings all over the city. He supervised the construction of many structures and remodeled many other buildings. Some of the buildings he built or remodeled include: Citizens Savings, Fall River National, and Metacomet Banks, which he remodeled; the Fall River Gas Works Co., building, North Main Street; Y.M.C.A. Boys' Club; Bennett Building; basement of St. Anne's church; St. Mathieu's church; Coughlin, Osborn Street, Hicks Street, Flint Street, and Cambridge Street schools; Bay View Hospital; the Columbian Building; Women's Union building; Union Hospital; Nurses' Home, Truesdale Hospital; St. Catherine's Convent; Horton Building; Brewer Building on Pearce street; chapel of the Central Congregational Church; and the E.L. Anthony Building, in which the Western Union office is located on Bedford street. His company had also done general construction work for the Fall River Electric Light Company for a number of years.

John and Anna Crowe had no children. Anna passed away on September 25, 1926, at the age of 74 of chronic myocarditis (long term inflammation of the heart muscle, which we understand today is usually caused by a virus).

The last big jobs Crowe did were the Masonic Temple, North Main and Elm Streets; the service station of the Fall River Electric Light Company on Hartwell Street; and the M.T. Hudner building at South Main and Borden Streets.

On April 30, 1927, John Crowe died at home at 736 High Street of chronic valvular heart disease at the age of 77. His obituary published in the *Fall River Herald News* features a large photo of Crowe, headlined:

Prominent Builder Summoned by Death

John Crowe Dies at High St. Home

Constructed Many Local Buildings – Among Them Masonic Temple – Native of Scotland – 78

John Crowe, president of the John Crowe Co., Inc., and one of the most prominent contractors in this section, died Saturday evening at his home, 736 High Street, after a brief illness. He was in his 78th year.

Funeral Services Tomorrow

Mr. Crowe is survived by a brother, Robert, of Springfield; and three sisters, Miss Janey S. Crowe, who came to this city from Scotland last December, and Mrs. Mary Little and Mrs. Margaret Pringle, both of Scotland.

Funeral services will be held from his late residence tomorrow afternoon at 2, with Rev. Dr. John E. LeBosquet, pastor of the First Congregational church, officiating. Burial will be in the Oak Grove cemetery.

Later, the following was published from the city of Taunton, Massachusetts:

The late John Crowe of Fall River left an estate valued in the inventory at $47,801.81 personal and $4500 real. The inventory has been filed by George W. Bowen, administrator. The personal estate consists of the following: 38 shares Massachusetts Light Co., $3876; 38 shares Massachusetts Light Co., common, $6118; five shares Arctic Ice and Cold Storage, $25; 63 shares Barnard Mfg. Co., $1575; 25 shares Flint Mills, $2175; 198 shares John Crowe, Inc., $14,850; 40 shares Masonic Hall Association, $400; 200 shares Mass. Lead and Zinc, of no value; automobile, 1925 model, $1400; household furniture, $500; Massachusetts Casualty insurance policy, $200; deposit in Fall River Saving (sic) bank, $2279.23; deposit in Citizens' Savings bank, $3325.18; deposit in Massasoit-Pocasset National bank, $5078.50; share of estate of Anna L. Crowe, wife of intestate, $5,000. The real estate consists of land and buildings at 736 High Street, Fall River, valued at $4500.

Sources:

Fall River Daily Herald 17 June 1893.

"I Have Found Lizzie Borden's Hatchet." *Fall River Daily News Bulletin* 15 June 1893.

"Obituary of John Crowe." *Fall River Herald News* May 1927.

Probate published inventory of the estate of John Crowe from the Fall River Historical Society.

Rebello, Leonard. *Lizzie Borden, Past & Present*. Fall River, MA: Al-Zach Press, 1999.

Widdows, Harry, Stefani Koorey, Kat Koorey, eds. *The Preliminary Hearing in the Lizzie Borden Case, New Edition*. Orlando, FL: PearTree Press, 2005.

Widdows, Harry, Stefani Koorey, Kat Koorey, eds. *The Trial of Lizzie Andrew Borden*. Orlando, FL: PearTree Press, 2005.

Possible Ellen Egan grave at St. John's Cemetery, Fall River, Massachusetts.

Ellen Eagan

1855 – January 21, 1929

Ellen Eagan was born in Ireland. Her parents were Jeremiah Hurley and Mary Carey. In 1874 she came to the United States. She married Owen Eagan, who was the son of John and Catharine (Hurley) Eagan. Owen Eagan was a laborer, clerk, and owner of a store at the corner of Hope and Mulberry Streets in Fall River. Ellen Eagan is described in the papers as a "big, good-natured Irish woman."

Between 10:30 and 11 a.m. on the morning of August 4, 1892, ice cream peddler Hyman Lubinsky said that he saw a lady in a dark dress walking from the direction of the barn to the house on the Borden property. He only knew that it was not Bridget Sullivan, for he had had dealings with her before.

Officers Harrington and Doherty found the woman Lubinsky saw that day. The policemen all but disregarded Lubinsky's possibly important claim. It could prove that Lizzie Borden did indeed go to the barn that hot morning while her father was being killed.

According to police, the woman Lubinsky saw was Ellen Eagan of Mulberry Street. She was not well and took something that gave her a nauseous or laxative effect after she left her home to pick up a few things in town. When she got to near 92 Second Street, she became suddenly ill and rushed into the Kelly's yard, the Borden's neighbor, to use their outdoor facility.

On August 11, Eagan testified briefly at the inquest. She was asked just three questions before her testimony was dismissed as meaningless to the case. She was not in the Borden yard at all, the court determined, but in the Kelly yard.

The Eagans were the parents of five children. Ellen's husband, Owen, died on October 9, 1901, at the age of 43. She continued living at the corner of Hope and Mulberry Streets. In 1910, she moved to 18 Branch Street, where she stayed until she died on January 21, 1929. Ellen Eagan was 74 years old. She died of nephritis (kidney disease) and endocarditis (infection of the heart, usually occurring in those who have a preexisting heart condition).

Ellen Eagan is buried at St. John's Cemetery in Fall River, Massachusetts. (Grave location: 114, Row 10, Plat 1.) No sign of a marker could be found. According to their burial cards, Owen Eagan is also buried at grave 114, Row 10, Plat 1. His monument in the cemetery is a large one. It is possible that Ellen Eagan is buried in her husband's grave, her casket resting upon his. Catharine Eagan, Owen's mother, who died on November 9, 1903, at the age of 70, is buried at grave 115, Row 10, Plat 1.

Sources:

Rebello, Leonard. *Lizzie Borden, Past & Present*. Fall River, MA: Al-Zach Press, 1999.

Henry Hawthorne Jr. grave at St. Patrick's Cemetery, Fall River, Massachusetts.

Henry J. Hawthorne Jr.

April 18, 1889 – November 1, 1978

Henry J. Hawthorne/Hawthornewaite Jr., was married to Ellen Eagan's daughter, Mary (see 'Ellen Eagan'). He and his mother-in-law, Ellen Eagan, together pieced together a true (to them) story of who killed Andrew and Abby Borden. They named as the murderer William S. Borden, a supposedly illegitimate son of Andrew Borden. Hawthorne had written the story in notes. Lewis "Pete" Peterson, Hawthorne's son-in-law, gave the story to Arnold Brown. From this Brown wrote his book *Lizzie Borden: The Legend, the Truth, the Final Chapter* (1991).

Writing the notes when he was 89 years old, Hawthorne used his years working on William S. Borden's farm and the story of Ellen Eagan coming across William Borden on the morning of the murder as the foundation of the story. Brown's book received a lot of criticism as he had no real proof to back up most of Hawthorne's claims, and it did not help any that Hawthorne got many of his facts wrong.

Henry Hawthorne Jr. was born in Fall River. His parents were Henry J. Sr., and Bridget Gillespie. His father was born in England and his mother was born in Ireland. He was one of seven children.

He lived most of his life in Fall River. He was a veteran of World War I. He worked as an oil inspector for the Charles Martin Company. Hawthorne married Mary Eagan, who predeceased him on September 26, 1975. She died at the age of 80 from colon cancer. At the time of her death, they were living at 29 Courtney Street in Fall River.

His last place of residence was at 217 Longhill Avenue in Somerset, Massachusetts. At 3:25 p.m. on November 1, 1975, he died in Middleboro, Massachusetts, at St. Luke's Hospital, of cardiac arrest due to congestive heart failure, which was caused by Ischemic heart disease. He also had chronic obstruction lung disease.

Henry Hawthorne, and his wife, are buried at St. Patrick's Cemetery in Fall River, Massachusetts. He is buried in section 16, lot number 156, grave 1. His wife is buried in grave 2. They are buried in the family plot of George Jenkinson.

Sources:

Rebello, Leonard. *Lizzie Borden, Past & Present.* Fall River, MA: Al-Zach Press, 1999.

James Johnston grave at North Burial Ground, Fall River, Massachusetts.

James Johnston

1827 – August 20, 1897

OBITUARY

Death of James Johnston

Mr. James Johnston died at his home, 904 Rock Street, the residence of his nephew, James H. Booth, about 7 o'clock Friday night, aged 70 years. This intelligence will convey sadness to thousands of citizens to whom the figure of Mr. Johnston has been familiar all their lives, and to whom he has been a cheery and intelligent presence. His fatal illness was Bright's disease, from which he suffered several months, but which did not confine him to the bed until a few days since.

The departed was a native of Scotland, and was born in 1827. Coming to this country in early boyhood, he, with his parents, settled in Taunton, after a residence of two or three years in that place, he and they removed to Fall River, where he has since resided. The crucial experience of his life, and that which colored and limited all his future, came at 15 years of age, while playing around a well in Charity Lane, one day, he fell into it and, striking on his head, received injuries so grave that it was feared he would die from them, he finally rallied, however, and ultimately regained all his powers except that of vision, his eyesight gradually left him, and for 55 years he has had to make his way about the city with no other personal guide than his cane. In the course of this long period he has experienced hundreds of narrow escapes from serious or fatal injury in travel, but has never been hurt to any extent. His carefulness and the close pace he has kept with the times have won him many friends, and increased the circle of his acquaintance throughout the city. He has always enjoyed hearing the best literature read, and has kept close track of public events by the courtesy of his relatives and friends. For a while after his misfortune came upon him he was at the Perkins Institute for the Blind in South Boston, where he took a course both in the school and in the work-shop. Returning from the institute, he entered the employ of Borden & Almy as a mattress maker, and his trade thenceforward was in that line, his services being with Borden & Almy, Wood & Raymond, and Wood & Hall. He was employed by the last named firm until its dissolution about two years ago.

Mr. Johnston was never married, nor was he ever for a length of time a member of any society. Three brothers – Alexander, Thomas and John Johnston – and four sisters – Mrs. George Sheen, Mrs. James Gilles, Mrs. Sarah Booth, and Mrs. Peter Hargraves – survive him. His funeral services will be held on Monday at 2 o'clock, and interment will follow in the North Burying Ground.

Sources:
Fall River Evening News 21 August 1897.

Joseph Lemay grave at Notre Dame Cemetery, Fall River, Massachusetts.

Joseph Octave Lemay

Died March 19, 1921

Joseph O. Lemay gave a statement to A. Perron regarding what he saw that could have been tied into the Borden murders. From the police *Witness Statements*:

> August 18, 1892. 8.30 o'clock P.M. Joseph Lemay of North Steep Brook reports that about 5.30 o'clock this afternoon, while in the woods about a mile form [sic] his house, he heard somebody say "too bad about Mrs. Borden". Looking around to his left, he saw a man sitting down on a stone. Mr. Lemay asked him if he was tried [sic]. The man made no reply, but took up a small hatchet and commenced to grind his teeth. Mr. Lemay says that "he had some spots of blood on what was once a white shirt, three drops." His coat sleeves were pulled up, so that the wrist bands of his shirt could be seen, and there was some blood on both of them. They looked at each other for some minutes, when the man got up, jumped a wall, and went in a northerly fashion.
>
> Description: 30 or 35 years of age, height about five feet three inches, 140 pounds weight, brown mustache, quite good size, face looked as though he had not been shaved in two or three weeks. Dressed in black coat, dark pants, laced shoes, black derby hat, torn on top. Looked as though he had been having hard times recently, as he was a hard looking customer. Investigated by A. Perron, August 17, 1892, and finds it as reported as above.

Lemay was called by the defense to testify at the trial. He spoke French, and an interpreter (George E. Jendren) served in that capacity.

Mr. Lemay lived in Steep Brook, an area in the north end of Fall River. His farm was four miles from City Hall on Wilson Road and was situated on 56 acres with woods on each side of his farm.

Hosea Knowlton objected to the testimony, and both sides of Counsel approached the bench. Andrew Jennings summed up Lemay's story well:

> This witness will testify that on the 16th day of August, at his farm, about four miles north of City Hall, while traveling into the woods for the purpose of cutting poles, just before he reached a turn in the road, he heard the words 'poor Mrs. Borden' repeated three times, and immediately saw sitting upon a rock behind a wall and some brushwood, a man. He spoke, to the man in French twice, but received no answer. On speaking to him the second time the man took up from the ground by his side a hatchet, such as is used in shingling houses, and shook it at him. He stepped back and put his own axe up in an attitude of defence. They remained in that position some few minutes, when the man turned, leaped over a wall and disappeared into the woods. He said nothing to the witness at any time. The witness noticed

upon his shirt spots of blood. He notified the police the same evening of what he had seen and heard.

Knowlton and Jennings laid their arguments before the judges. The next morning Judge Mason announced the decision of Lemay's testimony. Because the evidence he offered could not be brought within any of the rules of evidences, Lemay's testimony was excluded from the trial.

In 1914, Lemay made the *Fall River Evening News* when he was accused of watering milk. Lemay had operated a small dairy at his Steep Brook farm for the past twenty-five years. An average of 15% added water was found in samples taken at Lemay's farm. Lemay claimed someone else had sneaked in and watered his milk, but the court did not believe him. He was fined $100.

Joseph Lemay was born in St. Edouard, County Lotbiniere, Canada. He married Almina Belanger.

Joseph Lemay died after a short illness in the early morning hours of Saturday, March 19, 1921. He was 72 years old and at the time lived at 4677 North Main Street in Fall River. He had lived in Fall River since his youth.

His wife had died several years earlier. He was survived by his children, the Misses Octavia, Eugenie, and Josephine, and sons Remi and Ovide Lemay. Also surviving him was his brother, Hypolite Lemay of St. Edouard, Canada.

Joseph Lemay's funeral was held on Tuesday, March 22, 1921, at 8:00 a.m. A solemn high mass of requiem was celebrated for the repose of his soul at St. Mathieu's Church at 8:30 a.m. Mr. Lemay is buried in the Lemay family plot at Notre Dame Cemetery in Fall River, Massachusetts.

Sources:

Fall River Evening News 30 January 1914.

Widdows, Harry, Stefani Koorey, Kat Koorey, eds. *The Trial of Lizzie Andrew Borden*. Orlando, FL: PearTree Press, 2005.

The Witness Statements. Orlando, FL: PearTree Press, 2005.

Hyman Lubinsky

Unsure – January 3, 1923

Hyman Lubinsky was a Russian Jew. He was born in Russia and arrived in the United States in 1889. Mr. Lubinsky was one of ten children born to Jacob and Bessie Sinderhoff. In 1892, he was living on Spring Street in Fall River.

Lubinsky worked in 1892 for Charles A. and Agnes S. Wilkinson, Confectioners, at 42 North Main Street as a peddler and a packer. On the morning of the Borden murders, he got off to a late start peddling ice cream after he got a team of horses from Charles Gardner's livery stable. He had the horses at a light trot as he drove up Second Street.

He did not bellow out his wares but instead looked at the houses to see if anyone were at home. If someone was, he approached the house to see if they wanted to buy ice cream.

He passed the Borden's house after 11 a.m. and saw a woman in a dark colored dress nearing the side door and, since her back was facing the barn, assumed she had come from there.

He looked at the woman. He had sold ice cream before to Bridget Sullivan. This woman was not her. He told his boss about it, as word of the double murders spread quickly. He told Officer Michael Mullaly about it, but felt that the policeman ignored his information. This could have proved that Lizzie actually was in the barn as she claimed at the time of Andrew's murder.

Officer Mullaly testified that Lubinsky named the time of passing by the Borden house on August 4 as 10:30—too early for Lizzie to have walked to the barn.

Lubinsky testified at Lizzie Borden's trial. Under Hosea Knowlton's questioning, Lubinsky was confused because his English was poor. It was hard to tell at times if his testimony was reliable, considering the many errors he made as he spoke on the stand.

Mr. Lubinsky lived at several residences during his lifetime. At one time he lived in the Borden house at 92 Second Street (1917-1919).

He married, but, by 1920, was divorced. Divorce was not such a scandalous thing in Victorian times as we have always been told. In some churches, though, it could be cause for ex-communication.

Several different dates of his birth are given from different sources. *The Knowlton Papers* has his birth year as 1874. Rebello cites it at 1876. Various dates of birth were given for him in different censuses. His gravestone says "1883." This is very doubtful, because it would make him nine years old in 1892. The date given in *The Knowlton Papers* seems the most logical (1874).

Lubinsky was a packer in Fall River at the time of his death. He died on January 3, 1923, at the age of 49. He died of pulmonary tuberculosis. Mr. Lubinsky died in Fall River. He is buried in the Hebrew Cemetery in Fall River, Line 19, Lot 28.

Hebrew Cemetery is located at 59 Greenlawn Street in Fall River. When entering the cemetery, the line numbers are painted on the walk. Look for "19" then count 28 lots in the row. The monument is white marble, but does not look it from weathering.

Sources:

Martins, Michael and Dennis Binette, eds. *The Commonwealth of Massachusetts vs. Lizzie A. Borden, The Knowlton Papers*. Fall River, MA: The Fall River Historical Society, 1994.

Rebello, Leonard. *Lizzie Borden, Past & Present*. Fall River, MA: Al-Zach Press, 1999.

Weissman, Jeffrey, Chairman, Hebrew Cemetery, Fall River, Massachusetts. Personal correspondence. 2003.

Widdows, Harry, Stefani Koorey, Kat Koorey, eds. *The Trial of Lizzie Andrew Borden*. Orlando, FL: PearTree Press, 2005.

Hyman Lubinsky grave at Hebrew Cemetery, Fall River, Massachusetts.

Hannah B. Gifford

1836 – June 20, 1912

Hannah (Borden) Gifford was born in 1836, in Fall River. Her parents were Joseph Borden and Hannah Westgate. She was related to Andrew Borden through a common great-grandfather. She married Perry Gifford, a Fall River widower and dealer in dry and fancy goods. Perry Gifford's first wife was Lydia Westgate, who died in 1858.

In 1892, she lived at 39 Franklin Street. In 1898, Hannah was widowed. She was a cloakmaker. Almost every season Emma, Lizzie, or Abby Borden called on her for her services. She had never been to the Borden house on Second Street.

In the early spring of 1892, Lizzie was at Hannah's place of business getting a new cloak made. Making conversation, Mrs. Gifford mentioned Abby Borden and was surprised at Lizzie's hostile reaction to her stepmother.

At the inquest, she was asked, "How came she to say that?"

Hannah Gifford said,

It was some remark I made about her mother's garment, what would be becoming for her. You know Mrs. Borden was very fleshy; I spoke to her of what I thought would be becoming for Mrs. Borden. She says 'well she is a mean old thing.' I says 'O, you don't say that Lizzie?' She says 'yes, and we don't have anything to do with her, only what we are obliged to,' she says.

Q: She said that?

A: She said that, yes.

Q: Anything more?

A: Well, she says "we stay up stairs most of the time; we stay in our room most of the time." I says "you do, don't you go to your meals?" "Yes, we go to our meals, but we don't always eat with the family, with them; sometimes we wait until they are through," she says.

Hannah Gifford told her story to the police, and it is in the *Witness Statements*. She testified at the inquest and at the trial.

In 1904, Mrs. Gifford moved to Hanson, Massachusetts. She died there on June 20, 1912, at the age of 76, of valvula heart disease. She is buried at the Oak Grove Cemetery in Fall River, Lot 20, Myrtle Path.

Sources:

Inquest Upon the Deaths of Andrew J. and Abby D. Borden, August 9 – 11, 1892, Volume I and II. Orlando, FL: PearTree Press, 2005.

Martins, Michael and Dennis Binette, eds. *The Commonwealth of Massachusetts vs. Lizzie A. Borden, The Knowlton Papers.* Fall River, MA: The Fall River Historical Society, 1994.

Rebello, Leonard. *Lizzie Borden, Past & Present.* Fall River, MA: Al-Zach Press, 1999.

Widdows, Harry, Stefani Koorey, Kat Koorey, eds. *The Trial of Lizzie Andrew Borden.* Orlando, FL: PearTree Press, 2005.

The Witness Statements. Orlando, FL: PearTree Press, 2005.

Hannah Gifford grave at Oak Grove Cemetery, Fall River, Massachusetts.

John C. Milne

May 18, 1824 – October 10, 1918

John Milne was born in Millfield, Scotland. Moving to Nova Scotia, he learned to be a compositor in the trade of printing. When he moved to Fall River, he and his wife (Abby A. Gifford, of Fall River) had nine children together.

In 1845, he and partner Frank L. Almy started the *Fall River Weekly News*. The two put up the $500 bail for John Morse after the Borden murders to ensure his presence at the preliminary hearing.

Sources:

Hoffman, Paul Dennis. *Yesterday in Old Fall River*. Durham, NC: Carolina Academic Press, 2000.

John Milne grave at Oak Grove Cemetery, Fall River, Massachusetts.

Lucy Normand grave at Notre Dame Cemetery, Fall River, Massachusetts.

Lucie (Collet) Normand

October, 1874 – June 5, 1900

Lucie Collet was born in St. Henry, Quebec, Canada, to Peter A.A. Collet and Georgianna (Verrault) Collet. She testified at the preliminary hearing and trial of Lizzie Borden.

Lucie was French-Canadian and had a little difficulty with the English language. Her father was a doctor and owned a drug store. At the time of the Borden murders, she was 17 years old and lived at 22 Borden Street, between Second and Third Streets.

On August 4, 1892, the day of the Borden murders, Officers Harrington and Doherty interviewed Lucie:

> At Dr. Chagnon's house we found his assistant, but he was at Bowenville during the forenoon, and the Doctor and family were at Pawtucket R. I., leaving there about 5. A. M. When the Doctor's assistant was on his way to Bowenville, he called at Dr. Collet's, and requested his (Collet's) son to go and care for the house. He was busy at the Drug store, and could not go, so the assistant went off. Afterwards Dr. Collet's daughter Lucy was sent up to Dr. Chagnon's to await callers. She could not gain entrance, for the door was locked, so she remained in the yard from 9.45 A. M., or thereabouts, to 12 M, when the assistant returned. She is positive no one could go through the yard without being seen by her. She heard no noise.

On August 27, 1892, Lucie Collet gave this statement to Philip Harrington:

Fall River, Saturday Aug. 27, 1892. Statement of Lucy G. Collett, aged 18 years.

'John Normand, clerk for Dr. Chagnon, telephoned to our house, No. 22 Borden street, requesting me to attend Dr. Chagnon's house while he drove the Doctor and his wife to the depot. This message was received by father (Dr. Collett). When he repeated it to me, I looked at the clock, it was 10.45 A. M. As I knew there was a train for Providence, where they were going, or rather Pawtucket, through Providence, I hurried to get ready. While in the sitting room up stairs arranging my hat, I saw the Doctor, his wife, and Mr. Normand, drive by. I then went to Dr. Chagnon's, arriving there at 10.50 A.M. The door was locked, so I went into the yard to see if the hammock was there. It was not, so I walked around the yard a while, them (sic) sat down on the steps. While there two men called. The first, about ten minutes after I had arrived, which would be about 11. A. M. He waited about ten minutes, when he said, I must go. He gave me a bottle, and asked me to give it to the clerk and tell him to refill it, and he would call for it this afternoon. When the second man was informed the Doctor was not at home, he went away. Both men came up Third street from Borden street, and returned the same way. About 11.45 A.M. Mr. Normand returned. We both entered the house, talked a short while, and after having a drink of lemonade, I returned home arriving just as the clock was striking twelve M. It was by this I fixed the time of Mr. Normand's return. While there at

Dr. Chagnon's, no one came through the yard, nor could such be done without my knowing it. I heard no noise or cry. I first heard of the murder when I arrived home.

This interview took place at Dr. Collett's house, No. 22 Borden Street Saturday Aug 27, from 3.55 to 4.40 P. M. This is my second interview with Miss Collett.
(Phil Harrinton) (sic)

In 1896, Lucie married Dr. Chagnon's clerk, Mr. Normand. In 1900, she and her husband resided at 728 Slade Street in Fall River. On June 5 of that year, she died at the age of 26, of phthisis pulmonalis, meaning that she died a slow death, wasting away from tuberculosis. Lucie Collet Normand is buried in the Notre Dame Cemetery in Fall River, Massachusetts.

Note: Lucie Collet has had her name spelled in different ways. Used here is the spelling used on her death certificate.

Sources:

Martins, Michael and Dennis Binette, eds. *The Commonwealth of Massachusetts vs. Lizzie A. Borden, The Knowlton Papers*. Fall River, MA: The Fall River Historical Society, 1994.

Widdows, Harry, Stefani Koorey, Kat Koorey, eds. *The Preliminary Hearing in the Lizzie Borden Case, New Edition*. Orlando, FL: PearTree Press, 2005.

Widdows, Harry, Stefani Koorey, Kat Koorey, eds. *The Trial of Lizzie Andrew Borden*. Orlando, FL: PearTree Press, 2005.

The Witness Statements. Orlando, FL: PearTree Press, 2005.

John Newton

c. 1854 – October 20, 1893

John Newton was thought of as an unbalanced man—an eccentric. He worked at the B.M.C. Durfee Safe Deposit and Trust Company. It was thought that Andrew Borden kept the bulk of his fortune there. John Newton was a janitor at the company. He said that the former marshal of Fall River, David S. Brigham, murdered the Bordens. There was never any proof found to back up his claim.

On October 20, 1893, John Newton committed suicide by jumping off the Cunard steamship *Campania*. He was a steerage passenger on the ship. He was 39 years old. Coincidentally, David S. Brigham died on October 22, 1893.

Newton and his wife, Margaret Ann (Brewer) Newton, lived at 150 Second Street in Fall River. His body was sent back to Fall River in November 1893. She did not believe it was a suicide. Mrs. Newton had Dr. William Dolan examine her husband's body. The doctor found that Mr. Newton had a skull fracture. This could have been caused by his head striking something when he jumped from the ship. However, playing up the mystery angle of the Borden murders to the hilt, the *Fall River Globe* reported that, "The fractured skull might have been the cause of death, however, and this surprising find adds something more of the mystery to the case."

The official cause of his death was "drowning." John Newton is buried in Oak Grove Cemetery, Fall River, Massachusetts.

Sources:

Rebello, Leonard. *Lizzie Borden, Past & Present*. Fall River, MA: Al-Zach Press, 1999.

Part Five

Friends

Genevra Almy grave at Oak Grove Cemetery, Fall River, Massachusetts.

Genevra M. Almy

February 26, 1826 - April 4, 1903

Genevra Almy was the wife of William M. Almy, long-time business partner of Andrew Borden. Her parents were Abram and Rachel (Gardner) Allen. She was born in Tiverton, Rhode Island.

Mrs. Almy was a close friend of Mrs. Sarah Anthony Morse Borden, Andrew Borden's first wife. She was also well acquainted with Emma and Lizzie Borden.

The Almys owned property by the Bordens on Garner's Neck Road in Swansea, which they called "Landscape Place."

Mrs. Almy died on April 4, 1903, at her home in Fall River, Massachusetts. She is buried in the Almy family plot in Oak Grove Cemetery in Fall River.

Sources:

Hoffman, Paul Dennis. *Yesterday in Old Fall River*. Durham, NC: Carolina Academic Press, 2000.

Martins, Michael and Dennis Binette, eds. *The Commonwealth of Massachusetts vs. Lizzie A. Borden, The Knowlton Papers*. Fall River, MA: The Fall River Historical Society, 1994.

William M. Almy grave at Oak Grove Cemetery, Fall River, Massachusetts.

William M. Almy

November 13, 1821 – June 11, 1885

William M. Almy was Andrew Borden's longtime business partner. He was born in Portsmouth, Rhode Island. His family moved to Fall River when he was six years old. His parents were Langworthy and Edith Almy, both of Dartmouth, Massachusetts. His parents were Quakers.

For almost thirty-five years he and Andrew Borden were business partners in furniture and undertaking. The firm of Borden & Almy was in business from the time Almy was 23 years old (March 1, 1845 – March 1, 1878). The only competitor was Abner Westgate, and there was plenty of business for both of them.

Almy was not one for public life, though he did spend one year as a member of the City Government. He was a prominent mason, being a charter member of King Phillip Lodge. For ten years he was treasurer of this lodge and was always an active worker in its interests. According to his June 12, 1885, obituary, "He was a thorough business man whose integrity was never called in question." When Almy retired, he and Borden continued to team up in real estate deals.

One of his obituaries follows:

Mr. Wm. M. Almy, whose death was briefly announced in Thursday's News, belonged to a generation of men who are rapidly passing away, but who have seen long business life in this active city, and have been busy and interested in promoting its welfare and growth. Mr. Almy was born in Portsmouth, R.I., November 13th, 1821, and came to Fall River when a young lad. He continued to attend school for a short time, but as was customary in those days, was early put to work, and entered the Robeson Print Works, where many of Fall River's once prominent men have found employment. Shortly after he began to learn the cabinet maker's trade, beginning an apprenticeship with the late Stephen D. Cragin and Co. About the same time Mr. Andrew J. Borden completed a similar apprenticeship with Abner L. Westgate, now of Middleboro, but long a well known resident of Fall River. With less than a thousand dollars in capital these two young men purchased, in October, 1844, the now valuable business property at Nos. 5, 7 and 9 Anawan street, upon which they erected a three story building, 20x40 feet, in which they opened in March, 1845, a house furnishing store, or rather a furniture store, - for the house furnishing establishments of those days did not include the complete equipment of those of to-day. They also conducted an undertaking business, and were for many years the principal undertakers of the town. This partnership continued for nearly 35 years, Mr. T.D.W. Wood being admitted to the firm about 15 years before its dissolution. By close application to business both of the original members acquired large properties, and even to the date of Mr. Almy's decease Mr. Borden was interested with him as joint owner in considerable valuable real estate in different sections of the city. The firm also became interested in the manufacturing interests of the city, and their capital has aided in the construction of several of these enterprises. About four years ago failing health compelled Mr. Almy to relinquish all business cares, and the illness, from which he never recovered, terminated fatally on Thursday last. His funeral will be held from his late residence, on Franklin street, to-morrow afternoon.

Though in poor health for his last four years, he rapidly declined in his last year. He died from "paralysis of the heart" about 2:30 in the afternoon of June 11, 1885, at his home at 14 Franklin Street.

William Almy was survived by his wife, Genevra, daughters Genevra M., Rachel B. Dodge, Edith L. Raymond, and a son, William Forrester Almy. The Almy family plot is adjacent to the Bordens'.

Sources:

Fall River Daily Globe 12 June 1885.

Fall River Evening News 15 June 1885.

Martins, Michael and Dennis Binette, eds. *The Commonwealth of Massachusetts vs. Lizzie A. Borden, The Knowlton Papers*. Fall River, MA: The Fall River Historical Society, 1994.

Rebello, Leonard. *Lizzie Borden, Past & Present*. Fall River, MA: Al-Zach Press, 1999.

Almy headstones at Oak Grove Cemetery, Fall River, Massachusetts.
Note the location in relation to the Borden family plots.

David Mason Anthony Jr.

June 6, 1869 – December 4, 1924

David M. Anthony Jr., was named as the murderer of the Bordens by an elderly woman in Maine in 1985. Miss Ruby Frances Cameron called a newspaper one day and decided it was time to tell what she knew.

Ruby claimed that her parents worked for the Anthonys. She said that David wanted to marry Lizzie Borden, but Lizzie's father and stepmother were against it. ATR ("according to Ruby"), David went to the Borden house on the morning of August 4, 1892. A terrible argument occurred between David and the parents, he went out back to get an axe, and quickly murdered the Bordens.

Lizzie's maid, whom Ruby said was 'Nora Donahue,' a 16-year-old who came from Ireland only six months prior, ran to get Maggie and John Cameron, Ruby's parents, who were engaged to be married at the time. The three got in a meat wagon and went over to the Borden house, cleaned up what mess they could, then had David hide in the back of the meat wagon while they scurried him out of town.

Ruby, who said she was born in 1900, was asked by a doctor to be Lizzie's nurse during her last weeks at Maplecroft. Ruby's mother forbade it, so the doctor said that she could choose anyone she thought was up to the job herself. Ruby did go to see Lizzie at Maplecroft in 1927 (ATR) and Lizzie, recognizing Ruby as Maggie Cameron's daughter, told Ruby the whole story, which matched Ruby's mother's.

The discrepancies and contradictions in Ruby's story are many and incredible. Here are some of them:

- Ruby said David died in 1917, during the Influenza Pandemic, and that he is buried in her family plot in an unmarked grave.
- Bridget Sullivan does not exist in Ruby's telling. "Nora Donahue," if meant to be Bridget, had been in America over two years and was well into her 20s.
- Ruby has Lizzie's biological mother leaving Lizzie a great deal of money (including some textile mills) that the Borden parents had control of, even though Lizzie was 32 years old. They were against Lizzie marrying David because then they would not have this control of Lizzie's money anymore.
- She doesn't mention David's family. Here the Camerons scurried him out of town to hide him, and she left the Anthony family totally out of the story. They must have missed his presence and must have known where he was, if all of this occurred.

- Ruby says that David was supposed to be hiding out of town, but, ATR, he revved his motorcycle up and visited Maplecroft often (with Ruby in a sidecar).
- ATR, David left the arguing Bordens to go outside to get an axe (and he knew it was there because …). The Bordens waited for him inside and, as he butchered one the other stood and waited his or her turn. It all happened in a flurry, which does nothing to explain the obvious hour and a half or so lead that Abby had on Andrew in being dead.
- Lizzie's real last nurse was named Doris Humphrey and Lizzie left her $10,000 when she died.
- John Armour bought Mr. Cameron's meat recipes in 1905. Mr. Cameron and David set up a meat factory at their home, complete with a meat grinder engine that Cameron made himself and, ATR, she sold for $50,000 during the Depression. The small factory also included a cooler that Cameron made in the cellar.
- It was in this cooler that the Cameron family hid a German man for four years during WWII.

Her personal story is just as colorful. ATR, she worked at Massachusetts General Hospital; got her bachelor's of science degree as an RN in three months from Columbia University; got a master's degree in English lit from Florida; and a doctorate in biochemistry from Chapel Hill. She nursed FDR and told Eleanor to "just get out and enjoy yourself!" She put a Hebrew Clinic in Boston "on its feet," and then a doctor wanted her to meet Golda Meir. They wanted her to establish a clinic in Jerusalem. She declined, she said, because she was 68 at the time.

Ruby Cameron died on November 18, 1985, after she had made national headlines.

David Anthony Jr., was born at 368 North Main Street in Fall River in the year 1869. His father was one of the founders of Swift and Company. Anthony invited Swift to join him. Anthony owned a large wholesale meat and slaughterhouse company. Anthony, Swift and Company started business in 1885, in Fall River.

For a time, David Anthony Jr. worked as a clerk at the meat company. He was somewhat younger than Lizzie Borden (23 in 1892, when Lizzie was 32). As he got older, he seemed to spend his time leisurely.

David loved the outdoors. He had enjoyed sailing most of his life, regardless of the weather. His last address was at 28 Charlotte Street in Fall River. He also had a cottage on the water in Swansea. He enjoyed music and played the viola for friends and was said to be very good on the harmonica. He belonged to the Methodist Episcopal Church in Fall River, then later became a Christian Scientist.

David died following an accident. The afternoon it happened, November 25, 1924, he was out sailing. Later that day he was riding his motorcycle in South Somerset and was involved in an accident that left him with a fractured skull. He died at Truesdale Hospital on December 4, 1924.

LIZZIE BORDEN: RESURRECTIONS

David Anthony Jr. is buried in the family plot of his own family in Oak Grove Cemetery in Fall River, Massachusetts. He is in plot 1825, Tritoma Path.

Sources:

Carlson, Joe. "The REAL David Anthony: Did Ruby Tell a Fib?" *The Hatchet: A Journal of Lizzie Borden Studies* 1.5 (October/November 2004).

Griffiths, Diana. "What Did Ruby Know?" *The Hatchet: A Journal of Lizzie Borden Studies* 1.5 (October/November 2004).

Koorey, Kat. "Impressions of Ruby." *The Hatchet: A Journal of Lizzie Borden Studies* 1.5 (October/November 2004).

Rebello, Leonard. *Lizzie Borden, Past & Present*. Fall River, MA: Al-Zach Press, 1999.

Wiggins, John R. "A Solution to the 1892 Crime? Ruby Cameron Says David Anthony Murdered Lizzie Borden's Parents." *Ellsworth American* 3 January 1985. Reprinted in *The Hatchet: A Journal of Lizzie Borden Studies* 1.5 (October/November 2004).

David Anthony grave at Oak Grove Cemetery, Fall River, Massachusetts.

Cook Borden grave at Oak Grove Cemetery, Fall River, Massachusetts.

Cook Borden

January 18, 1810 – September 20, 1880

Cook Borden was an uncle of Andrew Jackson Borden. He was a prosperous lumber merchant in Fall River and supplied most of the large and manufacturing companies in Fall River, Massachusetts, with wood products such as crates, shingles, boards, etc.

Mr. Borden married Mary Ann Bessey on January 1, 1832. Their daughter, Mary J. Borden, married Dr. James W. Hartley on May 1, 1853. They were the parents of Grace Hartley Howe, making Cook Borden the maternal grandfather of Grace Howe. She and her husband Louis Howe are buried in the plot of Cook Borden at Oak Grove Cemetery in Fall River.

Cook Borden was a great uncle of Lizzie and Emma Borden. The Cook Bordens' youngest son, Jerome Cook Borden (first cousin of Andrew Borden), served as a pallbearer at Andrew Borden's funeral.

Sources:

Cook Borden and Company Account Books, 1863-1914. Three Vols. Special Collections and University Archives, W.E.B. Du Bois Library, University of Massachusetts Amherst. Web. 18 June 2014.

Hurd, D. Hamilton, ed. *History of Bristol County, Massachusetts: With Biographical Sketches of Many of its Pioneers and Prominent Men*. Philadelphia, PA: J.W. Lewis & Company, 1883.

Rebello, Leonard. *Lizzie Borden, Past & Present*. Fall River, MA: Al-Zach Press, 1999.

Mrs. Dr. Bowen, *Boston Globe*, June 17, 1893

Phoebe V. Bowen

1848 – 1907

Phoebe Bowen was the wife of Dr. Seabury Bowen, the Bordens' physician. The couple lived diagonally across the street from the Bordens. Both Phoebe and her husband were friends of the family, and Phoebe especially visited them in their home often.

The Bowens' home was a huge duplex, with two families and two other adults residing there: Mr. and Mrs. Southard Miller (parents of Phoebe Bowen); Dr. and Mrs. Bowen; Mrs. Wyatt; and artist Franklin Miller, also an offspring of the Millers. In addition, the Bowens had one daughter, Florence.

Phoebe Miller Bowen had lived in the house all her life. She knew Emma throughout her life. She had known Lizzie since the Borden family moved to Second Street, about twenty years.

The night before the murders, she went over to the Bordens to visit. She had supper first, at the usual hour of 6 o'clock. At that time, Abby said she felt better from their sudden, flu-like illness of the night before. Andrew, however, was still not feeling well.

Phoebe commented that she saw Lizzie going out and said she supposed she was feeling better. Abby replied that Lizzie had not been out all day and was going out to see Alice Russell.

The next morning, not long after 11 o'clock, the Bordens' maid, Bridget, came to the Bowens' door and asked for the doctor. Mrs. Bowen told her that he was out and that she would send him over when he got back. When Dr. Bowen came home, he went to the Bordens' and returned, telling his wife that Mr. Borden was dead.

Bridget went back to the Bowens' and said that Miss Lizzie wanted Phoebe to come over, which she did. Lizzie was in the kitchen rocking chair, her head on Alice Russell's shoulder. Mrs. Churchill was fanning her with a newspaper.

Alice said, "Rub her hands," and Lizzie shook her head no. Later, when Mrs. Bowen heard of Abby Borden's death, she made a sound and the women told her that she was not fit to stay.

Phoebe Bowen was the last witness for the defense called at the preliminary hearing. She also testified at the trial.

She testified that the dress Lizzie had on the morning of the murders was a dress that Mrs. Bowen saw her wear frequently before. She said that the blouse in court was probably not the one she remembers Lizzie wearing that morning.

She also testified that on the morning of August 4, 1892, she noticed that Lizzie's hands were very white. Hosea Knowlton, prosecuting attorney, asked her if it looked like Lizzie had been in the hot, dusty barn looking through a very dusty box (Lizzie's alibi).

Mrs. Phoebe Bowen died in 1907, about eleven years before her husband. She is buried in the Southard Miller family plot at Oak Grove cemetery in Fall River.

Sources:

Rebello, Leonard. *Lizzie Borden, Past & Present*. Fall River, MA: Al-Zach Press, 1999.

Widdows, Harry, Stefani Koorey, Kat Koorey, eds. *The Preliminary Hearing in the Lizzie Borden Case, New Edition*. Orlando, FL: PearTree Press, 2005.

Widdows, Harry, Stefani Koorey, Kat Koorey, eds. *The Trial of Lizzie Andrew Borden*. Orlando, FL: PearTree Press, 2005.

Mrs. Dr. Bowen grave at Oak Grove Cemetery, Fall River, Massachusetts.

Elizabeth Hitchcock Brayton

September 16, 1865 – September 8, 1935

Elizabeth Hitchcock Brayton was the daughter of successful businessman David Anthony Brayton and Nancy R. (Jencks) Brayton. She was one of the women who took the Grand Tour of Europe with Lizzie Borden in 1890.

Miss Brayton died in 1935, just eight days before her 70th birthday. She is buried in Oak Grove Cemetery in Fall River, in the family plot.

Sources:

Rebello, Leonard. *Lizzie Borden, Past & Present*. Fall River, MA: Al-Zach Press, 1999.

Elizabeth Hitchcock Brayton grave at Oak Grove Cemetery, Fall River, Massachusetts.

Mary Ella Brigham grave at Oak Grove Cemetery, Fall River, Massachusetts.

Mary Ella Brigham

1858 – 1942

Mary Brigham was born in Fall River to parents George Sheen and Euphemia (Johnston) Brigham. Both parents were born in England. After graduating from Fall River High School in 1875, she taught school until her marriage in 1885. George Brigham was a bookkeeper.

Mary was a friend since childhood of both Emma and Lizzie Borden. She had gone to the same school as Lizzie, the same church (Central Congregational), and was involved in much charitable work there.

Mary was one of the first people to arrive at the Borden house after the murders. She was supportive of Lizzie throughout the trial. Mary visited her often in jail and testified at both the preliminary hearing and the trial.

She testified that she had John Morse lay face down in the spot Abby Borden was found in, while she stood on the top landing to see if she could see his body. She could not.

She also testified about the locks on the Bordens' front door. Mrs. Brigham had experimented with the front door, and at the trial she said, "I found that unless the bolt was used that the spring lock was not sure. Unless the door was shut with a bang you could not depend upon the spring lock working."

She testified that she was in Lizzie's cell with her the day that Police Matron Hannah Reagan was told by Marshal Hilliard that Mrs. Reagan was not allowed to sign a paper written by Reverend Buck. Mrs. Reagan had said that she heard words between Emma and Lizzie, during which Lizzie said that Emma had given her away, and Emma said that no, she did not. According to Mrs. Reagan, Lizzie then laid on her bed facing the wall, and the sisters did not speak for the rest of Emma's visit, about two hours. The paper was a retraction of the matron telling that story.

Mrs. Brigham said at the trial,

I saw Mr. Buck with a paper in his hand. I saw Mrs. Reagan leave the room with Mr. Buck. Someone told me –

Q: You can't tell what someone told you. Did she come back after?

A: I don't know how long after.

Q: And how did she appear and what did she do or say when she came back?

A: She acted mad.

Q: Well, what did she say?

A: She sat down in the rocking chair as near me as she could sit. She said to me, "It is all a lie from beginning to end. I was willing to sign that paper but the Marshal wouldn't let me do it. He told me to go to my room and obey orders. I would rather leave a place than stay here where I have been so lied about.

Mrs. Reagan testified at the trial that she did tell *Fall River Globe* reporter Edwin Porter of the sisters' quarrel. She said that the story was true. She said she did not tell any other reporter. Knowlton asked her on the stand,

Q: Now, following that did you or did you not tell any other reporters?
A: No, sir, I did not.
Q: And was there any reason for that?

Andrew Jennings objected to the question. The answer Mrs. Reagan never gave could have been going to hurt Lizzie's case. It is a strange and confusing sub-plot in the Borden case.

After the trial, Mrs. Brigham visited Lizzie and Emma often at Maplecroft. However, when Emma left Maplecroft and Lizzie over some unknown disagreement in 1905, Mary Brigham cut off her friendship with Lizzie. She continued hers with Emma.

Mary's husband died in 1927. She remarried and enjoyed socializing with such things as reading clubs and whist.

Whenever anyone asked her about Lizzie or her part in her trial, Mrs. Brigham would say, "Lizzie Borden was my friend, she was tried and she was acquitted. We do not discuss that anymore."

Mary Brigham's last residence was at 240 Florence Street in Fall River. On Friday, October 23, 1942, she died in her home at the age of 84 of generalized arteriosclerosis/arteriosclerotic heart disease. Services were held at her home at 2 p.m., Monday, October 26, with Rev. Dr. Charles E. Hellens, pastor of Central Congregational Church, officiating.

Sources:

Fall River Herald News 24 October 1942.

Widdows, Harry, Stefani Koorey, Kat Koorey, eds. *The Preliminary Hearing in the Lizzie Borden Case, New Edition*. Orlando, FL: PearTree Press, 2005.

Widdows, Harry, Stefani Koorey, Kat Koorey, eds. *The Trial of Lizzie Andrew Borden*. Orlando, FL: PearTree Press, 2005.

Alice Lydia Buck

1855 – 1944

Alice Buck was one of five daughters born to the Reverend Edwin Buck of Fall River. Her sisters were Miss Eliza Buck, Miss May Buck, Miss Anna E., and Miss Clara Buck.

Alice was a friend of Lizzie Borden's before the murders and supported her through her ordeal.

The *Fall River Daily Globe* reported that Lizzie did attend the 1893 Chicago World's Fair some time after her trial. Her traveling companions were Miss Caroline Borden and Alice Buck.

From the years 1912 – 1918, Emma Borden lived in the Buck home, which was around the corner from Maplecroft at 114 Prospect Street.

Alice Buck died in 1944, at or about the age of 89.

Sources:

Rebello, Leonard. *Lizzie Borden, Past & Present*. Fall River, MA: Al-Zach Press, 1999.

Alice L. Buck gravestone at Oak Grove Cemetery, Fall River, Massachusetts.

Rev. Buck, *Boston Globe*, June 16, 1893

Rev. Edwin Augustus Buck

May 31, 1824 – March 9, 1903

Lizzie Borden had been a member of the Central Congregational Church in Fall River since 1885, where she made the acquaintance of "Father Buck." Lizzie was active in the church and taught Sunday school.

On the morning of the Borden murders, Rev. Buck went into the office of C.H. Wells (a clerk in town and parishioner at Central Congregational) and told him of the occurrence. He said he was on his way to call on Lizzie, and Wells went along.

The two walked to the Borden house, and Rev. Buck pulled the bell. Alice Russell let both of them in. Mr. Buck went up the stairs with Miss Russell, as C.H. Wells observed Andrew's body on the sofa downstairs.

On Monday, August 8, Rev. Buck was interviewed by the Fall River Herald:

> City Missionary Buck in an interview expressed himself as a firm believer in Lizzie Borden's innocence. He said, 'Aside from her Christian character, her actions at the time of the murder count with me as indicating ignorance of the crime. I called on her in less than one hour after the discovery of her father's body. I asked her if there was anyone she suspected, and she replied in tears that she did not know of a person in the world who would have a motive for murdering her father. She highly endorsed the character of the Swede farm hand to Mr. Borden's employ, and said he was above suspicion. A guilty person takes every opportunity to throw suspicion on the innocent. Lizzie Borden did not do that.'

Reverend Buck visited Lizzie in jail and offered spiritual guidance and brought her books. He attended both the preliminary hearing and the trial. He and the pastor of Central Congregational, Rev. William Walker Jubb, hardly ever left her side throughout her entire ordeal. It left Robert Sullivan, in his book *Goodbye, Lizzie Borden*, to describe their attentiveness as "almost sickening."

After Lizzie's acquittal in June, 1893, Mr. Buck and Mr. Jubb seemed to have dropped her from their lives, as did so many in Fall River.

Emma's famous interview in 1913 with the *Boston Post* took place in the Buck family parlor. Emma had gone to him when she made her split with Lizzie in 1905. To Emma, Rev. Buck was "My best friend in the world, the one who advised me when matters reached such a pass that I could not stay longer in the same house with Lizzie."

Edwin Augustus Buck was born at Bucksport, Maine. His parents were James and Lydia (Treat) Buck, and he was the second of seven children. His great-grandfather, Jonathan Buck, settled the town of Bucksport.

Buck graduated from Yale, then entered Bangor Theological Seminary, took his second year at Andover Seminary, and returned to Bangor to complete his course, graduating in 1851. In September 1852, he entered upon his work as a preacher in Pownal, Maine, where he remained until May 1854. On May 31, he was ordained and installed pastor of the First Congregational Church in Bethel, Maine. After five years of service he was dismissed, and settled over the Congregational Church in Slatersville, Rhode Island.

In December 1867, Buck was appointed Missionary of the Fall River City Missionary Society. This work soon came to be supported by the Central Church alone. In 1892, he published a most interesting report of the work accomplished during twenty-five years of whole-hearted service, largely among those outside of the churches. He was instrumental in establishing in that city the Young Men's Christian Association and the Boys' Club, and the Pastors' Ministerial Association. In his last few years he had been Missionary Emeritus.

He married, on January 19, 1853, Elmira Rebecca Walker, daughter of Dean and Rebecca (Wright) Walker, of Medway, Massachusetts, and sister of a classmate, Augustus Walker. They had one son and five daughters: Augustus Walker (1866-1924); Elizabeth R. (1853-1924); Alice L. (1855-1944); Mary R. (1857-1913); Nancy Evelyn (1861-1944); and Clara F. (1868-1924).

The family lived at 114 Prospect Street in Fall River. Mrs. Buck died in February 1877, at the age of 49.

Their son graduated at Williams College in 1888, and from the Medical Department of the University of Pennsylvania in 1892, and one of the daughters graduated from Wellesley College in 1892.

Mr. Buck published an "Historical Discourse," delivered at the Semi-Centennial Anniversary of the Slatersville Congregational Church, "Tribute to the Memory of Mrs. Ruth Slater," and a small book titled *Infant Baptism*.

He always kept in touch with his old class at Yale and, in 1899, he attended its 50th reunion, when only fifteen of the original number were present, and only thirty-three were still living.

Mr. Buck died of pneumonia at his home in Fall River, on March 9, 1903, at the age of 78.

Rev. Edwin A. Buck

The tolling of the Central Congregational church bell at 11 o'clock this morning gave public notice of the death of Rev. Edwin A. Buck, the city missionary, who was missionary emeritus at the Central church for the past few years. He passed away shortly before that hour of pneumonia, after an illness that confined him to his home about three weeks, and to his bed about two weeks. His sufferings were not great and his passing away was as gentle as the life he led, and in keeping with all that his thousands of well wishers would hope for.

… until a very short time he called at the police station to do what he could in the way of Christian aid to prisoners.

He was the man who initiated the work which has developed into the Fall River Boys' club, and was president of the club from its organization. … His labors were among the poor, the despondent, and the outcasts of the community, and he was known among the people as "Father Buck", their helper and friend when all else was turned against them. As an instance of the amount of work he performed, it is recalled that he officiated at nearly 3000 funerals, and performed 1635 marriages. When he conducted the Pleasant street mission it was a haven for the thousands who nowadays find refuge with the Salvation Army and the other charitable and church organizations of the city.

No one can measure the good done by Mr. Buck in the community, but all who have _ in contact with the poor in the past generation are aware of the profound friendship that was manifested among them for this gentle and devout man. The police who have been on the force for many years speak of him as one of the salt of the earth and they were always ready to help him in any way they could in the performance of his peculiar labors.
...

Mr. Buck was a constant correspondent of the Congregationalist, and he wrote a treatise on baptism which went through two editions. Until late years he never took a vacation but for a few summers past he has visited his old home in Bucksport regularly. It is probable that the funeral will take place at the Central Congregational church Thursday.

Tidings of the death of Rev. Mr. Buck were telephoned to the pastor, Rev. Dr. Swift, at the Central church, while the Fall River Ministerial association was in session. At the close of the reading of the paper, then in progress, announcement was made of the fact. Later appropriate remarks were made and an expression of the sympathy of the association and of its sense of loss was sent to the family. A committee, consisting of the president of the association, Rev. J.E. Enman, and Rev. Messrs. Martin, Jutten, Kaufman and Lyman was appointed to draft suitable resolutions and to make any needful arrangements for proper representation and it was decided to attend the funeral in a body, notice to that effect to be sent to the different members.

Services were conducted at Central Congregational Church. He is buried in the Buck family plot at Oak Grove Cemetery in Fall River.

His church paper, for which he was long a correspondent, in commenting upon his death, said:

His ministry was whole-hearted and consistent. He was daily in the homes of the people, their minister, counselor and friend. The funeral evinced the esteem in which Mr. Buck was held by all classes in the community. Men who have attended the burial services of leaders of national renown say that they never witnessed such a spontaneous outburst of love and gratitude as came to the surface in connection with the gathering in Central Church and at Oak Grove Cemetery. Humble people by the hundred welcomed the opportunity to look at his remains, and the tears shed told of the indebtedness of the poor, the discouraged, and the outcast, to their constant benefactor.

Sources:

Fall River Daily Herald 9 March 1903.
Fall River Herald 8 August 1892.

Fall River Historical Society Newsletter 14.3 (Fall 2002).

Hoffman, Paul Dennis. *Yesterday in Old Fall River*. Durham, NC: Carolina Academic Press, 2000.

Hurd, D. Hamilton, ed. *History of Bristol County, Massachusetts: With Biographical Sketches of Many of its Pioneers and Prominent Men*. Philadelphia, PA: J.W. Lewis & Company, 1883.

Kent, David, ed. *Lizzie Borden Sourcebook*. Boston: Branden Publishing Company, 1992.

Obituary Record of Graduates of Yale University, Deceased during the Academic Year Ending in June 1903. Yale University Library, Manuscripts & Archives. Web. 18 June 2014.

Rebello, Leonard. *Lizzie Borden, Past & Present*. Fall River, MA: Al-Zach Press, 1999.

Sullivan, Robert. *Goodbye, Lizzie Borden*. NY: Penguin Books, 1989.

Rev. Buck grave at Oak Grove Cemetery, Fall River, Massachusetts.

Mrs. Churchill, *Boston Globe*, June 9, 1893

Adelaide Buffinton Churchill

1850 – February 16, 1926

Adelaide "Addie" Churchill was the Borden's next door neighbor to the north (toward town) at 90 Second Street in Fall River, Massachusetts. She had lived in the "Buffinton House" all of her 43 years at the time of Lizzie Borden's trial. The house was so named after her father, Edward P. Buffinton, who was a very popular mayor of Fall River. Her father was born in Westport, Massachusetts, and lived from 1814 – 1871. Her mother, Comfort (Tabor) Buffinton, was born in Tiverton, Rhode Island, in 1819, and died in 1899. Adelaide Churchill was born in 1850, in Fall River, one of nine children.

Adelaide was married to Charles H. Churchill, who worked at the Water Works as a clerk and registrar. On February 6, 1879, he died at the age of 35. They had one son, Charles Henry Churchill, who lived from 1878 – 1952.

Mrs. Churchill was active in the First Congregational Church. The Buffinton House was large and, besides herself and her mother, she also lived with her sister, her son, her niece (see Addie Cheetham), and a man who worked for them. She also had two lodging rooms.

On the morning of the Borden murders, Mrs. Churchill saw Andrew Borden about 9 a.m. out of her kitchen window. He was standing by the steps as if he were about to go downstreet, as was his usual habit on a weekday.

Later, at perhaps 10 a.m., she saw Bridget Sullivan rinsing ("throwing water up onto") a downstairs parlor window. Contrary to popular belief, it was not unusual at all for Bridget to be washing windows that day. As Mrs. Churchill testified at the inquest, "I don't think she washed the windows but once a week, and Thursday was generally the day."

At about 11 a.m., Adelaide went to M. T. Hudner's Market on South Main Street to pick up fresh meat for dinner. She did not stay long and it was but a short, perhaps five minute, walk to the store. While there, she also talked to her brother, who worked at Hudner's. On her return home, she saw Bridget running from Dr. Bowen's house (diagonally across from the Borden's). To her, Bridget looked scared.

She went into her house, laid her parcels from Hudner's on a bench in the kitchen, and, through her kitchen window, saw Lizzie standing by the screen door "as if she were in great distress".

"What is the matter, Lizzie?" inquired Mrs. Churchill.

Lizzie replied, "O, Mrs. Churchill, do come over, somebody has killed Father."

Mrs. Churchill went out her front door immediately in answer of Lizzie's plea. Lizzie was then sitting on the second stair, at the right of the screen door as one comes in the back stairs.

Mrs. Churchill put her hand on Lizzie's arm and said, "Lizzie, where is your father?"

Lizzie said, "In the sitting room."

"Where was you when it happened?"

"I went to the barn to get a piece of iron." She said Dr. Bowen was not at home, "but I must have a Doctor." Adelaide offered to go and find one. She had left Lizzie alone while she went on her errand. Her handyman, Thomas Boulds, was at Mr. Hall's yard, she knew, and she went there. She told him that somebody had killed Mr. Borden and to go get a doctor.

When Mrs. Churchill returned to the Borden house, she found that Lizzie had not moved from the step she was sitting on. "I shall have to go to the Cemetery myself," Lizzie said. Adelaide assured her that "the undertaker will attend to all such things as that for you; they generally do."

Enter Dr. Bowen.

Addie Churchill said, "He is in the sitting room."

Bridget, who had been sent out a second time by Lizzie, had come back from going to get Alice Russell. Dr. Bowen came out of the sitting room and shook his head. He said, "That is awful." He told Mrs. Churchill he was very much confused. "Addie," he says, "won't you go in and look at Mr. Borden?" She answered, "O, no, doctor, I don't want to see him. I looked at him out in the yard this morning, he looked nice to me, I don't want to see him."

By that time Alice Russell had arrived. She was comforting Lizzie, who had her head on Alice Russell's shoulder. Dr. Bowen's wife, Phebe, came in and Lizzie did not seem to know who she was. Alice told her, "That is Phebe Bowen."

Dr. Bowen asked for a sheet to cover up Andrew Borden. Mrs. Churchill accompanied Bridget upstairs to comply. Bridget was afraid to go upstairs alone. When they reached the bureau where the sheets were kept, Bridget asked her if two were enough, to which Adelaide replied, "I should think a plenty."

This is where the myth comes from that, upon hearing Dr. Bowen ask for a sheet to cover her father with, Lizzie supposedly replied, "Better get two." It didn't happen.

For the second time, Lizzie said she wished someone would go upstairs to find Mrs. Borden as "I thought I heard her come in." Up went Adelaide with Bridget again. This time they went up another staircase and Bridget took the lead. When she got on a certain step, Mrs. Churchill could see a prostrated form lying on the floor as she looked into the guestroom. The door was open, and Addie did not know where Bridget went but she turned around post haste. Once downstairs she let out a sound of distress.

"Is there another?" Alice Russell asked.

"Yes. She is up there." When Dr. Bowen returned from sending a telegram to Lizzie's sister Emma who was visiting in Fairhaven, Addie told him, "Dr. Bowen, you must go upstairs in the spare bed room," and he went.

After the discovery of Mrs. Borden's body, Mrs. Churchill said there was a great deal of confusion. It was about 12 noon by this time when Mrs. Churchill told Lizzie that she had to go home and told her that if there was anything she wished her to do to let her know later on. "She said, there will be plenty to do bye and bye."

Adelaide Churchill testified at the inquest, the preliminary hearing, and at the trial. Perhaps the most important thing she said at the trial was about the dress Lizzie had on the morning the Bordens were bludgeoned.

She described it as a cotton dress with a blue and white background with navy blue diamonds printed on it. She said that it was not the dress that Lizzie had turned in to the police, which was an exhibit in the courtroom.

When Alice Russell testified at the trial, she was asked to describe the dress that Lizzie burned in the kitchen stove three days after the murders. Miss Russell's description, "a cheap cotton dress with a light blue background with a dark figure on it," closely matched the dress Mrs. Churchill described Lizzie wearing on that Fatal Fourth.

Adelaide Churchill continued her good works at the First Congregational Church. She never remarried. She died at 216 Second Street (renumbered in 1896), the home she had lived in all her life, at the age of 76 on February 16, 1926, of a cerebral hemorrhage.

She is buried at Oak Grove Cemetery in Fall River, Massachusetts.

Sources:

Hoffman, Paul Dennis. *Yesterday in Old Fall River*. Durham, NC: Carolina Academic Press, 2000.

Inquest Upon the Deaths of Andrew J. and Abby D. Borden, August 9 – 11, 1892, Volume I and II. Orlando, FL: PearTree Press, 2005.

Kent, David, ed. *Lizzie Borden Sourcebook*. Boston: Branden Publishing Company, 1992.

Martins, Michael and Dennis Binette, eds. *The Commonwealth of Massachusetts vs. Lizzie A. Borden, The Knowlton Papers*. Fall River, MA: The Fall River Historical Society, 1994.

Rebello, Leonard. *Lizzie Borden, Past & Present*. Fall River, MA: Al-Zach Press, 1999.

Widdows, Harry. "1892 & 1896 City Directory Entries." *The Hatchet: A Journal of Lizzie Borden Studies* 5.2 (May 2008).

Widdows, Harry, Stefani Koorey, Kat Koorey, eds. *The Preliminary Hearing in the Lizzie Borden Case, New Edition*. Orlando, FL: PearTree Press, 2005.

Widdows, Harry, Stefani Koorey, Kat Koorey, eds. *The Trial of Lizzie Andrew Borden*. Orlando, FL: PearTree Press, 2005.

The Witness Statements. Orlando, FL: PearTree Press, 2005.

Adelaide Churchill grave at Oak Grove Cemetery, Fall River, Massachusetts.

Lurana and Hiram Harrington grave at Oak Grove Cemetery, Fall River, Massachusetts.

Lurana (Borden) Harrington & Hiram C. Harrington

August 10, 1826 – December 28, 1898

February 26, 1829 – January 30, 1907

Lurana Harrington was the sister of Andrew Borden and the last survivor of their father, Abraham Borden. Born in Fall River, she was a member of the Second Baptist Church. In 1854, she married Hiram Harrington. The couple lived in Fall River.

They had one son, George B. Harrington. He died instantly of a brain disease at the age of 9 on March 4, 1867, at home (then 13 Ferry Street). He is buried in the Harrington plot at Oak Grove Cemetery in Fall River. An illegible child's gravestone in all probability marks his grave.

Lurana Harrington died at the age of 72 of peritonitis and complications on December 28, 1898. Peritonitis is a serious disorder—an inflammation of the peritoneum, most often due to a bacterial infection. The peritoneum is a two-layered membrane that lines the abdominal cavity and encloses the stomach, intestines, and other abdominal organs. This membrane supports the abdominal organs and protects them from infection. Infection usually spreads from organs within the abdomen. Peritonitis is a medical emergency. The muscles of the walls of the intestine become paralyzed and the forward movement of intestinal contents stops.

Usual symptoms are: Sudden, steady severe pain throughout the abdomen or in one spot, which may persist for hours and is worsened by movement or pressure on the abdomen; board-like rigidity of the abdomen due to contraction of the abdominal wall; bloated or swollen abdomen; nausea; fever and chills with profuse perspiration; pale, cold skin; weakness; and shock.

Lurana (Borden) Harrington is buried at Oak Grove Cemetery in Fall River, next to her husband, Hiram.

Hiram C. Harrington was born on February 26, 1829, in East Greenwich, Rhode Island, to parents George Harrington and Mercy C. Green. Before settling in Fall River, he traveled to California to search for sudden wealth. He then became a machinist and blacksmith in Fall River. He worked at the Crystal Springs Bleachery in Assonet (Freetown), Massachusetts from 1885 – 1888. Afterwards, he operated a blacksmith shop in Fall River at the corner of Fourth and Borden Streets. In 1860, he served on the Fall River city council, and again in 1864. He served as High Priest for the Royal Arch Chapter of the Masons. At the time of the murders, he and his wife lived at 12 Turner Street in Fall River. He testified at the inquest, but was not a witness at the preliminary hearing or the trial itself.

When Emma Borden testified at the inquest, she was asked if she knew if Andrew Borden had anyone that was he on bad terms with, and she named her uncle, Hiram Harrington. The two men did not speak. Harrington was on good terms with Abby, Lizzie, and herself. Aunt Lurana was on good terms with them and Andrew Borden. Lurana would visit their home, but Hiram would not. He would sometimes come to their door to call on Emma or Lizzie.

Hiram Harrington said pretty much the same thing that Emma testified to at the inquest. Under oath, he said: "We never had no words or nothing of that kind. Some years ago I thought he was hard, and I cut his acquaintance; that is, he came to my house, and I would leave the room, and he very soon saw I cut his acquaintance; and he did mine."

He said, "I did not go to the house; any more than sometimes on business, that is, sometimes my wife wanted to send a letter or to invite the girls, or something of that kind, I would go to the house; sometimes I met him at the door, and have spoken."

Lizzie had spoken to the Harringtons about the trouble between her and Emma and their stepmother, sometimes in a joking way; sometimes in an unfriendly, sneering way. The last time before the murders that he had heard anything Lizzie say about it was that winter, probably the last time he saw her before August 4. He had not seen her since the winter. He asked his wife why Lizzie hadn't been to their home to see them. Emma had always come. He said at the inquest, "And the reply I would get from her was that Lizzie was into everything; that is, she works in the church, and her time was occupied; that is what I would get from her."

Harrington also testified, "For several years, I guess, of his early marriage with her, everything was very, very pleasant, uncommonly so for a step-mother." He added that there had been trouble in the house for "quite a number of years."

An interview Hiram Harrington gave to the *Fall River Herald* shortly after the murders is, in part, revealing of life between the sisters and the father and stepmother:

> Hiram Harrington, 40 Fourth street (sic), is married to Laurana, Mr. Borden's only sister. A reporter who interviewed him gathered the following story: 'My wife, being an only sister, was very fond of Mr. Borden and always subservient to his will, and by her intimacy with his affairs I have become acquainted with a good deal of the family history during years past. Mr. Borden was an exceedingly hard man concerning money matters, determined and stubborn, and when once he got an idea nothing could change him. He was too hard for me.
>
> 'When his father died some years ago he offered my wife the old homestead on Ferry street for a certain sum of money. My wife preferred to take the money, and after the agreements were all signed, to show how close he was, he wanted my wife to pay an additional $3 for water tax upon the homestead.'
>
> 'What do you think was the motive for the crime?' asked the reporter.
>
> 'Money, unquestionably money,' replied Mr. Harrington. If Mr. Borden died, he would have left something over $500,000, and all I will say is that, in my opinion, that furnishes the only motive, and a sufficient one, for the double murder. I have heard so much now that I would not be surprised at the arrest any time of the person to whom in my opinion suspicion

strongly points, although right down in my heart I could not say I believed the party guilty.

'Last evening I had a long interview with Lizzie Borden, who has refused to see anyone else. I questioned her very carefully as to her story of the crime. She was very composed, showed no signs of any emotion or were there any traces of grief upon her countenance. That did not surprise me, as she is not naturally emotional. I asked her what she knew of her father's death, and, after telling of the unimportant events of the early morning, she said her father came home about 10:30. She was in the kitchen at the time, she said, but went into the sitting room when her father arrived. She was very solicitous concerning him, and assisted him to remove his coat and put on his dressing-gown; asked concernedly how he fell (sic), as he had been week from a cholera morbus attack the day before. She told me she helped him to get a comfortable reclining position on the lounge, and asked him if he did not wish the blinds closed to keep out the sun, so he could have a nice nap. She pressed him to allow her to place an afghan over him, but he said he did not need it. Then she asked him tenderly several times if he was perfectly comfortable, if there was anything she could do for him, and upon receiving assurance to the negative she withdrew. All these things showed a solicitude and a thoughtfulness that I never had heard was a part of her nature or custom before. She described these little acts of courtesy minutely.

'I then questioned her very carefully as to the time she left the house, and she told me positively that it was about 10:45. She said she saw her father on the lounge as she passed out. On leaving the house she says she went directly to the barn to obtain some lead. She informed me that it was her intention to go to Marion on a vacation, and she wanted the lead in the barn loft to make some sinkers. She was a very enthusiastic angler. I went over the ground several times, and she repeated the same story. She told me it was hard to place the exact time she was in the barn, as she was cutting the lead into sizable sinkers, but thought she was absent some 20 minutes. Then she thought again, and said it might have been 30 minutes. Then she entered the house and went to the sitting room, as she says she was anxious concerning her father's health. "I discovered him dead," she said, "and cried for Bridget, who was upstairs in her room."

'Did you go and look for your stepmother?' I asked. 'Who found her?' But she did not reply. I pressed her for some idea of the motive and the author of the act, and, after she had thought a moment, she said, calmly: "A year ago last spring our house was broken into while father and mother were at Swansey, and a large amount of money stolen, together with diamonds. You never heard of it because father did not want it mentioned, so as to give the detectives a chance to recover the property. That may have some connection with the murder. Then I have seen strange men around the house. A few months ago I was coming through the back yard, and, as I approached the side door, I saw a man there examining the door and premises. I did not mention it to anyone. The other day I saw the same man hanging about the house, evidently watching us. I became frightened and told my parents about it. I also wrote to my sister at Fairhaven about it." Miss Borden then gave it as her opinion that the strange man had a direct connection with the murder, but she could not see why the house was not robbed, and did not know of anyone who would desire revenge upon her father.'

Mr. Harrington was asked if he knew whether or not there were dissensions in the Borden family. 'Yes, there were, although it has been always kept very quiet. For nearly ten years there have been constant disputes between the daughters and their father and stepmother. Mr. Borden gave her some bank stock and the girls thought they ought to be treated as evenly as the mother. I guess Mr. Borden did try to do it, for he deeded to the daughters, Emma L. and Lizzie A., the homestead on Ferry street, an estate of 120 rods of land with a house and barn, all valued at $3000. This was in 1887.

'The trouble about money matters did not diminish, nor the acerbity of the family ruptures lessen, and Mr. Borden gave each girl ten shares in the Crystal Spring Bleachery company, which he paid $100 a share for. They sold them soon after for less than $40 per share. He also gave them some bank stock at various times, allowing them, of course, the entire income from them. In addition to this he gave them a weekly stipend, amounting to $200 a year.

'In spite of all this the dispute of their not being allowed enough went on with equal bitterness. Lizzie did most of the demonstrative contention, as Emma is very quiet and unassuming, and would feel very deeply any disparaging or angry word from her father. Lizzie, on the contrary, was haughty and domineering with the stubborn will of her father and bound to contest for her rights. There were many animated interviews between father and daughter on this point. Lizzie is of a repellant disposition, and after an unsuccessful passage with her father would become sulky and would refuse to speak to him for days at a time. She moved in the best society in Fall River, was a member of the Congregational church, and is a brilliant conversationalist. She thought she ought to entertain as others did, and felt that with her father's wealth she was expected to hold her end up with others of her set. Her father's constant refusal to allow her to entertain lavishly angered her. I have heard many bitter things she has said of her father, and know she was deeply resentful of her father's maintained stand on this matter.

'This house on Ferry street was an old one, and was in constant need of repairs. There were two tenants paying $16.50 and $14 a month, but with taxes and repairs there was very little income from the property. It was a great deal of trouble for the girls to keep the house in repair, and a month or two ago they got disgusted and deeded the house back to their father.'

On January 30, 1907, Hiram Harrington died at the last home he and Lurana shared, at 266 Franklin Street, at the age of 77, of organic valvular disease of the heart. He is buried next to his wife in Oak Grove Cemetery.

Sources:

Hoffman, Paul Dennis. *Yesterday in Old Fall River*. Durham, NC: Carolina Academic Press, 2000.

Inquest Upon the Deaths of Andrew J. and Abby D. Borden, August 9 – 11, 1892, Volume I and II. Orlando, FL: PearTree Press, 2005.

Kent, David, ed. *Lizzie Borden Sourcebook*. Boston: Branden Publishing Company, 1992.

Rebello, Leonard. *Lizzie Borden, Past & Present*. Fall River, MA: Al-Zach Press, 1999.

Anna Covell Holmes

March 5, 1861 – November 9, 1943

Anna Covell Holmes was one of three children born to Mr. and Mrs. Charles J. (Mary Anna) Holmes. She was born on March 5, 1861, in Fall River, Massachusetts.

She helped form the Central Congregational Church's Chinese class. She and her family were active members of the church.

Anna Holmes was a schoolmate of Lizzie Borden. Anna was one of the young ladies who was at Dr. Handy's cottage in Marion, expecting Lizzie's presence on Monday, August 8. Lizzie never realized that vacation plan, as the Borden murders occurred on August 4.

Anna Holmes' parents were staunch supporters of Lizzie throughout and after her trial. It was to their home that Lizzie was honored at a reception on the night of her acquittal.

Anna was a friend of Emma's. In her will, Emma left Anna "my gold lorgnette chain." (A 'lorgnette' is a pair of eyeglasses or opera glasses with a handle.)

In 1906, after the death of her father, she, her mother, and her sister, Mary L., moved to Rochester, Massachusetts. Anna returned to Fall River in 1937. She died after a long illness in Fall River. Anna C. Holmes is buried in the family plot at Rochester Center Cemetery in Rochester, Massachusetts. Surviving her were two nephews.

Sources:

Hoffman, Paul Dennis. *Yesterday in Old Fall River*. Durham, NC: Carolina Academic Press, 2000.

Rebello, Leonard. *Lizzie Borden, Past & Present*. Fall River, MA: Al-Zach Press, 1999.

Anna C. Holmes grave at family plot in Rochester Center Cemetery, Rochester, Massachusetts.

Charles Jarvis Holmes, from Edwin Porter, *Fall River Tragedy*, 1893.

Charles Jarvis Holmes

March 4, 1834 – February 26, 1906

Charles Jarvis Holmes was born in Rochester, Massachusetts, on March 4, 1834. His parents were Charles Jarvis and Louisa Haskell Holmes, both from Rochester. Both his father and grandfather were lawyers. When he was 5 years old, he moved with his parents to Taunton, Massachusetts. At the age of 9, his family moved to Fall River. He was a member of the first class formed in the Fall River High School, graduating in 1853.

After completing high school, he worked for the Massasoit Bank. At the age of 31 he was elected treasurer of the Fall River Five Cent Savings Bank and remained so until his death. That same year he was elected cashier of the Wamsutta, afterward the Second National Bank, and he held that position until the bank went out of business in 1903.

Charles J. Holmes was an important man in Fall River and an historical figure who is very much a part of the city's growth and prosperity. It is said that he saved the city from one of the worst financial disasters ever. He was one of those rare combinations—one having great executive ability, who could take on remarkable responsibilities, and willing to apply these talents in public service.

Holmes was president of the King Philip Mills, the Sagamore Manufacturing Company, and a director of the Border City Mills. He served in the Board of Aldermen in 1885, 1888 – 1889. He was on the school committee for sixteen years, exerting a strong influence in Fall River's educational affairs. He was a trustee of the public library for forty-three years. He was a member of the board of overseers of the poor, from the time of the change made in that body under Mayor James F. Jackson, until the time of his death.

Charles Holmes also served as treasurer of the Fall River Hospital for a number of years. He was for many years chairman of the Civil Service Commission. He served in the House in 1873, and in the Senate in 1877 – 1878. He was chairman of the Committee of Associated Savings Banks of the State for over thirty years. And when it was proposed to tax the savings banks' deposits for internal revenue, he alone represented Massachusetts at the hearing in Washington in protest of the measure.

Mr. Holmes was prominent in the affairs of the Central Congregational Church, which he joined in 1857. In 1877, he was elected deacon, which office he held until his decease.

There was scarcely a life in Fall River that has not in some measure felt the stimulus of his abounding energy, his devotion, and his ardent faith.

Mr. Holmes married Mary Anna Remington on May 4, 1858. She was the daughter of Joshua and Joanna Remington of Fall River. They had three children: Mary L., Anna C., and Charles L. Holmes.

Charles Holmes and his wife were two of the few mourners allowed to attend the funeral services of the Bordens at 92 Second Street. The Holmes were staunch supporters of Lizzie Borden all through her trial. Charles Holmes accompanied Lizzie, along with Reverend Buck, every day and sat right next to her. He testified for the defense during the trial concerning the alleged quarrel between Lizzie and Emma Borden (where Lizzie said, "You have given me away...") and what he saw and heard for himself regarding Matron Hannah Reagan and the did-she-or-didn't-she witness any argument at all.

On the evening of Lizzie's acquittal, she attended a gathering of friends, including Dr. Bowen, at Holmes' Pine Street home. She gave an interview there to the *Fall River Globe*, which was the last interview she gave.

Charles J. Holmes died at the age of 71, after a five-year battle with heart disease, and arteriosclerosis that set in the last three months of his life. He is buried in Rochester, Massachusetts.

Sources:

Fenner, Henry M. *History of Fall River*. NY: Smiley Publishing Company, 1906.

Hoffman, Paul Dennis. *Yesterday in Old Fall River*. Durham, NC: Carolina Academic Press, 2000.

Widdows, Harry, Stefani Koorey, Kat Koorey, eds. *The Trial of Lizzie Andrew Borden*. Orlando, FL: PearTree Press, 2005.

Holmes family plot in Rochester Center Cemetery, Rochester, Massachusetts.

Mary Anna Holmes (Marianna)

March 13, 1834 – June 5, 1916

Mary Anna Holmes (also known as 'Marianna') was the wife of Charles Jarvis Holmes, an accomplished banker and citizen of Fall River, Massachusetts. She was born in Fall River on March 13, 1834, to parents Joshua and Joanna (Lawton) Remington.

Mary Anna married Charles J. Holmes on May 4, 1858. They had three children: Mary L., Anna C., and Charles L. Holmes.

The Holmes' daughter, Anna, was a schoolmate of Lizzie Borden, and Mrs. Holmes knew Lizzie since childhood. They attended the same church (Central Congregational), of which Lizzie had belonged for some five years at the time of the Borden murders in 1892. Mary Anna was a member of the Bible class of the Sunday school, while Lizzie taught in the "Chinese department." Lizzie and Mrs. Holmes were both members of The Woman's Board of the Fall River Hospital (sometimes called the Hospital of the Good Samaritan).

Both of the Holmes' daughters, Anna and Mary, were two of the several women who planned to meet Lizzie at Dr. Handy's cottage in Marion, Massachusetts, on August 8, but Lizzie's plans were aborted when the murders of her father and stepmother occurred on August 4th.

Mary Anna and her husband were staunch supporters of Lizzie from almost the moment of the murders until and after her acquittal. Mrs. Holmes arrived at the Borden home on the day of the murders at about 1 p.m. She left that night about 8:30 p.m.

While there, she was up in Lizzie's room with her during the time policemen searched Lizzie and Emma's rooms. She attended the funerals for the Bordens, which took place at 11 a.m. on Saturday, August 6th.

Mary Anna Holmes testified for the defense at Lizzie's trial. She told the court that there were some handkerchiefs that were ironed in the Borden house. She said that Lizzie did shed tears the day of the funeral. She said the dark dress that was a court exhibit was worn by Lizzie on Friday morning, August 5, and for a short time on the morning of August 6. Lizzie wore a black dress to the funeral, she said, and that when Lizzie came downstairs on that morning she went to the casket her father lay in and kissed him.

The night of Lizzie's acquittal, the Holmes gave a party in her honor at their home (67 Pine Street in 1892; renumbered to 381 Pine Street in 1896).

After husband, Charles, died in 1906, Mary Anna moved to Rochester, Massachusetts, with her daughters, neither of whom married.

Mary Anna Holmes died on June 5, 1916, at the age of 83. She is buried in the Holmes family plot at Rochester Center Cemetery in Rochester, Massachusetts.

The following is from the obituary for Mary Anna Holmes, printed in a Fall River newspaper from June 1916. (Mary Anna Holmes' grave monument gives her birth year as 1834. The obituary below gives her birth year as 1833.):

MRS. MARY A. HOLMES DEAD

Was an Active Worker in the Central Church – And in Hospital Affairs

Mrs. Mary Anna Holmes, one of the oldest and most respected ladies interested in the welfare of Fall River, was called by death in her 83d year, at her home in Rochester, Monday night, after a short illness. Mrs. Holmes was the daughter of Joshua and Joanna (Lawton) Remington. She was born in this city in 1833 and resided here continuously until the death of her husband, Charles J. Holmes, in 1906, when she removed to Rochester, where she had resided with her daughters ever since. She married the late Charles J. Holmes in this city May 4, 1858 and to them three children were born, two daughters, Mary L. and Anna C. and one son, Charles L., treasurer of the Five Cents Savings Bank in this city. Mrs. Holmes leaves, in addition to the children, two sisters, Mrs. William K. Covell of Newport and Mrs. John G. Dexter of Rochester.

After attending the public schools of the city she entered the Fall River High school, and was one of the first students to graduate from that institution. After leaving high school, she attended the Greenwich Academy for a short time, after which she took up the study of music. Mrs. Holmes always retained her interest in the Alumni association of the Fall River High school, and only as recently as May 12 of this year contributed the leading article in Nucleus, a magazine published in the interests of the association. Mrs. Holmes was secretary of the alumni classes of 1849 – 52, from the inception of the reunions until her death.

Mrs. Holmes was particularly interested in church work and had been a member of the Central Congregational church of this city since early childhood. She was always known as one of the most active and efficient workers connected with the church and was always willing to give her services to aid a good cause. She held many offices in church organizations, several of which she was instrumental in organizing. The Old Colony Branch of the Woman's Board of Foreign Missions was one of these and Mrs. Holmes ably filled the office of president for many years.

She was always a leader in social affairs of the church and her presence at any meeting or entertainment was always welcome.

In 1904 the members of the church decided to have a history of the church from its incorporation written, and Mrs. Holmes with Mrs. Eli Thurston and Mrs. William Carr were chosen to do the work. The book was completed and published in 1905. Both her co-workers said after the (sic) had been accomplished that Mrs. Holmes had been the cheering power during the long hours of hard and tedious labor.

Mrs. Holmes was also deeply interested in hospital work and on Feb. 18, 1888, when the Woman's Ward of the Fall River hospital (late the Union hospital) was formed she was chosen as a member of the board of trustees. Later she served as a chairman for several years and was always one of the most efficient and cheerful workers in behalf of the organization.

Mrs. Holmes was deeply beloved by her children, and found her greatest happiness in her home circle. Her beautiful character will live long in the memories of all who had the pleasure and honor of her friendship. She will be remembered as a friend of all that was good and pure in life and an enemy of the base.

Sources:

Hoffman, Paul Dennis. *Yesterday in Old Fall River*. Durham, NC: Carolina Academic Press, 2000.

"Mrs. Mary A. Holmes Dead." Unknown Fall River newspaper June 1916.

Rebello, Leonard. *Lizzie Borden, Past & Present*. Fall River, MA: Al-Zach Press, 1999.

Widdows, Harry, Stefani Koorey, Kat Koorey, eds. *The Trial of Lizzie Andrew Borden*. Orlando, FL: PearTree Press, 2005.

Holmes family plot in Rochester Center Cemetery, Rochester, Massachusetts.

Holmes family plot in Rochester Center Cemetery, Rochester, Massachusetts.

Mary Louisa Holmes

1859 – 1934

Mary Louisa Holmes was one of three children born to Mr. and Mrs. Charles J. (Mary Anna) Holmes of Fall River, Massachusetts.

Mary was among the group of young ladies vacationing at Dr. Handy's cottage in Marion the week of the Borden murders and, prior to August 4th, all had expected Lizzie to join them on August 8. Of course, Lizzie never came.

Mary was a former teacher at the Nathaniel B. Borden School. She died in 1934, and is buried in the family plot at Rochester Center Cemetery in Rochester, Massachusetts.

Sources:

Hoffman, Paul Dennis. *Yesterday in Old Fall River*. Durham, NC: Carolina Academic Press, 2000.

Rebello, Leonard. *Lizzie Borden, Past & Present*. Fall River, MA: Al-Zach Press, 1999.

Grace Hartley Howe

Grace Hartley Howe

November 9, 1874 – June 14, 1955

Grace Hartley Howe was a second cousin of Lizzie Borden. She is one of two persons who was left the largest portions of Lizzie's estate. The following comes from Lizzie's will:

> To my cousin, Mrs. Grace H. Howe, my diamond and amethyst ring and I direct that she shall have second choice of my rugs, books, china, pictures and furniture, and I also give to her the privilege, so far as I have the same, to use the Oak grove Cemetery lot for burial purposes. I also give and devise to her one-half of my share in the A.J. Borden Building in said Fall River, to her, to her heirs, executors, administrators and assigns forever.

Her estimated inheritance from Lizzie's will was $36,000.

Grace was born in Fall River on November 9, 1874, to parents Dr. James W. Hartley and Mary Jane Borden Hartley. She was the granddaughter of Cook Borden and Mary A. Bessey, his wife. Grace was the great granddaughter of Richard Borden and Hope Cook, his wife, and Nathan Bowen and Hannah Cook, his wife.

Grace graduated from B.M.C. Durfee High School then attended Vassar College. During the summer of 1896, while at Dr. Strong's Sanitarium in Saratoga, New York, she met her husband-to-be, Colonel Louis McHenry Howe. Grace and her mother were there to remove Grace from the advances of an Irish suitor.

They were married in a Vermont village on November 9, 1889. Their marriage produced two children: Hartley Edward Howe and Mary (Howe) Baker.

Louis Howe was a master of politics and was Franklin Delano Roosevelt's right-hand man. The Howes were with the Roosevelts at Campobello Island in New Brunswick during the summer of 1921, when FDR contracted polio.

Roosevelt spent short vacations at the Howe's summer place at Horseneck Beach in Westport, Massachusetts, while he was assistant secretary of the Navy.

After Roosevelt's election to the presidency, Grace attended White House teas and had a large acquaintance with politicians in the nation.

When Louis Howe died in Washington D.C. on April 18, 1936, Eleanor Roosevelt phoned Grace in Fall River to break the news gently. From then on, every year on Louis's birthday, Mrs. Roosevelt sent Grace a dozen white roses. Eleanor and Grace's friendship continued after the death of Louis, with Grace being invited to the White House on occasion.

Franklin and Eleanor Roosevelt came to Oak Grove Cemetery in Fall River for Louis Howe's funeral. After his death, Grace stayed in Fall River. Louis Howe left an estate of less than $20,000.

During the Democratic National Convention in 1936 (which Louis Howe had been at work on for Roosevelt), Grace was a delegate at large for the state of Massachusetts. The convention was held on June 27, 1936, in Philadelphia. The convention held a tribute of silence for Louis Howe.

There it was announced that Grace Hartley Howe would be appointed Post Mistress of the Fall River post office by Postmaster General James Farley, which would take place in July. The entire Democratic party stood to applaud. She was the first woman postmaster of Fall River. Franklin Roosevelt knew that, with a salary of $4,000 as postmaster, she would be assisted in her years as widow. She was one of four women to head Class One post offices in the nation in 1936. Grace was 60 years old. She held the position until her retirement in 1951, at the age of 75.

Grace was on a long list of committees. She was a director of Fall River's Family Welfare Association, Historical Society, Ninth Street Day Nursery, and the League of Nations Association; advisory board member of the Consumers' League of Massachusetts and of various local WPA projects; trustee of the Bristol County Agricultural School and Fall River Public Library; secretary of Massachusetts' Democratic State Committee and vice chairman of Fall River's Democratic City Committee; member of the Fall River Women's Club, American Association of University Women, Massachusetts Horticultural Society, New England Farm and Garden Club, English-Speaking Union, League of Women Voters, D.A.R. (Daughters of the American Revolution), Fall River Vassar Club, and the Society for the Preservation of New England Antiques. She maintained a personal interest in the annual Roosevelt Birthday Ball which won the support of Fall River.

Grace talked to a reporter twice about Lizzie Borden. In 1942, she said Lizzie was not a recluse. She said Lizzie still did charity work after 1893 but did not want it known. She also told of Lizzie financing some young persons through college.

In 1951, when a reporter visited Grace in her home at 141 Martha Street, he noticed one of Lizzie's gorgeous rugs from Maplecroft, along with some of Lizzie's books. During that interview, Grace said she had gone to a Boston restaurant with Lizzie and Lizzie ordered "tripe and mushrooms." Tripe is stomach tissue of a hoofed animal such as cattle, oxen, and deer. Lizzie's tripe probably came from a cow.

Grace loved plants and her home always had a smell of flowers. She had books in every spot available.

On March 16, 1955, Grace Howe suffered a cerebral hemorrhage and remained in a coma until her death on June 14, 1955. She was 80 years old.

Grace was a member of the Church of Ascension on Rock Street (the same church which its pastor, Edmund Cleveland, in 1927, conducted the burial services for Lizzie Borden). Grace's funeral was held at the church at 2:30 p.m. on Friday, June 17, and burial took place in Oak Grove Cemetery in Fall River. The service was performed by Rev. Irving A. Evans, rector of St. Mark's Episcopal Church.

On December 17, 1996, the Howe's son, Hartley E. died at the age of 85 at Horseneck Road in Westport. He was survived by his wife, Rosella S. (Senders) Howe; their children David S., Edward H., and Rosemary Howe Camozzi; his daughter-in-law Edith C. Howe; and his son-in-law Robert Camozzi. Hartley Howe's sister, Mary (Howe) Baker, predeceased him (June 4, 1900 – May 5, 1965). Mr. Howe was cremated and a Graveside Committal

Service was held privately at Oak Grove Cemetery in Fall River.

GRACE HARTLEY HOWE
LAST WILL AND TESTAMENT

I, Grace Hartley Howe, of Fall River, in the County of Bristol and Commonwealth of Massachusetts, do make this my LAST WILL AND TESTAMENT, hereby revoking all Wills and Codicils heretofore made by me.

After the payment of my debts, funeral and administration expenses, and all State and Federal estate, inheritance and succession taxes, I give, devise and bequeath as follows:

1. To my daughter, Mary Howe Baker, all of my jewelry, silverware, and personal effects, for her own use, and I request, but do not direct, that she may distribute such of the same as she shall, in her uncontrolled discretion, determine to be in accordance with my wishes.

2. To my son, Hartley E. Howe, my household furniture, for his own use.

3. To each of my grandchildren living at my death the sum of One Thousand ($1,000.00) Dollars.

4. To the Union Hospital in Fall River, a charitable corporation, the sum of One Thousand ($1,000.00) Dollars, to be known as the "Dr. James W. Hartley and Dr. Richard Cook Borden Hartley Fund," the income to be used for the work of the Infantile Paralysis Foundation at the Hospital.

5. To the Fall River National Bank, of Fall River, Massachusetts, all the rest and residue of my estate, both real and personal, and wherever the same may be situated, but as Trustee, in trust, to be held and administered by it as additions to and part of the Trust Fund now held by it as Trustee under an Indenture between me and said Bank dated September 10, 1926, or under any amending or substitute provisions in respect thereto, and for the purposes therein specified, prior to the date hereof.

I nominate and appoint the said The Fall River National Bank to be Executor of this my Will, and direct that it be not required to furnish surety upon its official bond as such.

In Testimony Whereof I hereunto set my hand, and in the presence of three witnesses declare this to be my last Will this 31st day of March, in the year one thousand nine hundred and fifty-four.

Grace Hartley Howe (signed)

On this 31st day of March A.D. 1954, Grace Hartley Howe, of Fall River, Massachusetts, signed the foregoing instrument in our presence, declaring it to be her last Will: and as witnesses thereof we three do now, at her request, in her presence, and in the presence of each other, hereto subscribe our names.

(signed)

Richard K. Hawes
Richard K. Hawes, Jr.
Lodivine LeMoyne

Sources:

Curry, Judith Paula. "What's in a Name?: Cousin Grace Hartley Howe." *Lizzie Borden Quarterly* 4.1 (January 1997).

"Death Takes Mrs. Howe." *Fall River Herald News* 15 June 1955.

"Democrats: Relict's Recompense." *Time Magazine*. Web. 18 June 2014.

Hetzel, Susan Riviere, General Historian. *Lineage Book, National Society of the Daughters of the American Revolution, Vol. XIV (1896)*. Harrisburg, PA: Harrisburg Publishing Company, 1902.

Last Will and Testament, Grace Hartley Howe.

Rebello, Leonard. *Lizzie Borden, Past & Present*. Fall River, MA: Al-Zach Press, 1999.

Howe family grave at Oak Grove Cemetery, Fall River, Massachusetts.

Louis McHenry Howe

January 14, 1871 – April 18, 1936

Louis McHenry Howe was Franklin Delano Roosevelt's political strategist or, as he was also known, his "right hand man." He first met Roosevelt in 1911, when Howe was a newspaper reporter. He steered FDR through his political career, remaining close and calling most of the shots. Howe had a brilliant political mind, and Franklin Roosevelt was the man he was most confident would in time be President of the United States.

Howe was born in Indianapolis, Indiana. He married Grace Hartley on November 9, 1898, when they eloped to a little town in Vermont. There they were married by a justice of the peace. Grace was a second cousin to Lizzie Borden, and it is said he often quipped about it while he lived in the White House. Grace's mother was not fond of Louis Howe and did not think him suitable as a husband for her daughter, but what was done was done. She insisted the two have a proper wedding, and on May 6, 1899, they did so at the Church of the Ascension in Fall River, Massachusetts, Grace Hartley's home town. Mrs. Hartley purchased a large home for them, not far from Louis's father and newspaper business in Saratoga Springs, New York.

Louis had their house heavily mortgaged within the first year to try to save the family business, but to no avail. He never seemed to get a steady job after that. He would have liked to have been able to make a living as a freelance writer, and he did get his share of bylines, but jobs were only here and there with nothing entirely steady.

His wife, Grace, did not do well when she was carrying their first baby. She was often ill that year (1900) and she went home to Fall River to await the new arrival. On June 4, their daughter Mary was born.

In the spring of 1910, Louis was chosen by the head of the New York State Commission, Spencer Trask, to do a study in Europe on the chances of profit in state-controlled "watering holes." The Howes traveled happily in Europe for months. Upon their return, Spencer Trask had been killed in a train accident that Louis Howe had bought the ticket for, Louis's mother died, and both Howes were ill. Louis was sick from a chronic heart ailment. Grace was pregnant again.

In November of 1910, she gave birth to a son. The son died within a week of meningitis.

In 1908, the Howes rented a cottage on Horseneck Beach. The ocean was right there, and they had no road access, which made it most private. They ended up purchasing the cottage as a summer home. In 1933, at last a road of packed sand was put in along with electricity. This cottage was destroyed by a hurricane in 1938.

At the time FDR and Howe's paths crossed, Louis was a correspondent in Albany of the *New York Herald*. He was sent to interview Roosevelt for the paper. As chairman of the Wilson Conference Committee, Roosevelt hired him to handle its publicity. He was impressed by Howe's skill, industry, and sardonic wit.

Roosevelt worked for Woodrow Wilson and was at the 1912 Democratic convention in Baltimore that Wilson got the nomination. Louis Howe sent Roosevelt a congratulatory telegram which started with, "Beloved and revered future President!"

Howe stayed with Roosevelt through his burgeoning political life. When FDR was appointed by Wilson as Assistant Secretary of the Navy, he took Howe with him. Through the Senate, as Governor of New York, to the White House, Louis Howe told him what moves to make and what to say in his speeches—and the pairing of the two whom Grace and Eleanor called "Mutt and Jeff" was sheer political genius.

Would there have been an Eleanor Roosevelt as we knew her, had it not been for Howe? It was he who coached her on public speaking and helped her lose her fear of shyness of those events.

Louis Howe was a strange looking man. He was 5'5" and a chain smoker. "He looked sickly with his bulging eyes, pockmarked face and chronic cough. He was never without a vile cigarette between his blistered lips." The scarred face were the result of a fall from a bicycle when he was young. The press called him "The Medieval Gnome." He would often answer his phone with, "This is the Medieval Gnome speaking." He called himself "one of the four ugliest men in the state of New York." He enjoyed hearing an apt remark about his appearance. He would grimly joke how children would flee from his protruding eyes.

Some were appalled at his appearance, which stood out among the highly groomed. Usually he had his jacket off, sleeves rolled up, clothes wrinkled, and his Sweet Caporal hanging from his mouth while the destination of its ashes were unimportant to him. His secretary described his office in 1931 as "the most disorderly office in New York." He would open his mail, take a quick look at it, and if he didn't like it, he pitched it over his head where a pile grew daily.

Howe often used "Luhowe" in his telegrams. He was always calm in a crisis. When hearing that Roosevelt's 1932 presidential nomination was clinched, he said, "That is fine."

Although Louis and Grace Howe were often apart due to his work, they seemed to have a good marriage. Louis was a self-taught painter and enjoyed doing seascapes from Horseneck Beach. He loved to read mysteries. He adored his children (in 1911 their son Hartley was born). His poor health (a heart murmur and asthma aggravated by bouts of bronchitis) was an always-hovering obstacle.

When FDR was elected President in 1932, he made Louis Howe his #1 secretary. He had an office next to Roosevelt. Many visitors whom Roosevelt could not or did not see at least got to speak to the man closest to the President, and he had every confidence that Howe knew exactly what to say to each one. Howe could not tolerate a lie, though. If he discovered someone had been untruthful, he never forgot it. Roosevelt also gave him the Lincoln bedroom, which had a dressing room and private bath with it. Howe looked at the massive room and said to just give him a small bed in that dressing room.

Louis Howe did have a theory as to who killed the Bordens of Fall River. Fulton Oursler said in his autobiography that Howe had said that Lizzie didn't do it. He said Emma "stole back from Marion" [it was Fairhaven, Massachusetts, where Emma was supposed to be during the murders] and committed the murders. He told him Emma was crazy and had epileptic fits. Howe said that Lizzie discovered Emma and sent her back to Marion.

Fulton Oursler knew Edmund Pearson and arranged for him to meet Howe. Pearson did not agree with his theory, though it was published in Pearson's "Legends of Lizzie" in the April 22, 1933, issue of the *New Yorker*.

Howe had been critically ill times before in his life, but in January of 1935 he was facing his last crisis, which lasted sixteen months. He still worked from his bed in the White House, but eventually he was admitted to Bethesda Naval Hospital.

Louis Howe died in his sleep on April 18, 1936, of coronary artery disease at the age of 65. Roosevelt canceled his plans for a week and lowered the White House flag to half-staff. He was given a State funeral in the East Room, then sent by train to be buried in Fall River. The Roosevelts attended his funeral there. Children were given the day off of school, and they lined the streets of the President's route.

In 1945, a cargo ship was named for him, the USS *Louis McHenry Howe*, and launched from Vancouver, Washington.

Roosevelt had written a note to Eleanor shortly after Howe died. "I suggest the following to be put on Louis' tombstone: 'Devoted friend, adviser and associate of the President'. FDR."

His stone is an exact, but smaller, replica of FDR and Eleanor's, enshrined at the Rose Garden at Hyde Park.

Sources:

"Advocate from the Doom: The Diaries and Papers of James G. McDonald, 1932-1935." *American Magazine*, 1933.

Davis, Kenneth S. *FDR: The Beckoning of Destiny, 1882-1928*. NY: History Book Club, 2004.

Fenster, Julie M. *FDR's Shadow: Louis Howe, the Force that Shaped Franklin and Eleanor Roosevelt*. NY: Palgrave Macmillan, 2009.

Lovinger, Robert. "Fall River FDR Advisor Left Legacy of Secrecy." SouthCoastToday.com 24 October 2000. Web. 18 June 2014.

Rebello, Leonard. *Lizzie Borden, Past & Present*. Fall River, MA: Al-Zach Press, 1999.

Rollins, Alfred B. *Roosevelt and Howe*. NY: Alfred A. Knopf, 1962.

Roosevelt, David B. and Manuela Dunn Mascetti. *Grandmere: A Personal History of Eleanor Roosevelt*. NY: Warner Books, 2002.

Steinberg, Alfred. *Mrs. R.: The Life of Eleanor Roosevelt*. NY: Putnam, 1958.

Stiles, Lela. "The Man Behind Roosevelt," Coronet Book Condensation. *Coronet*: June 1958.

Lucy Macomber stone and burial card at Oak Grove Cemetery, Fall River, Massachusetts.

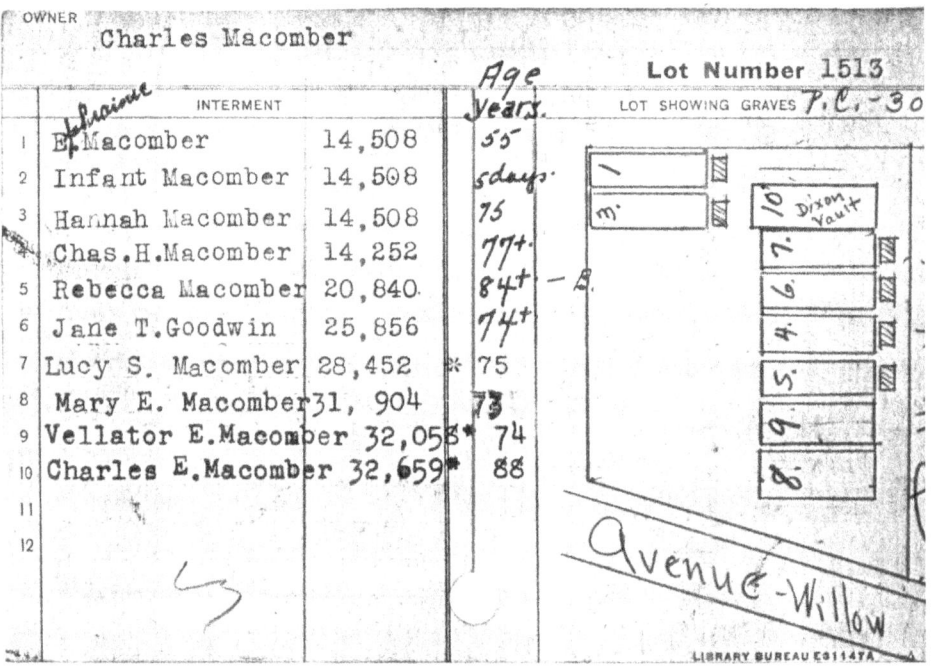

Lucy S. Macomber

1858 – June 3, 1933

Lucy Macomber was a schoolmate of Lizzie Borden's and is mentioned in Lizzie's will. She was born in Fall River, one of five children to parents Charles H. Macomber and Rebecca W. Russell. In 1878, she graduated from B.M.C. Durfee High School. Lucy (or "Lou") graduated in three years, taking a course called "Select Course – Three Years." She attended the New England Conservatory of Music, Emerson College, and State College in Amherst, Massachusetts.

Lucy boarded in North Westport, Massachusetts, from 1888 – 1917. She taught for forty years at the Davis School, retiring in 1923. She also taught elocution at the Borden Block at some time. She moved back to Fall River and lived with her brother. She was one of Lizzie Borden's supporters through the trial.

It sounds like Miss Macomber was well-off and probably in a social class that Lizzie (pre-Maplecroft) aspired. The name "Macomber" was prolific in Fall River and Westport. On the first floor of the A.J. Borden Building, at 41 South Main Street, was a store called Charles E. Macomber & Company. It is uncertain whether this was Lucy's father or another Macomber.

Lucy Macomber died at the age of 75. Her estate was valued at $22,000. Her funeral was handled by Winward's. She is buried at Oak Grove Cemetery, Fall River, in the family plot.

From Lizzie Borden's will: "To my old schoolmate, Lucy S. Macomber, of said Fall River, the sum of one thousand dollars."

Sources:

Rebello, Leonard. *Lizzie Borden, Past & Present*. Fall River, MA: Al-Zach Press, 1999.

Franklin Miller grave at Oak Grove Cemetery, Fall River, Massachusetts.

Franklin Harrison Miller

January 7, 1843 – March 19, 1911

Franklin H. Miller was born on January 7, 1843, at home at 219 Second Street, a double house that stood across the street diagonally from the Borden residence. His parents were Southard H. and Esther G. (Peckham) Miller. His father was one of Fall River's leading and most influential citizens, a contractor in a large way, builder of mills, and also prominent in public affairs.

Franklin Miller was a noted artist, specializing in landscapes and marine paintings but also produced portraits. His early work indicates that he probably first studied with Robert S. Dunning. The two were very close friends and associates.

Early in his career, Miller studied with Benjamin Champney of Boston, one of America's leading artists. Later he went abroad and traveled in England, France, and, in a more limited way, Switzerland. He worked to develop his talent and gained a breadth which was always afterwards a valuable attribute in his work.

Miller never sought out a prominent place in the art world. The Millers were well off, thanks to Southard Miller's business, and Franklin Miller was not a starving artist. He continued to create beautiful paintings as a steady, hard worker.

Unlike his father, Franklin Miller was in no way a public figure, and left his paintings to speak for themselves. He was known as a very kindly, likable man, once one got to know him, but to know him one had to seek him out. He had little to say about his art, unlike fellow artists who could speak about paintings when they can be induced to speak of little else.

Miller taught art in the Fall River Evening School for two years.

Almost from the time the Academy Building was finished, Miller had his studio there. Robert Dunning had a studio at first on the top floor, but shortly came down to the third floor to a room on the northeast corner. Miller went in with him early in the 1880s, and they remained together there as long as Mr. Dunning lived, a curtain separating the two studios. Miller stayed with the studio after Dunning's death. This room was a favorite gathering place for other artists and those that were interested in painting but were not painters themselves.

After his father's death, Franklin kept his residence in the south section of the double house on Second Street, of which the north half was occupied by the Dr. Seabury W. Bowens and their daughter, Florence. Mrs. Bowen was Miller's sister.

Franklin Miller also had a studio at his house. Mrs. Florence (Bowen) Hathaway, his niece, visited it daily. When she was little, as she shared with Mrs. Edward B. Lovell, she went in the studio and decided to try painting. She ended up ruining one of Miller's paintings and was thereafter banned from her uncle's studio.

Miller never married. He enjoyed playing the violin and was said to be fond of animals.

Franklin Miller gave up his studio a few weeks before his death. He had been in failing health for about two years, due to cancer of the throat, and for the last eight weeks of his life he was confined to his home.

Franklin Miller died on Saturday afternoon, March 19, 1911, at his home. He was 68 years old.

Mr. Miller is buried at Oak Grove Cemetery in Fall River in the Miller family plot.

The following was published in one of the Fall River newspapers after his death:

THE LATE F. H. MILLER

To the editor of the News. Some facts relative to the late Franklin H. Miller, artist, have not yet been published. His pictures stood high, and though they were little appreciated and known here, were shown and commended both in New York and Philadelphia. The Knights and other Rhode Island families admired them and were generous purchasers.

Mr. Miller, when in his early twenties, studied art for nearly two years in Paris, where he lived with B.M.C. Durfee. Since his return to this city he had lived a very quiet, secluded life, with visits of a month or two each summer to the wilds of Maine or Nova Scotia, 'to hear the songs of the birds and to catch the colors of the sea.'

He was a man of few friends, but those whom he favored with his acquaintance valued it highly. Though an elusive personality, he was one of the purest, cleanest men of his day and generation.

A.

The Fall River Historical Society has a little red velvet book that Miller kept a list of frames he ordered for different paintings and to whom some of his paintings were being sold. Two of his paintings were purchased by Stephen A Chase and were given to the Fall River Library: "Under the Apple Tree" and "September Afternoon," completed in 1906.

Mrs. Dwelly bought his "Willows and Brook" in 1895. A painting of pansies was done for Mrs. Gifford; "Peaches and Leaves" for G. Ballard; and a painting of cherries for Mr. Robertson.

The Historical Society displays two of Franklin Miller's paintings: "Cherries" and "Concord Grapes." A portrait of Franklin Miller by Robert Dunning hangs in the music room.

Sources:

Fall River Evening Herald 20 March 1911.

Lovell, Mrs. Edward B. "Early Painters of Fall River." Manuscript presented before the Fall River Historical Society,1944.

Martins, Michael, Curator, Fall River Historical Society. Personal correspondence. 5 June 2008.

Southard Miller and family grave at Oak Grove Cemetery, Fall River, Massachusetts.

Southard Harrison Miller

November 30, 1811 – October 29, 1895

Southard Miller was born in Middleboro, Massachusetts, on November 30, 1811. His parents were Alden and Millicent (Lovell) Miller. They married on February 9, 1809. Alden Miller was a farmer and had a mill business on the family property. They had six children: Hannah P., born September 9, 1809, who married Alexander Hackett of Middleboro; Southard Harrison; Alden, born August 3, 1814, who was engaged in various jobs and died in Middleboro; Lucy Ann, born March 20, 1816, died February 14, 1897, and was married to Andrew Cobb Wood; Samuel, born in 1819, died in 1821; and Lorenzo Theodore, born December 8, 1821, and died in 1900 in Middleboro.

Their first child, Hannah, was born seven months after they married. One can conclude that either her birth was premature or that life was not so dull in the early 1800s.

Southard Miller married Esther G. (Peckham) Miller of Newport, Rhode Island, in 1836. They had three children. Reuben Morton who was in the lumber business in Fall River (1839 – 1884). Reuben married twice in his lifetime, first to Sarah J. Gifford, then later to Jamesetta Carson. His only surviving child, Charles S. Miller, was born to his first marriage. His other two children were Franklin Harrison Miller, a well-known artist; and Phoebe Vincent Miller, the wife of Dr. Seabury Bowen. The Dr. Bowens had one daughter, Florence G., who married Horace M. Hathaway.

At the age of 16, he moved to Fall River and learned the trade of carpentry and builder under a "Mr. Chaloner." He worked for a short time as a journeyman, then formed the building contractor company of Ford & Miller with James Ford. Their business was located at the southwest corner of Borden and Second Streets. Their partnership only lasted a few years. Miller then continued on alone for many years.

Miller was known as a very good mechanic as well as a man that had splendid executive ability and business methods, which made him hugely successful. He was known for his high-class work and honorable methods, of which he was rewarded by the patronage of largely well-to-do clientele.

After the fire of 1843, he had a large share of the work of rebuilding Fall River. Among the buildings his business built were: the almshouse in Bridgewater, Massachusetts; the U.S. Marine Hospital in Portland, Maine; some of the original buildings at the State Farm in Bridgewater, Massachusetts; in Fall River the Laurel Lake Mills, the Baptist Temple, and the Unitarian Church; the Union, Tecumseh, Davol, Granite No. 1, and Mechanical Mills. His firm also did carpentry at City Hall.

Andrew Borden worked for Mr. Miller for two years as a carpenter when the City Hall (Market Building) was completed in 1844 – 45.

Southard Miller built the house at 92 Second Street, completed in December of 1845, for Charles Trafton. Miller's own large house was across the street diagonally from it, and was considered one of the finest residences in Fall River in its day.

In April of 1872, Andrew Borden and his family purchased the home at 92 Second Street. The Borden family lived there until the murders in 1892. Built as a duplex, Andrew Borden had it converted into a single family dwelling. The layout of the home interior has always been interesting to read about, and is often noted for its lack of hallways (each room opens into another). Most houses in Fall River do not contain hallways, and multiple family homes ("two-deckers" and "triple-deckers") save space by avoiding this interior feature. One can not truly appreciate the spaciousness of the Borden house until one is actually inside. It is not a claustrophobic design and quite comfortable for a family of four and one domestic.

Miller ran unsuccessfully for mayor in 1868. He was fire chief of his Fall River community from 1860 – 1869. In 1875, he was a member of the Legislature and a member of the first board of aldermen. Miller was a Democrat, serving twice as a member of the General Court, in 1852 and again in 1875. He was director of the Massasoit National Bank for almost forty years. He retired in 1893, due to his progressing age.

On the morning of the murders, between 10:15 and 10:30 a.m., Southard Miller was at Whitehead's Market and saw Andrew Borden walking, turning the corner onto Spring Street.

From Albert Chase's notes in the *Witness Statements*:

Alexander B. Coggeshall, a stable keeper on Second street, left his stable at 11.10 to go to diner. He stopped to talk with Mrs Buffington, and she told him that there had been trouble in the next house. Just then Bridget Sullivan came out of the house on the run, and went over to Southard H. Miller's house, and went in. Soon after Mr. Miller came to the door, and called him over, and said "Here Alex, I want you to listen to what this girl says," Bridget then told them that Mr. Borden and his wife had both been murdered. Mr. Coggeshall then went to dinner at Mrs. Tripp's No. 80 Second street, and he told her of the murder. It was then 11.20 by the clock in the restaurant.

Moulton Batchelder of the District Police interviewed Southard Miller, along with others, for prosecuting attorney Hosea Knowlton in regard to any insanity known on Lizzie's maternal side of the family (the Morses).

S. H. Miller 93 Second St. Fall River opp. The Bordon (sic) House. I have lived in Fall River 64 years. Bordon use to work for me. I know the Bordons and all of the Morses, the father of Lizzie's mother was Anthony Morse. I use to know his two brothers. Know the brothers of Mrs. Morse, Lizzie's mother. One is now supposed to be out West. I never knew or never heard that any of the Morses is or was Insane. Know they were somewhat peculiar. Anthony Morse had two brothers George and Gardiner Morse. I was not a witness at the trial. I did not intend to be. I saw Mr. Borden a little while before the murder. Bridget, the Servant girl came running into my house and said both was dead just then a man was passing. I called him and told Bridget to tell him what she told me. She did and that man was a witness. I did not want anything to do with it and I did not go near the house.

Southard Miller died at the age of 83 years, 11 months on October 29, 1895, of old age. He is buried in the Miller family plot at Oak Grove Cemetery in Fall River.

Note: Southard Miller's death certificate fixes his age at death as "84 years, 11 months"; however, he was born in the month of November of 1811, and would not have turned 84 until the month following his death. His age given on his grave monument is correct.

Sources:

Caplain, Neilson. "Lizbits." *Lizzie Borden Quarterly* VI.3 (July 1999).

Martins, Michael and Dennis Binette, eds. *The Commonwealth of Massachusetts vs. Lizzie A. Borden, The Knowlton Papers*. Fall River, MA: The Fall River Historical Society, 1994.

Rebello, Leonard. *Lizzie Borden, Past & Present*. Fall River, MA: Al-Zach Press, 1999.

Representative Men and Old Families of Southeastern Massachusetts, Volume I. Chicago: J.H. Beers & Co., 1912.

The Witness Statements. Orlando, FL: PearTree Press, 2005

Alice Russell, unknown newspaper, n.d.

Alice Russell, *Boston Globe*, August 30, 1892

Alice M. Russell

1852 – January 21, 1941

Alice Maria Russell was the only child of Frederick W. and Judith Manley Russell. She was born in New Bedford, Massachusetts. Her father was born in Nantucket, Massachusetts, and was a clerk. He lived from 1810 – 1878. Her mother was born in 1833, in Little Compton, Rhode Island. She worked as a domestic and was a well-known nurse in Fall River.

In 1873, the family lived on Whipple Street in Fall River until the death of Alice's father on May 31, 1878. It was then that Mrs. Russell and Alice moved to 96 Second Street, next door to the Bordens. In 1891, Alice moved to 33 Borden Street, while Mrs. Russell moved to Maple Street, as she continued her work as a nurse.

Alice worked for the Leander D. Wilbur Clothing Store, which was located at the corner of Pleasant and South Main. There she worked as a clerk and bookkeeper. In 1896 both Alice and her mother moved to 232 Third Street.

Alice worked as a sewing assistant to Annie Hoyt for the fourth and fifth grades in the city in 1896. She became the supervisor of sewing in 1908. Past curator of the Fall River Historical Society, Mrs. Florence Brigham, was one of her students. She remembered her as a gentle woman with "lovely white hair." She believed that Alice "would not have told the story about the burning of the dress if her conscience hadn't bothered her."

Alice and her mother lived in a duplex at 18 Hillside Street. Mrs. Russell died in 1913. The following year Alice retired. She continued to live in the Hillside Street house until 1930, when she moved into the Home for Aged People (today called Adams House) at 1168 Highland Avenue.

Alice Russell was probably the most important witness for the prosecution at the trial of Lizzie Borden in June of 1893. On the morning of August 4, 1892 ("The Fatal Fourth"), Lizzie sent Bridget for Dr. Bowen allegedly as soon as she found her father's still-warm body. When Dr. Bowen proved not to be home, Bridget was then sent for Alice Russell. It was not far.

The very night before the murders on Wednesday, August 3, Lizzie had paid a visit to Alice Russell. Alice had been friends with Emma and Lizzie for years, and exchanging visits was not unusual. But what Lizzie said was.

At about 7 p.m. that evening, Lizzie walked over to Alice Russell's home. Lizzie had decided to join a group of friends at Dr. Handy's cottage in Marion after all and told Alice of it. Alice wished her a good time, and Lizzie hesitated before saying,

> Well, I don't know; I feel depressed. I feel as if something were hanging over me that I cannot

throw off, and it comes over me at times, no matter where I am. When I was at the table the other day, when I was at Marion, the girls were laughing and talking and having a good time, and this feeling came over me, and one of them spoke and said, 'Lizzie, why don't you talk?'

She filled Alice in on the sicknesses the day before of Andrew and Abby. Bridget was not sick, she said. And Lizzie herself said she was not sick enough to vomit. She talked about someone having poisoned them, but Alice Russell dissuaded her from the theory.

"I feel afraid sometimes," said Lizzie, "that father has got an enemy. For he has so much trouble with his men that come to see him." She told of one man who got argumentative with her father when he came to the Borden house recently. She told Alice of the barn break-ins, the daylight robbery, and seeing someone hanging around the house one night.

"I feel as if I wanted to sleep with my eyes half open … for fear they will burn the house down over us," she ended dramatically. Of course, the next morning both Andrew and Abby were murdered, right in their house, in broad daylight.

When Alice Russell went back to the Borden house with Bridget, she would be there for four nights. She spent Thursday, August 4 and Friday, August 5 in Mr. and Mrs. Borden's bedroom. The next two nights she spent in Emma's room.

On Thursday night she and Lizzie went down to the cellar. Alice carried a lamp. Lizzie took a slop pail. Alice went into the water closet. The bloody clothing from the victims was in the washroom. Lizzie went into the washroom alone. She went to the sink and rinsed out a pail and the two friends went back upstairs. Alice did not know that Lizzie returned to the cellar by herself. Officer Joseph Hyde could see her through the window but could not see what she did.

If not for Alice Russell, no one would have ever known that on Sunday, August 7, Lizzie burned a dress in the kitchen stove. As it was, it did not come out at the first two hearings where she testified. And she did not volunteer it. It wasn't until the Grand Jury hearing in December that she gave her testimony about the event.

"I went into the kitchen," Alice testified at Lizzie's trial, "and I saw Miss Lizzie at the other end of the stove. I saw Miss Emma at the sink. Miss Lizzie was at the stove, and she had a skirt in her hand, and her sister turned and said, 'What are you going to do?' and Lizzie said, 'I am going to burn this old thing up; it is covered with paint'."

Alice then left the room and when she returned, "Miss Lizzie stood up towards the cupboard door, -- the cupboard door was open, and she appeared to be either ripping something down or tearing part of this garment. … I said to her, 'I wouldn't let anybody see me do that, Lizzie.' She didn't make any answer. … She stepped just one step farther back up towards the cupboard door."

On Monday she talked with an official in the Borden parlor. It is obvious that Miss Russell did not divulge the dress burning incident to him. When she saw the sisters in the dining room she remarked, "I am afraid, Lizzie, the worst thing you could have done was to burn that dress. I have been asked about your dresses." To which Lizzie replied, "Oh, what made you let me do it? Why didn't you tell me?"

Her trial testimony reveals that the dress she saw Lizzie burn was "light blue [back] ground with a dark figure – small figure," the same description Adelaide Churchill gave in her testimony regarding the dress Lizzie wore on the murder morning.

LIZZIE BORDEN: RESURRECTIONS

Alice had nothing to do with the Misses Borden afterwards. She seldom spoke of the murders. But once she did tell her cousin (Mrs. Ida Russell Minor) that she thought Lizzie was innocent, until she saw her burn the dress in the stove.

Alice Russell died at the Home for Aged People of chronic myocarditis on January 21, 1941. She was in her 89th year (88 years, 1 month and 16 days old according to her death certificate).

Services were held at the Home on January 22. She is buried at the Beech Grove Cemetery in Westport, Massachusetts.

Her passing made news in the papers, referring to her as the last witness in the trial of Lizzie Borden.

Sources:

"Death of Miss Russell Recalls Borden Murders." *Fall River Herald News* 25 January 1941.

Fall River Herald News 21 January 1941.

"Lizzie's Turncoat Friend." *Fall River Historical Society Newsletter* 14.1 (Spring 2002).

Rebello, Leonard. *Lizzie Borden, Past & Present*. Fall River, MA: Al-Zach Press, 1999.

Widdows, Harry, Stefani Koorey, Kat Koorey, eds. *The Preliminary Hearing in the Lizzie Borden Case, New Edition*. Orlando, FL: PearTree Press, 2005.

Widdows, Harry, Stefani Koorey, Kat Koorey, eds. *The Trial of Lizzie Andrew Borden*. Orlando, FL: PearTree Press, 2005.

Alice Russell grave at Beech Grove Cemetery, Westport, Massachusetts.

Ellen Shove grave and family plot at Oak Grove Cemetery, Fall River, Massachusetts.

Ellen ("Nellie") M. Shove

August 13, 1851 – July 2, 1932

Nellie Shove was born in Fall River. Her parents were Charles O. Shove of Fall River and Rachel E. (Haines) Shove of Lockport, New York. She graduated from the Fall River High School. She was a friend of Lizzie Borden and was one of the ladies who went on the Grand Tour of Europe with Lizzie in 1890.

Miss Shove was most likely a respected lady from a fairly well-to-do family. Her father was an agent and the treasurer of the Granite Mills. He was also president of Shove Mills. There were two Shove Mills on Laurel Lake; one in Globe Village large, the other over the line in Tiverton, Rhode Island.

For sixty years, Nellie Shove attended the First Baptist Church in Fall River and was in charge of Bible classes for many of them. (Doctor Seabury Bowen attended the same church.) She was also secretary of the board at the Children's Home in Fall River. Her last residence was at 446 Highland Avenue in Fall River.

Miss Shove died of a cerebral hemorrhage at the age of 80 on Saturday, July 2, 1932. Funeral services were held at her home. Officiating was Rev. Dr. Albert C. Thomas of the First Baptist Church. Bearers were Richard Osborn, Sr., Richard Osborn, Jr., Arthur Reynolds, Ackley Shove, Robert R. Borden and Edward S. Borden. She was buried in the large Shove family plot at Oak Grove Cemetery in Fall River.

(Note: An error on Nellie Shove's death certificate states her date of death as July 1, 1932, and that has been picked up by other writers. Her grave monument gives the date as July 2, 1932, and her funeral write-up in the *Fall River Herald News* notes that she died on Saturday, which July 2 was.)

Sources:

"Funerals: Ellen M. Shove." *Fall River Herald News* 6 July 1932.

Rebello, Leonard. *Lizzie Borden, Past & Present*. Fall River, MA: Al-Zach Press, 1999.

Adelaide Whipp grave and family plot at Oak Grove Cemetery, Fall River, Massachusetts.

Adelaide B. Whipp

October, 1859 – April 1, 1941

Addie Whipp was a schoolmate of Lizzie Borden. She attended one year of high school with Lizzie. For some years her family was a neighbor of the Bordens. She held various jobs with local printers and publishers. She attended Central Congregational Church and was a member of the Fall River Historical Society.

Her mother was Sarah (Mowry) Whipp. Her father was Thomas R. Whipp and was a native of England. He came to the United States in 1849. He worked as a weaver, laborer and janitor at various times during his life in Fall River.

Lizzie left Adelaide Whipp $1,000 in her will. Miss Whipp died at her brother's home in Fall River. Survivors were two brothers, Elmer E. and Thomas R. Whipp. She is buried at Oak Grove Cemetery in Fall River, Massachusetts.

Sources:

Rebello, Leonard. *Lizzie Borden, Past & Present.* Fall River, MA: Al-Zach Press, 1999.

Lizzie Borden's Boston bull terriers grave at Pine Ridge Pet Cemetery, Dedham, Massachusetts.
Photograph courtesy of Hannah and Mark Amarantes.

Lizzie's Pets

Lizzie Borden loved animals. Books tell us that people remembered seeing her outside on the grounds of Maplecroft feeding the animals. In her will, Lizzie left $30,000 to the Animal Rescue League of Fall River.

> To the Animal Rescue League of said Fall River, the sum of thirty thousand dollars, also my shares of stock in the Steven Manufacturing Company. I have been fond of animals and their need is great and there are so few who care for them.

Emma Borden left the Fall River Animal Rescue League $20,000 in her will.

Inside the building in the lobby of the Animal Rescue League of Fall River today hangs framed photographs of Lizzie and Emma Borden.

Lizzie purchased a lot in the Pine Ridge Pet Cemetery in Dedham, Massachusetts, in 1927, the year of her death. Her registration card at the cemetery reads: "Miss E. A., 306 French Street, Fall River, Mass." It is possible that Lizzie sent one of her servants to tend to the business at the pet cemetery, as she may have been too ill, or have passed away, when the card was made out.

Three dogs of Lizzie's, Boston bull terriers, were buried in the lot at the pet cemetery the following year. There is one headstone listing their Scottish-sounding names: Donald Stuart, Royal Nelson, and Laddie Miller. The last two share their surname with servants of Lizzie. The name "Borden" is in large letters at the base, and the words "sleeping awhile" are on the monument.

The Pine Ridge Pet Cemetery is located at 238 Pine Street in Dedham, Massachusetts, and is managed by the Animal Rescue League of Boston. It opened in 1907, becoming an addition of the League, which started their operations in 1899. It was first called The Country Annex and Home of Rest for Horses, where overworked and older horses were brought for a restful vacation or to spend their last days.

A small house at the entrance was the summer home of founder Anna Harris Smith. The barn that is there today is a replica of the one that had originally come with the property.

The League's regular newsletter, "Our Four Footed Friends," is still published today and can be found Online at their website. In the July 1908 edition it was noted that eighteen burials of animals took place in their first year. It is the oldest pet cemetery in the United States owned and operated by an animal welfare agency.

It is estimated that there are twenty to thirty thousand animals buried at the cemetery. They do four or five burials a week and up to five-thousand cremations a year. Today the cemetery charges $900 for a grave, and raised granite monuments are about $500.

According to an interview for WBUR radio in Boston, burying a pet in your back yard is illegal and a Board of Health ordinance. It is unclear if that means the entire state or just the county or city.

The cemetery offers a self-guided walking tour that includes the grave of the dog of Admiral Byrd that is in the shape of an igloo and the pets of actor George Arliss, a benefactor of the cemetery. A printout is handed out for the purpose. Admission is free.

To get to the Lizzie Borden pet monument: When you reach the cemetery, go up the hill past the house and behind the barn. Go down this hill and look for the stone shed. Take the right fork. At the curve in the road, walk toward the woods. The Borden pet grave is at the edge of the woods near a stone wall.

Sources:

Brady-Myrov, Monica. "Pet Cemetery," Online radio interview. WBUR, Boston, 6 May 2008.

"Our Four Footed Friends." Animal Rescue League. Boston (Spring 2008).

Rebello, Leonard. *Lizzie Borden, Past & Present*. Fall River, MA: Al-Zach Press, 1999.

Lizzie Borden's Boston bull terriers are buried here, at Pine Ridge Pet Cemetery, Dedham, Massachusetts.
Photograph courtesy of Hannah and Mark Amarantes.

Part Six

The Hired Help

Mathilda Anderson grave and burial card at Oak Grove Cemetery, Fall River, Massachusetts.

Mathilda Anderson

September 22, 1852 – August 16, 1935

Matilda Wilhemina Johnson (Anderson) Anderson was a housekeeper at Maplecroft for at least five years and was there until the death of Lizzie Borden in 1927.

She was born in Sweden and came to the United States in the mid 1880s. Her parents were Anna K. Johnson and John A. Anderson. Her husband, Otto Leonard Anderson, was a shoemaker. He died in 1923. They had two children. After her husband's death, Mrs. Anderson lived at 94 Turner Street in Fall River.

Matilda Anderson received the sum of $3,000 from Lizzie Borden's will.

She died at the age of 82, and is buried at Oak Grove Cemetery in Fall River, Massachusetts.

Sources:

Rebello, Leonard. *Lizzie Borden, Past & Present.* Fall River, MA: Al-Zach Press, 1999.

Gertrude Callow grave and burial card at Oak Grove Cemetery, Fall River, Massachusetts.

Gertrude Callow

1889 – 1968

Gertrude (Russell) Callow worked for Lizzie Borden as a live-in domestic from 1912-1913. She was born in New Bedford, Massachusetts. Her husband, John W. Callow, worked as a weaver, gardener, and a sexton at the Church of the Ascension in Fall River, the city in which the Callows lived.

Gertrude Callow died at Fall River's Home for the Aged. She and her husband are buried at Oak Grove Cemetery in Fall River. She left behind her daughter, Mrs. Virginia (Harold) Taylor and her son, John R. Callow.

Sources:

Rebello, Leonard. *Lizzie Borden, Past & Present*. Fall River, MA: Al-Zach Press, 1999.

Charles C. Cook grave at Oak Grove Cemetery, Fall River, Massachusetts.

Charles C. Cook

March 28, 1854 – September 28, 1934

Charles Cook was born in Fall River, Massachusetts. His parents were Alexander Otis Cook and Mary (Bronson) Cook. His wife was Wealthy (Winslow) Cook. With her he had one child, Benjamin A. Cook. He died of dysentery when he was just four years old on August 20, 1882.

Cook's father had a shop in Globe Village—Cook & Grew, known as plumbers and tinsmiths. They were at 31 South Main and later moved to 43 Second Street not far from the Bordens' home. Charles Cook worked as a clerk in his father's store from 1873 until 1884. He then became an insurance and claims agent and conveyancer (taking care of legal papers that transferred the ownership of property) and worked in the Granite Block in Fall River. He soon engaged in handling stocks, bonds, and real estate. He later had an office in the A.J. Borden Building at 109 South Main, which he was occupying at the time of the murders.

Charles Cook testified at the preliminary hearing. He was in the habit of seeing Andrew Borden three or four times a week. On Tuesday, August 2, 1892, he talked in his office with Borden but did not reveal what was said. He testified that they did not talk about the subject of a will. On August 3, 1892, he saw Mr. Borden walking down Main Street, on the other side of the street, as Cook stood in the doorway of his office. And on Thursday, August 4, Cook saw him only after he was dead.

The subject of a will did come up two or three weeks before Borden's death. According to Cook: "He simply told me that he had not one."

Q: Told you what?

A: That he had not any will.

He and Lizzie were close friends. He had managed her father's financial affairs before Lizzie became his client. She mentioned him in her will: "To Charles C. Cook, of said Fall River and Tiverton, for his long and faithful services to me the sum of ten thousand dollars, and my so-called Baker Lot on French Street, across from where I live."

She also named Cook as her executor.

Cook still had the 'Baker Lot' when he died. Its value in 1927, when Lizzie died, was $3,000. He asked for $10,000 as his executor's fee. Grace Howe and Helen Leighton (two major legatees mentioned in Lizzie's will) contested this and his fee was lowered to $5,000.

In a memorandum Lizzie wrote, she also gave her 1923 Lincoln sedan to Cook, which was valued at $1,000.

Two months before his death, Charles Cook wrote his last will and testament:

BE IT REMEMBERED that I, Charles C. Cook of Fall River in the County of Bristol in the Commonwealth of Massachusetts, being of sound mind and memory, do make this my last will and testament.

After the payment of my just debts and funeral expenses, I give, devise and bequeath as follows:

1. I give and bequeath to Grace M. Walsh, of said Fall River, the sum of Five Thousand (5,000) Dollars.

2. I give and bequeath to Thirley (sic) L. Andrews of Tiverton, Rhode Island, if she is in my employ at the time of my death, the sum of Five Hundred (500) Dollars.

3. I give and bequeath to Elwood Burns of Tiverton, Rhode Island, if he is in my employ at the time of my death, the sum of Five Hundred (500) Dollars.

4. I give and bequeath to Phyllis M. Bonner, of said Fall River, the sum of Five Hundred (500) Dollars.

5. I give and bequeath to Louise C. Cheetham, of said Fall River, the sum of Two Thousand (2000) Dollars.

6. I give and bequeath to my cousin Mary H. Burgess of Boston, Massachusetts, the sum of Two Thousand (2000) Dollars.

7. I give and bequeath to my cousin Caroline Bronson the sum of Two Thousand (2000) Dollars.

8. I give and bequeath to Doris Titcomb, to Helen C. Titcomb and Louise C. Titcomb, children of my late sister, Charlotte Titcomb, the sum of Five (5.00) Dollars each.

9. All the rest and residue of my estate, of whatever kind, real and personal and wherever found, I give, devise and bequeath to my trustee herinafter named, upon trust nevertheless to pay the income thereof, for and during the term of ten years from and after the date of my death, to the Second Baptist Society of Fall River, said payments to be made semi-annually on such dates as my said trustee shall determine; and at the end of said term of ten years to transfer, convey, and pay over the principal of the said trust, with all accumulations theron, to the said Second Baptist Society, absolutely; the said income and principal to be used for the general purposes of the said society; and I give to my said trustee full power to invest and re-invest the said truste (sic) estate and to make changed in the form of investment thereof, as in its descretion it may deem advisable and for the best interests of the trust estate, and I authorize and empower my said trustee to make sale of my real estate at public auction or private sale and give effectual deeds of conveyance thereof, without first securing license for the sale therefor from any court, and the purchaser at any sale of any real or personal property from my said trustee, shall not be answerable for the disposition of any of the proceeds thereof.

10. I nominate and appoint Fall River National Bank, of said Fall River, trustee under this will and request that it be excused from furnishing surety or sureties on its official bond.

11. I nominate and appoint said Grace M. Walsh, executrix of this will and request that she be excused from furnishing surety or sureties on her official bond.

In witness whereof I hereunto set my hand and in the presence of three witnesses declare this to be my last will and testament this 10th day of July in the year one thousand nine hundred and thirty-four.

(signed)
Charles C. Cook

Cook died on September 28, 1934, only four months after his wife, Wealthy Winslow Cook. At that time he was living on Main Road in Tiverton, Rhode Island. His estate was valued at over $69,000. Charles Cook is buried with his wife at Oak Grove Cemetery in Fall River, Massachusetts.

Sources:

Last Will and Testament of Charles C. Cook.

Last Will and Testament of Lizzie A. Borden. LizzieAndrewBorden.com. Web. 16 June 2014.

Rebello, Leonard. *Lizzie Borden, Past & Present.* Fall River, MA: Al-Zach Press, 1999.

Widdows, Harry, Stefani Koorey, Kat Koorey, eds. *The Preliminary Hearing in the Lizzie Borden Case, New Edition.* Orlando, FL: PearTree Press, 2005.

Winifred F. French grave and burial card at Oak Grove Cemetery, Fall River, Massachusetts.

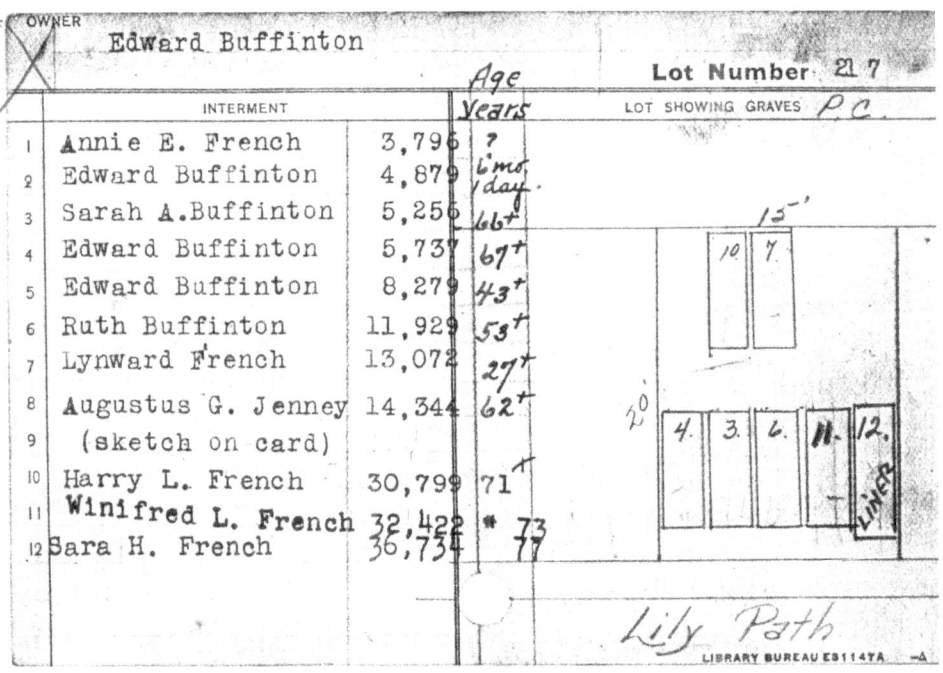

Winifred F. French

June, 1869 – January 25, 1943

    Winifred French was born in Brooklyn, New York. Her parents had four children: two daughters and two sons. None of them ever married. Her father was John French of Hopkinton, Massachusetts, and her mother was Anna Buffinton of Fall River, Massachusetts.
    She was a member of the Central Congregational Church in Fall River for many years. She worked for Lizzie Borden and was remembered in her will with a $5,000 bequest.
    Miss French was a stenographer until 1933. She remained in Fall River until her death after a brief illness.
    Winifred French is buried next to her sister, Sara H. French, at Oak Grove Cemetery. Their brothers are buried near them.

Sources:

Rebello, Leonard. *Lizzie Borden, Past & Present.* Fall River, MA: Al-Zach Press, 1999.

Catherine McFarland grave and burial card at Oak Grove Cemetery, Fall River, Massachusetts.

Catherine Mary McFarland

January 12, 1858 – January 17, 1947

Catherine McFarland (name spelled "Mc" and "Mac" in different sources) was born in Nova Scotia. Her husband, John L. McFarland, was a shipper and receiver for Allen & Slade Company. He died in 1918, at the age of 57.

The McFarlands had one child, James Donald McFarland, who died at the age of 26 of pneumonia. He had just started employment as high school principal in Cape May, New Jersey.

Catherine McFarland was a nurse for Lizzie Borden until 1927. In her will, Lizzie left her $5,000. She died at the age of 89 in Taunton, Massachusetts, of generalized arteriosclerosis. Mrs. McFarland is buried at Oak Grove Cemetery in Fall River.

Sources:

Rebello, Leonard. *Lizzie Borden, Past & Present*. Fall River, MA: Al-Zach Press, 1999.

Helen Smith gravestone at Oak Grove Cemetery, Fall River, Massachusetts.

Helen Smith

1883 – January 8, 1923

Helen Smith was a housekeeper for Lizzie Borden at Maplecroft from 1917 – 1920. She was born in Scotland and came to the United States in 1909. She died at the age of 39 in Fall River of tuberculosis. She is buried at Oak Grove Cemetery in Fall River, Massachusetts.

Sources:

Rebello, Leonard. *Lizzie Borden, Past & Present*. Fall River, MA: Al-Zach Press, 1999.

Bridget Sullivan

Bridget Sullivan

1875 – March 25, 1948

If the Bridget Sullivan buried in Olivet Cemetery in Butte, Montana, is the same Bridget Sullivan who worked for the Borden family during the time of the murders, her death certificate may be interesting.

This Bridget Sullivan had lived in the city of Butte, Montana for twenty-two years when she died. She had moved there, or to her last residence, around 1926.

She was born in Ireland. Her parents were Eugene Sullivan and Margaret Leary, both born in Ireland. The year of her birth is given as 1875 – it does not say "around" 1875 or anything else to qualify it; it simply states "1875." This means that she would have had to be about 17 at the time of the Borden murders. Something is not right with this date. Bridget herself tells the court that she was 25 years old in 1892.

From *The Preliminary Hearing in the Lizzie Borden Case:*

Q: How old are you?
A: Twenty-five.
Q: When was your last birthday?
A: I do not know.
Q: You do not know?
A: No Sir.
Q: Then how do you know you are twenty-five; because you have been informed so?
A: Yes Sir.

She lived at 112 East Woolman Street, Butte, Montana, in Silver Bow County. Her usual occupation was "housewife." She was a widow at the time of her death.

Bridget died in the county of Silver Bow at County Hospital in Butte, Montana, at the age of 73.

She died of exhaustion, cardiac failure, chronic myocarditis, arterial sclerosis, and senility. The death certificate required the doctor to underline the cause of death that should be charged statistically, and he underlined "senility".

Bridget was also blind. The cause was unknown. There is nothing to indicate the duration of her blindness on the death certificate.

She died at 2:20 p.m. on March 25, 1948. She was taken to Duggan's Merrill Mortuary in Butte, Montana, and buried at Mt. Olivet Cemetery on March 29, 1948. This may suggest that she had visitation and a funeral. She was not given an autopsy.

Signs point to this not being the correct death certificate for the Bridget Sullivan that worked for the Bordens, even though it was being sold as such through various web sites.

Sources:

Rebello, Leonard. *Lizzie Borden, Past & Present*. Fall River, MA: Al-Zach Press, 1999.

Widdows, Harry, Stefani Koorey, Kat Koorey, eds. *The Preliminary Hearing in the Lizzie Borden Case, New Edition*. Orlando, FL: PearTree Press, 2005.

Bridget Sullivan, *Boston Globe*, August 27, 1892

Bridget Sullivan, unknown newspaper, n.d.

Ernest Alden Terry grave and burial card at Oak Grove Cemetery, Fall River, Massachusetts.

Ernest Alden Terry

January 26, 1885 – October 11, 1955

Ernest Terry was Lizzie Borden's chauffeur from 1920 until her death in 1927. He was born in Fall River, Massachusetts, and was one of nine children. His parents were George C. Terry, who was a ship's carpenter, and Mary M. Gifford.

Before working as Lizzie's chauffeur, Terry was a farmer, laborer, salesman of boots and shoes, and a clerk. He had also worked as a chauffeur for Anna Howland Borden.

Terry was married to Ellen Hodgson. They had two children: Grace L. (later Mrs. Grace L. Gross) and Ernest Alden Terry Jr. Their son was a doctor and died in 1960. Grace Terry was an assembler and also worked in Children's Hospital in Boston. She died at the age of 60. After Ellen's death, Terry married Annie Robinson.

The Terrys lived on New Boston Road, within walking distance of Maplecroft. When Ernest worked as Lizzie's chauffeur he was always in full uniform.

When Lizzie died, she left Terry $3,000; another $2,500 in cash that she gave him a few hours before she died; and her 1924 Buick sedan, valued at $425. Terry claimed $2,380 for expenses incurred after Lizzie's death, but it was denied him by the court.

Grace Terry received $2,000 from Lizzie Borden's will. Ernest Terry Jr. received $2,000 and a piece of land on Belmont Street.

After Lizzie's death, Mr. Terry worked for a family by the name of Burke in Fall River as a driver for their textile business.

Ernest and Ellen Terry are buried at Oak Grove Cemetery in Fall River.

Sources:

Kelly, Jacques. "Dorothy Klug, 93, Volunteer, College Chemistry Teacher." *Baltimore Sun* 12 April 2006.

Rebello, Leonard. *Lizzie Borden, Past & Present*. Fall River, MA: Al-Zach Press, 1999.

Vida Turner grave and burial card at Oak Grove Cemetery, Fall River, Massachusetts.

Vida L.P. Turner

1887 – December 31, 1979

Vida Turner sang "My Ain Countrie" at Maplecroft when Lizzie Borden died, at Lizzie's prior request. It is unclear whether Lizzie asked for her by name, but it is most likely that Lizzie asked for it to be done in a generic way.

I had the good fortune in 2003 to meet a woman whose family knew Vida Turner well. She said that Vida Turner was asked to go to Maplecroft for this task. She was soloist at the Central Congregational Church. She went and sang the song Miss Borden requested from a separate room that shared a door with the room in which Lizzie laid in her casket. Mrs. Turner was nervous. Not a sound could be heard. It was too quiet. She sang and then was asked, probably by the undertaker, if she would like to see Lizzie Borden's body. She said no. When she left the big house, she did so with a great feeling of relief. She was told to not tell anyone about her first, and last, visit to Maplecroft.

Apparently this is not quite the correct story of Vida Turner's solo at Maplecroft. Somewhere along the line, this story started going around, whether started by Mrs. Turner or not. I am quite sure the lady I talked to did not make up what she was saying. Mrs. Turner was at the funeral at Maplecroft and she sang in front of the guests and, I presume, the body (per conversation with Michael Martins, Curator, Fall River Historical Society).

Vida Louise Pearson was born in Topsfield, Massachusetts. Her parents had a farm there. She came to live in Fall River as an infant. She married Alfred G. Turner (a Fall River native resident) on September 11, 1907, at her residence at 611 Walnut Street.

Alfred Turner worked in Joe Taylor's Fall River store in 1910, as a clothing salesman. Retired in 1951 from Besse Russell's and The Hub in Fall River, he then was a night watchman at Truesdale Hospital.

The Turners made their home at 1307 President Avenue. They had two sons: David Pearson Turner of Wilmington, Delaware, and Hartwell Alfred Turner of Holyoke, Massachusetts. They had six grandchildren.

Vida and Alfred Turner were members of Central Congregational Church for more than fifty years. Vida was soloist there for thirty-two years. She also was organist for the Order of the Eastern Star, Fall River Chapter, for years.

She was a member of the Golden Age Club, the Fall River Grange, and for years was a delegate to the Council of Women's Organizations from the Women's Association of the Church. Later she served as an alternate.

Her husband was a patron of the OES Chapter in Fall River and held the office of tyler in the Massasoit Lodge, AF and AM, for ten years and also belonged to the grange.

Alfred Turner died in 1971. Vida died on December 31, 1979, at the age of 92. The couple is buried in Oak Grove Cemetery in Fall River, Massachusetts. Their double headstone is on Lot Number 2726, on Tacsonia Path.

Sources:

Fall River Historical Society files.
"Mr. and Mrs. Turner Feted on 60th Anniversary." *Fall River Herald* 21 August 1967.
Personal interview with friend of Vida Turner, Spring 2003.
Rebello, Leonard. *Lizzie Borden, Past & Present*. Fall River, MA: Al-Zach Press, 1999.

Theodore Dwight Weld Wood

August 21, 1836 – February 19, 1914

Theodore Dwight Weld Wood was a clerk at Borden & Almy in 1862. Two years later he was a business partner. Borden & Almy became Borden, Almy & Company. When Andrew Borden and William Almy retired in 1878, Andrew Borden's interest in the business was sold to Theodore D.W. Wood. William Almy's share was sold to Edward S. Raymond, Almy's son-in-law. The company was then called Wood & Raymond. This partnership dissolved in 1883.

Wood & Hall was then formed when Wood and Henry A. Hall became partners. Wood & Hall was located in the A.J. Borden Building until a fire occurred there and they then moved to Market Square. The A.J. Borden Building survived four Fall River fires: 1893, 1905, 1916, and 1928. Wood & Hall was later called the Eastern Furniture Company and was owned by William Wood, T.D.W. Wood's son.

Theodore Dwight Weld Wood died on February 19, 1914. His obituary from the *Fall River Evening News* of February 20, 1914 follows:

DIED SUDDENLY IN HIS CHAIR

DEMISE OF THEODORE D. W. WOOD, LONG IN FURNITURE AND UNDERTAKING BUSINESS

Theodore D. W. Wood, who was for many years in the furniture and undertaking business in this city, and who had a wide circle of acquaintants in Fall River and adjoining, by all of whom he was held in high esteem, died peacefully in his chair at the home of his son, T. Elton Wood, in Tiverton, about 11 o'clock Thursday morning. He had been failing for some years, and suffered a shock a short time ago, but was apparently in his usual health Thursday morning. He was 77 years of age.

Theodore Dwight Weld Wood was the son of William Southworth and Diana Coe (Gray) Wood, and was born in Little Compton Aug. 31, 1836. He came to this city when a young man and entered the employ of Borden & Almy, who carried on a furniture and undertaking business at the northwest corner of South Main and Anawan streets. He was later admitted to the firm, which became Borden, Almy & Co. Subsequently, in partnership with Edward Raymond, he carried on the business under the name of Wood & Raymond, and finally in partnership with Henry A. Hall as Wood & Hall. The store was burned while he was located at South Main and Anawan streets. Wood & Hall's last location was in the Mason building, next north of City Hall. The partnership was dissolved about 1897, and Mr. Wood afterward carried on the undertaking business alone until about five or six years ago.

Mr. Wood was much interested in boating, and was a charter member of the Anawan Boat Club, of which he was president for a long period. He was also a member, and for a time president of the Fall River Yacht Club, whose regatta committee for many years consisted of himself, Lyman W. Deane and George W. Rankin. He was secretary and treasurer of the old Choral Union, and had been a member of Mt. Hope Lodge of Odd Fellows and Anawan Lodge, Knights of Pythias. He was also for some years a trustee of the Union Savings Bank. He was one of the original members of the Church of the New Jerusalem, and superintendent of its Sunday school for a long period.

His wife, who was Miss Mary Ann Taber of New Bedford, died some years ago. He leaves six children; William S. and T. Elton Wood of the Eastern Furniture Co., who are well known yachtsmen; Frank T. Wood, a customs house inspector in Boston; Lieut. Clarence E. Wood of the battleship Georgia, now in Mexican waters; Mrs. Alice G. Dunn, wife of Hartwell H. Dunn of this city, and Mrs. Amelia J. Hope of Providence.

And this, taken from a Fall River newspaper of February 24, 1914:

His services were conducted by Rev. Fred E. Mayer. Several hymns were sung. Interment was in the North Burial ground. The pall-bearers were his sons, Frank F. Wood of Boston, William S. Wood, T. Elton Wood, and a son-in-law, Clarence Hope of Providence. The floral tributes were numerous and very beautiful.

Mr. Wood was a direct descendant in the eighth generation of John Alden and Priscilla Mullins, through their daughter Elizabeth, who married William Pabodie. Her grave stone still stands in the old church yard in Little Compton.

Note: Tiverton, Providence and Little Compton are in the state of Rhode Island

Sources:

"Died Suddenly in His Chair/Demise of Theodore D.W. Wood." *Fall River Evening News* 20 February 1914.

Rebello, Leonard. *Lizzie Borden, Past & Present*. Fall River, MA: Al-Zach Press, 1999.

T.D.W. Wood grave and burial card at North Burial Ground, Fall River, Massachusetts.

Part Seven

All in the Family

Abraham Bowen family at Oak Grove Cemetery, Fall River, Massachusetts.

Abraham Bowen Borden, Wives and Daughters

Abraham Bowen Borden was the father of Andrew Jackson Borden. He is buried between the two wives he had in life, and next to them are two daughters that died young he had with his first wife. They are laid to rest at Oak Grove Cemetery in Fall River, Massachusetts, in the Borden family plot.

1. Bebe Wilmarth, Wife of Abraham B. Borden, July 5, 1801 - July 2, 1883

Bebe Borden was the second wife of Abraham Borden. She was the stepmother of Andrew Borden. In her will, she left Lizzie "a small breakfast shawl." Bebe and Abraham were married at the Second Baptist Church in Fall River on November 23, 1854. It was Bebe Borden's first marriage.

2. Abraham Bowen Borden, July 8, 1798 - December 6, 1882

Abraham Borden was the father of Andrew Borden and grandfather of Lizzie and Emma Borden.

3. Phebe Davenport, Wife of Abraham B. Borden, August 25, 1789 - October 13, 1853

Phebe Borden was Abraham Borden's first wife. She bore all children of Abraham Borden.
Phebe was first buried in "Town Lot," which meant North Burial Ground in Fall River. It is possible that she is still buried there and her gravestone at Oak Grove is an ornamental memorial.

4. Phebe Ann, Daughter of Abraham B. & Phebe D. Borden, February 19, 1829 - August 29, 1855

5. Lurana, Daughter of Abraham B. & Phebe D. Borden, November 5, 1824 - August 25, 1825

Lurana had a twin sister, Charlotte Borden, who died on August 20, 1828. There is no gravestone for Charlotte.
There is nothing on file at Oak Grove Cemetery or North Burial Ground in Fall River to say she is buried at either cemetery. Records before 1828 are almost non-existent.

Abraham and Phebe Borden also were the parents of Lurana / Laura Ann Borden, who was born on August 10, 1826. She lived to be 72 and is buried with her husband, Hiram Harrington, at Oak Grove Cemetery. Andrew Borden was Abraham's oldest child and only son.

Sources:

Mautinho, Tammy, Oak Grove Cemetery, Fall River, Massachusetts. Written correspondence. 17 September 2008.

Rebello, Leonard. *Lizzie Borden, Past & Present*. Fall River, MA: Al-Zach Press, 1999.

Alice Esther Borden

May 3, 1856 – March 10, 1858

Alice Esther Borden was the second of three daughters born to Andrew and his first wife, Sarah Morse Borden.

Alice died of "dropsy" on the brain, an accumulation of watery fluid or "water on the brain." It is possible that this changed her physical appearance by the swelling of the head since, in infants, that is usually the first sign that gives an alert that something is wrong.

It can be caused by a number of things including a genetic source, meningitis, a tumor, premature birth or a traumatic head injury. (Hmm ... Emma would have been five when Alice was born ...)

Other symptoms in infants can include vomiting, sleeplessness, irritability, downward deviation of the eyes ("sunsetting"), and seizures. Symptoms vary in individuals.

If left untreated, it is fatal. Today a shunt can be inserted to redirect the fluid from the brain to other parts of the body where it is absorbed, or a fiber optic camera can help to do it. In 1858, there may have been nothing that could have been done.

Alice Borden's record of death lists "brain displazia" as the cause of her death. "Displasia" is when a part of the body does not grow correctly. Alice Borden was one year and ten months old when she died.

Sources:

"Definition of Dropsy." MedicineNet.com. Web. 22 June 2014.

Rebello, Leonard. *Lizzie Borden, Past & Present*. Fall River, MA: Al-Zach Press, 1999.

Sarah Anthony Morse Borden, birth mother to Lizzie and Emma Borden.

Sarah Anthony Morse Borden

September 19, 1823 – March 26, 1863

Sarah Anthony (Morse) Borden was the daughter of Anthony Morse and R. Morrison (Rhoda or Rhody). Sarah was born in Somerset, Massachusetts. Both of her parents were from Somerset.

Sarah Morse married Andrew Jackson Borden on Christmas Day, 1845, at the Central Congregational Church of Fall River, then located at the corner of Rock and Bedford Streets.

Sarah was a seamstress at the time of their marriage and Andrew was a cabinet maker.

They had three children. Emma Lenora (March 1, 1851 – June 10, 1927); Alice Esther (May 3, 1856 – March 10, 1858); and Lizzie Andrew (July 19, 1860 – June 1, 1927).

Sarah was a friend of Mary Rice Livermore. Mary and Daniel Livermore (a Universalist minister) lived in Fall River in 1845. Sarah Borden and her father were parishioners of the church.

Mary Rice Livermore (1820 – 1905) was later a national figure in the womens' suffrage movement. Livermore was a reformer, lecturer, writer, editor, and the key organizer of the U.S. Sanitary Commission. When Lizzie was making the news with the murders of Andrew and Abby Borden, Mary Rice Livermore was also making the news with her staunch public defense of Lizzie.

Sarah Borden had suffered from uterine congestion the last four months of her life—an enlarged, or over-full uterus. There is not enough information available to know what it was from or to give us any details about it. Uterine congestion varied greatly from person to person. She could have had very pronounced symptoms such as fullness and weight, pain, and hemorrhages or have hardly any symptoms at all. Since we know she suffered with this condition for four months tells us that she probably had some symptoms to make her aware that something was wrong.

In the 1800s, uterine congestion was sometimes treated with iodine locally applied, or a mix of iodine with nitrate of silver solution. It was also treated with arsenic locally in large doses every 15-20 minutes. The condition had the capacity to invade the stomach and other organs and to even cause spinal irritation. The subject was quite broad in old medical books, but there was one thing the doctors could agree on— it caused "hysteria."

In 1863, Sarah Borden died of uterine congestion and disease of the spine. Lizzie was just two and a half and would never remember her.

Sources:

The American Journal of Medical Sciences: October 1859. Web. 19 June 2014.

"A Gentle Girl." *Boston Daily Globe* 18 June 1893.

James, Edward T, Janet Wilson James, Paul Boyer, eds. *Notable American Women: A Biographical Dictionary, 1607-1950*. Volume II. Cambridge, MA: Belknap Press of Harvard University Press, 1971.

Phillips, Charles D.F. *Material Medica and Therapeutics, Inorganic Substances*. NY: William Wood & Co., 1882. Web. 19 June 2014.

Rebello, Leonard. *Lizzie Borden, Past & Present*. Fall River, MA: Al-Zach Press, 1999.

Robinson, Byron. "The Abdominal and Pelvic Brain." McMillinMedia.com. *Early American Manual Therapy, 5.0*, 1907. Web. 19 June 2014.

Shwell, Samuel A. *A Practical Treatise on the Diseases Peculiar to Women*. Philadelphia, PA: Blanchard & Lea, 1855.

Simple headstone of Sarah Borden.

George B. Fish

Died January 3, 1894

George B. Fish was the husband of Priscilla S. Gray and brother-in-law to Abby Borden. His parents were Cook and Mary B. Fish, both of Rhode Island. George Fish was born in Franklin, Connecticut.

George Fish believed that Lizzie and John Morse conspired to have Abby and Andrew Borden murdered and that they hired someone to do it. He shared his comments with the press of the day.

The Fish's may have known quite a bit about the goings on between the Borden sisters and Abby. Sarah "Bertie" Whitehead, Priscilla and Abby's half-sister, told the papers that, "She and my sister, Mrs. Fish of Hartford, were on even more confidential terms than she was with me, as Mrs. Fish was nearer her age. I imagine she told her a great deal about the family matters in the correspondence between them."

George Fish's last address was at 27 Pavillion Street, a duplex in Hartford, Connecticut. He died at the age of 75, of lobar pneumonia. Priscilla followed him to the grave just twenty-two days later.

Sources:

Rebello, Leonard. *Lizzie Borden, Past & Present*. Fall River, MA: Al-Zach Press, 1999.
"To Whom Property?" *Boston Daily Globe* 12 August 1892.

Sherry Chapman

Priscilla S. Fish

1820 – January 25, 1894

Priscilla S. Fish was Abby Borden's sister. Both Priscilla and Abby's parents were Oliver Gray and Sarah S. Sawyer. Priscilla was born in Connecticut and was about eight years older than Abby.

Priscilla married George B. Fish. Their wedding took place at the home that would later be a source of trouble between Abby and the Borden sisters—45 Fourth Street in Fall River. The couple lived in Hartford, Connecticut. Abby Borden's estate was split between her sister, Priscilla, and her half-sister, Sarah Bertha "Bertie" Whitehead.

Her last place of residence was a duplex at 27 Pavilion Street in Hartford, Connecticut. She died at the age of 73 of Bright's Disease and pneumonia. Bright's Disease is a class of diseases of the kidney, having protein in the urine. Symptoms are usually severe. Pain in the back, vomiting, and fever are usually the first signs, followed by a puffiness of the face and accumulation of fluid in the body. According to her death certificate, she had been seriously ill for five days. Her husband had predeceased her about three weeks earlier.

Sources:

Rebello, Leonard. *Lizzie Borden, Past & Present.* Fall River, MA: Al-Zach Press, 1999.

"To Whom Property?" *Boston Daily Globe* 12 August 1892.

Oliver Gray family plot at Oak Grove Cemetery, Fall River, Massachusetts.

Oliver Gray Family

Oliver Gray was Abby Borden's father. He was born in Tiverton, Rhode Island. He first married Sarah Sawyer Gray, and the couple had two children. Priscilla Gray was born in 1820. She married George H. Fish. George Fish died on January 4, 1894. Priscilla followed him in death on January 25, 1894.

Abby Durfee Gray was born on January 21, 1828. She married Andrew Jackson Borden and became the step-mother of Emma and Lizzie Borden. Abby was murdered on August 4, 1892.

Abby's mother, Sarah, died on December 22, 1860 at the age of 66.

Oliver Gray remarried to Jane Eldredge D. Baker, a widow whose husband was lost at sea in 1857. Oliver was about 25 years older than his second wife. Jane Gray, Abby and Priscilla's step-mother, was born in 1826 in Bakersville, Massachusetts.

Jane Gray was about six years younger than step-daughter Priscilla Gray Fish and only 14 months older than Abby Gray Borden.

Jane Gray had two children with her first husband. Henry H. Eldredge died of consumption at the age of 32 in South Dartmouth, Massachusetts on April 16, 1882. Their other child was a daughter, Lucy J. (Eldredge) Cahoon.

Jane and Oliver Gray had one daughter, Sarah Bertha Gray, who was born in 1864 and became Abby Borden's beloved half-sister.

Jane Gray died on November 11, 1916 at the age of 89. Oliver Gray and both of his wives are buried at Oak Grove Cemetery in Fall River.

Sources:

Rebello, Leonard. *Lizzie Borden, Past & Present*. Fall River, MA: Al-Zach Press, 1999.

John V. Morse, *Boston Globe*, June 8, 1893

John Vinnicum Morse

July 5, 1833 – March 1, 1912

John V. Morse was the maternal uncle of Emma and Lizzie Borden. Their mother, Sarah Anthony Morse, was his sister. His parents were Anthony and Rhody Morrison Morse. Morse was born in Fall River, Massachusetts. (Note: His birthplace is given as Somerset, Massachusetts, in *The Knowlton Papers*.) Early in his life, he became a butcher and worked for Charles and Isaac C. Davis in that capacity in South Dartmouth, Massachusetts.

When he was 22 years old, John moved in with his brother, William Bradford Morse, who lived in Minnesota. After a year there, he spent fourteen years farming in Illinois. In 1869, John Morse moved to Hastings, Iowa, purchasing land which later proved a wise investment. Morse boarded or lived with others in Iowa.

He traveled to New England frequently, his major stopping places being Fall River and New Bedford, Massachusetts; Warren, Rhode Island, and Boston. He stored a boat in New Bedford and had relatives and friends there.

On a visit to Andrew Borden's house on July 10, 1892, Mr. Borden asked him if he knew of anyone that would be a good candidate for a job running his farm. Morse said he would send a man to him, but Andrew wanted to see Morse again before meeting the possible employee.

John Morse arrived at the Borden home unannounced on Wednesday, August 3, 1892, the day before the murders, about 1:30 in the afternoon. The noon meal was over but Abby Borden fixed him something to eat. Morse left the Bordens between 3 and 4 o'clock to go over to the Borden Swansea farm and returned that evening at about 8:30 p.m. Morse had been visiting with Abby and Andrew in the sitting room and heard Lizzie come in the front door and go up to her room. Abby went up to bed about 9 p.m., and Andrew and Morse retired a little after 10 p.m. Morse noticed that Lizzie's bedroom door was closed. He slept in the guest room, where Abby would be murdered the next morning, with his door open.

Morse was up and dressed at about 6 a.m. and went to the sitting room. He did not have occasion to go back to the guest room, and he left its door open when he went downstairs. When Andrew and Abby got up that morning, they joined Morse in the sitting room until breakfast was served about 7 a.m. in the dining room. Two or three times during the meal, Abby summoned their servant girl, Bridget, for more coffee by ringing a bell. While they were eating, Abby told Bridget that she wanted her to wash the windows "today," and Bridget said that she would.

After a breakfast of mutton, bread, "sugar cakes," bananas, and coffee, they returned to the sitting room. Both Mr. and Mrs. Borden were still ill from their sickness on Tuesday night, which Dr. Bowen diagnosed as "summer complaint" and Mrs. Borden diagnosed as being "poisoned."

Abby Borden dusted the sitting room with a feather duster. John Morse last saw her alive when she was in the front hall. He did not think she had anything in the form of a dust cap on her head.

John Morse left the Borden home about 8:45 a.m. He unhooked the side door and Andrew, who was still inside, re-locked it.

Morse first went to the post office. He then walked to Weybosset Street to visit a nephew and niece. Weybosset was about a mile east of Pleasant Street; his destination was about 1 ¼ miles from the Bordens. He visited with his niece and left about 11:20 a.m., taking a horse car, then walking the rest of the way to the Borden home from the corner of Pleasant and Second Streets. He went to the back of the house to a pear tree and picked up two or three from the ground, eating part of one before he went into the house.

John Morse was a suspect in the Borden murders and to this day remains under suspicion as to what role, if any, he played in the events.

After Lizzie Borden's indictment from the Grand Jury on December 2, 1892, Morse returned to Hastings, Iowa. He had testified at the inquest, preliminary hearing, and he went to New Bedford in June of 1893, to testify at the trial.

Morse died on March 1, 1912, at the age of 78 in Hastings, Iowa. His funeral was held at the Methodist church with the Reverend M. A. Gable officiating. He is buried in Hastings Cemetery, Row 23. Survivors included a brother, William B. Morse of Excelsior, Minnesota, and Mrs. Arabella Davidson of Hastings, Iowa, a half-sister.

Just ten days before he died, Mr. Morse wrote his will, which left his estate of about $23,000 to his nieces and nephews.

Part of his will states:

> I direct that the real estate of which I am now possessed in Mills County, Iowa, which is now leased to W. E. Van Ausdale shall at the expiration of said lease be sold and the proceeds be divided equally between my nephew and nieces, not named, except those named Borden, who are not in need of it.

In 1913 a court ruled that Lizzie and Emma Borden were to receive a portion of Morse's will. Emma refused her part and it was put in an account in Iowa. When Emma died her executors had the money returned and put in with her estate.

Sources:

Martins, Michael and Dennis Binette, eds. *The Commonwealth of Massachusetts vs. Lizzie A. Borden, The Knowlton Papers*. Fall River, MA: The Fall River Historical Society, 1994.

Rebello, Leonard. *Lizzie Borden, Past & Present*. Fall River, MA: Al-Zach Press, 1999.

Widdows, Harry, Stefani Koorey, Kat Koorey, eds. *The Preliminary Hearing in the Lizzie Borden Case, New Edition*. Orlando, FL: PearTree Press, 2005.

Widdows, Harry, Stefani Koorey, Kat Koorey, eds. *The Trial of Lizzie Andrew Borden*. Orlando, FL: PearTree Press, 2005.

Above: John V. Morse, *Boston Globe*, June 17, 1893

Below: John Morse grave in Hastings, Iowa.

Abbie Borden Potter gravestone at Oak Grove Cemetery, Fall River, Massachusetts.

Abbie Borden Potter

July, 1884 – May 9, 1974

Abbie Borden (Whitehead) Potter was the niece of Abby Borden. Abbie's mother was Abby's beloved half-sister, Sarah Bertha "Bertie" Gray.

"Little Abbie" was 8 years old when the Borden murders took place. She remembered Abby well and knew how explosive the incident of Andrew Borden giving Abby the half house stepmother Jane Gray owned was to Lizzie. She attended the funerals of Abby and Andrew. She thought Lizzie Borden was their murderer.

In 1972, Robert Sullivan interviewed Abbie Borden, and she relayed a famous story about Lizzie to him. In her words, spoken into Sullivan's tape recorder, she said:

> Lizzie Borden had company and my aunt had a tabby cat and the cat was trained so that it would touch the latch – you know, it was (sic) latches in those days – she'd touch the latch and the door would open. So the cat went in where Lizzie was entertaining and she took it out and shut the door again, and it came back so this is what she told Aunt Abby and Abby told my mother … Lizzie Borden finally excused herself and went downstairs – took the cat downstairs – and put the carcass on the chopping block and chopped its head off. My aunt … for days wondered where the cat was – all she talked about. Finally Lizzie said, 'You go downstairs and you'll find your cat.' My aunt did.

Abbie Borden Potter died on May 9, 1974. She is buried at Oak Grove Cemetery in Fall River, Massachusetts.

Sources:

Martins, Michael and Dennis Binette, eds. *The Commonwealth of Massachusetts vs. Lizzie A. Borden, The Knowlton Papers*. Fall River, MA: The Fall River Historical Society, 1994.

Rebello, Leonard. *Lizzie Borden, Past & Present*. Fall River, MA: Al-Zach Press, 1999.

Sullivan, Robert. *Goodbye Lizzie Borden*. Brattleboro, VT: Stephen Greene Press, 1974.

Sarah Gray Whitehead gravestone at Oak Grove Cemetery, Fall River, Massachusetts.

Sarah Gray Whitehead

1864 - 1932

Sarah Bertha "Bertie" Gray was the daughter of Oliver Gray and Jane Gray, Abby Borden's father and stepmother, making her Abby's half-sister.

Sarah was born in 1864. She was thirty-six years younger than Abby. Her mother, Jane Gray, was just fourteen months older than Abby Borden. Sarah and Abby were very close. Some say they were like mother and daughter. Abby knew she could not be a mother to her own stepdaughters, and it is often said that she lavished her maternal instincts on her much younger half-sister.

Sarah married George Whitehead. He was born in 1861 and would die in 1898, at the age of 38.

The couple had two children. Their daughter, Abby B. Whitehead, was born in July of 1884. Abby married Charles E. Potter. She died May 9, 1974, in Warwick, Rhode Island, at the age of 89. Their son was George O. Whitehead and was born in March of 1887.

In 1887, there was much todo over mother Jane Gray's decision to sell her half of the house Sarah had lived in all her life at 45 Fourth Street in Fall River. When Oliver Gray died, the house was given to Oliver's wife, Jane, and his three daughters, each having a fourth. Abby gave her share to Sarah. It is unclear how Jane Gray came to own Priscilla Gray Fish's share in the house, too. Abby Borden appealed to her husband, Andrew, to let her purchase it so that her half-sister and family would not be without a home. Andrew bought the half house and put it in Abby's name.

Andrew's daughters, Emma and Lizzie, were angry when they heard what had happened. The daughters said that what Andrew did for Abby's people he ought to do for his own. Andrew gave them his father's house at 12 Ferry Street, which allowed them to collect rent from the tenants there.

Things between the daughters and Abby remained volatile nonetheless. Lizzie stopped calling Abby "mother" and tensions were thick in the house. It would seem as if Andrew's daughters were quite cruel to Abby. It seems even crueler when we realize that in the year 1887 (The Year of The House) Sarah Whitehead was probably either pregnant or had just given birth to her baby boy, George.

Sarah lived until 1932. She and her husband, George Whitehead, are buried at Oak Grove Cemetery in Fall River, Massachusetts.

Sources:

Inquest Upon the Deaths of Andrew J. and Abby D. Borden, August 9 – 11, 1892, Volume I and II. Orlando, FL: PearTree Press, 2005.

Rebello, Leonard. *Lizzie Borden, Past & Present*. Fall River, MA: Al-Zach Press, 1999.

Sullivan, Robert. *Goodbye Lizzie Borden*. Brattleboro, VT: Stephen Greene Press, 1974.

Part Eight

The Girls

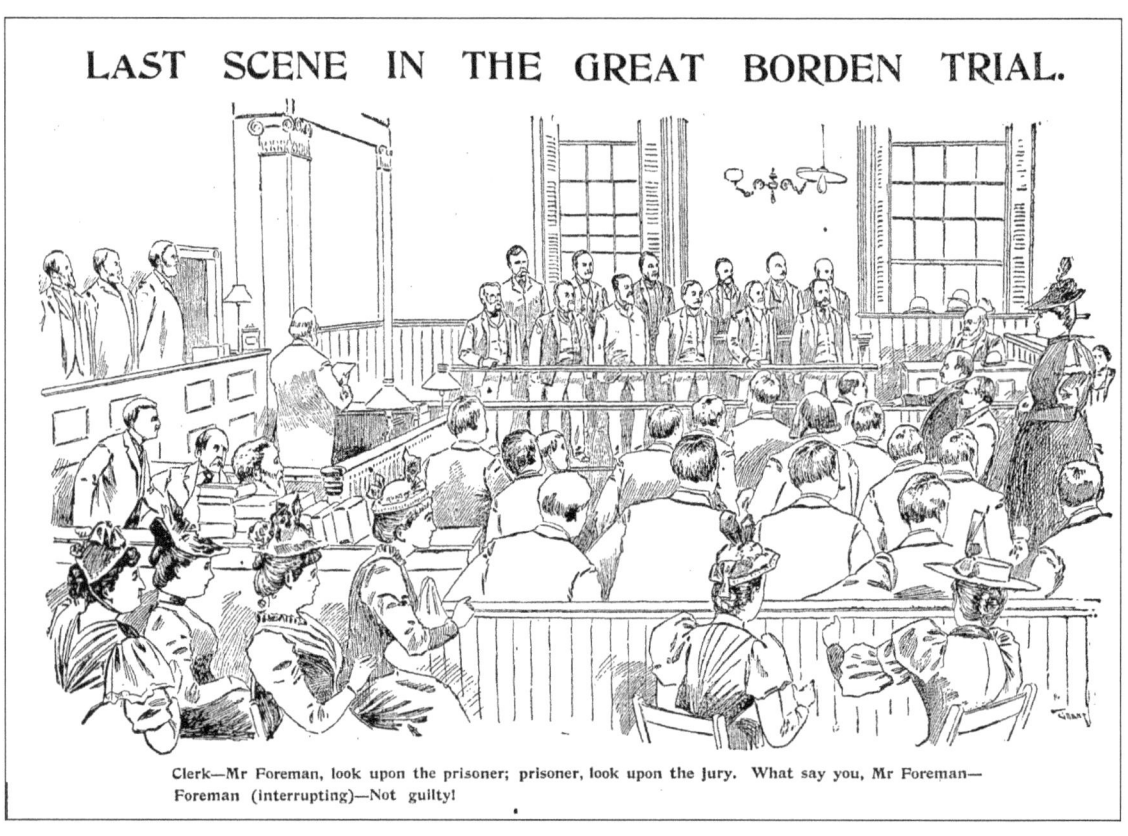

"Not Guilty," *Boston Globe*, June 21, 1893

The Acquittal

The trial of Lizzie Borden lasted from June 5, 1893, until June 20, 1893. It had been hot in that New Bedford courtroom throughout the trial, and this last day was said to be the very hottest of them all.

At 3:25 p.m. on the afternoon of June 20, Hosea Knowlton asked that the jury retire. The jury was out for 1 hour and 10 minutes. At 4:25 they returned.

CLERK: Lizzie Andrew Borden, stand up.

Lizzie, dressed in black that day, rose.

CLERK: Gentlemen of the jury, have you agreed upon your verdict?

FOREMAN: We have.

CLERK: Please return the papers to the Court.

This was done.

CLERK: Lizzie Andrew Borden, hold up your right hand. Mr. Foreman, look upon the prisoner; prisoner, look upon the Foreman. What say you, Mr. Foreman ---

FOREMAN: (interrupting) Not guilty.

The courtroom erupted in sound, ecstatic and agreeable to the verdict. Lizzie sank into a chair, rested her forehead upon the rail in front of her, and cried. Deputy Sheriff Kirby used his hand gently, but firmly to bring her to her feet to hear the court's last words, which were hardly audible, some catching the phrase "and go thereof without delay."

Her sister, Emma, her counsel, spectators—everyone it seemed—rushed to greet her. She buried her head in Emma's arms and said, "Now take me home."

A crowd waited outside the back of the courthouse to watch Lizzie board the carriage that had brought her back and forth from the jail to the Superior Courthouse for so many days. Here it finally was, brought from its shed to the door. The crowd pushed forward, shoving. The door of the building opened, and Deputy Sheriff Kirby and another man came out, hurried into the carriage and drove away.

A policeman told the crowd that Lizzie would be coming out of the front door so they all ran there.

An express wagon pulled up to the back entrance. Several boxes were loaded into it, a trunk, and the sofa that Andrew Borden was murdered on. These were the exhibits for the Borden trial, which was no more in the courthouse in New Bedford. For the next 120 years and counting, the case of Lizzie Borden would still be fascinating to the public, who would continue looking for an answer to who killed Andrew and Abby Borden.

The evening of Lizzie's acquittal, members of the Wamsutta Club played croquet behind the courthouse. The jury went to a photographer's studio to have their group picture taken, which they planned to give to Miss Lizzie. Then the jury went to the place they were sequestered during the trial, the Parker House, and had one last meal on the government.

Melvin O. Adams and Governor Robinson were having their supper at the hotel. Andrew Jennings waited to catch the 5:45 train leaving New Bedford for Fall River. The depot was crowded with people from the trial—typists, reporters, stenographers—all going home.

A handsome landau with a lovely pair of horses fitted with a new harness from bit to breeching was being readied at the stable for Lizzie. At 5:32 it started out with its passengers. Lizzie, Emma, and Mr. and Mrs. Charles J. Holmes were inside. Deputy sheriff Kirby handled the reins.

The windows were tightly closed as it drove out of the stable. Its departure was not particularly noticed. In just a few minutes it was on the peaceful road to Fall River.

Mary Rice Livermore sent Lizzie a telegram from her home in Melrose, Massachusetts: "Thank God, Lizzie, that you are acquitted. Everybody is rejoicing, and the wires all over the country are freighted with the good news. I kiss you in my heart."

A crowd was gathered at the Fall River depot, to meet the 6:15 train from New Bedford. They expected Lizzie, but instead got Andrew Jennings and Reverend Buck. They lauded the two with congratulations.

By 8 p.m., a crowd of several hundred waited outside the Borden home at 92 Second Street. They would not see Lizzie that night.

About the same time the train from New Bedford arrived in Fall River, the grand landau carrying Lizzie stopped at the front door of the home of Charles J. Holmes on Pine Street. The large home was brightly lit, where about twenty of Lizzie's closest friends were gathered for an impromptu reception. The daughters of Reverend Jubb, Dr. and Mrs. Bowen, and Andrew Jennings were but a few of the invited guests.

Lizzie sat in full view of the people outside on the street, occupying a seat by the door. Cuts and clippings from the papers about the trial were entertaining for a time. The affair ran until a late hour.

Lizzie spent the night at the Holmes house at Charles Holmes' behest. He thought she would probably be swarmed upon with reporters if she went home that night.

At 10:00 a.m. the next morning, Lizzie and Emma left the Holmes' house and returned to their own on Second Street. The streets were almost empty and they were not much noticed, if at all, when they arrived.

Already the press was mentioning that some of the public did not agree with her acquittal. The police of Fall River would not talk to the papers and appeared lackluster about searching for the murderer of the Bordens, now that the court had decided it was not Lizzie Borden who did the deed.

Jennings talked to a reporter, for a change, and said Lizzie and her sister will leave no stone unturned to find out who the murderer is. In fact, he said, the hunt is already on.

By Saturday, June 24, neighbors were saying they have not seen Lizzie out in the yard, but they have noticed her moving from room to room. Surely some would see her at church tomorrow.

Sunday morning service came, and no Emma, no Lizzie. Their home showed no sign of life—the gate was shut and all the doors were closed. One or two of the windows facing Mrs. Churchill's house were open, but the white painted blinds inside were partially closed. A parlor window had its outside green blinds that faced the street open a bit, so that one could see out, but not in.

Reverend Jubb's sermon was from Jeremiah, about trouble.

Reporters talked to Charles Holmes, a member of Lizzie's church. He said that people should not expect Lizzie to be attending things in public just yet; it would be weeks before she probably would.

No, he commented, there is nothing to a rumor that she is going to Europe.

"Will Lizzie and Emma continue to live in Fall River?"

"They expect to do so, living in a quiet, unobtrusive way and trying to win the respect of everybody in the city."

"Will they stay on the old homestead on 2d st.?"

"No! In fact, after the murder and before Lizzie's arrest the sisters were looking for another house; they are looking for one now."

What about Bridget? Will she continue working for them?

"... Bridget Sullivan and the Borden sisters have had no communication with each other since the trial. Furthermore, Bridget is superstitious enough not to be willing to return to a house where murder has been committed. Why, she wouldn't stay there last August; was kept there by the police a day or two, I believe, and then departed for good."

"Who is with Lizzie now?"

"No one except her sister and the housekeeper. A man goes to the house to do the chores. Neighbors make calls."

Someone said Bridget was visiting relatives in Newport. She may be going back to work for jailer Hunt in New Bedford.

Reverend Buck was at his mission house, back to business as usual.

Dr. and Mrs. Bowen were in Waterbury, Connecticut, visiting Salter C. Paine.

The church was having a childrens' service that night. Charles Holmes was to be one of the readers. Lizzie would not be there.

Some time after the trial, Lizzie and Emma went to Newport for a couple of weeks to rest and recoup. They stayed at the home of Mrs. William King Covell, the sister of Charles Holmes' wife, Mary Ann. The home is at 45 Farewell Street. It is inland, one of many houses in the residential part of Newport. The house is a bed and breakfast today and is called "Covell Guest House."

On July 2, the newspapers reported that Emma and Lizzie had purchased a new home on High Street on 'The Hill,' the most fashionable part of Fall River. The sisters never purchased that home. Maybe a deal fell through.

On July 12, the papers correctly had it that the sisters bought a home that later was to be named "Maplecroft." This large white home was located on French Street, and is best described as a large house, not a mansion, like the rest of the houses up and down the road there. The Borden sisters paid $14,000 for the home. It was on 'The Hill' and had the modern conveniences Second Street never had.

Lizzie eventually did attend her church, Central Congregational. On July 23, 1893, she was seen at both the morning and evening services. Charles Holmes and Dr. Bowen escorted her to her pew for the morning service. The minister that day was Rev. Dr. Michael Burnham. Lizzie had joined the church under his pastorship, and he was in the sea of faces at the last day of her trial in New Bedford. Close friend Mary Brigham accompanied Lizzie to the evening service.

The house on Second Street was not vacant long. The sisters moved into their house on 'The Hill' in September 1893. In October, 92 Second Street was rented by a grocer, W. B. Peckham, and a livery stable keeper, Lewis Hall.

The Manse

On Friday, January 11, 1895, the A.J. Borden family monument was erected on the family plot at Oak Grove Cemetery in Fall River. Until that day, there were no markers at all to indicate who was buried where.

The monument is made of Westerly granite. It is about ten feet high. Its base is 4' x 5'. It was described then as "artistic," but not "elaborate."

Facing south on the base, in large letters it tells us that it is the monument of "A.J. Borden." There is an inscription on its north side:

ANDREW JACKSON BORDEN
1822 – 1892
His Wife,
SARAH ANTHONY BORDEN, 1823 – 1863
His Wife,
ABBY DURFEE BORDEN
1828 – 1892

On its west side, so far, it read:

Children Of
ANDREW J. AND SARAH A. BORDEN
ALICE ESTHER
1856 – 1858

This was the Borden baby girl that tragically died of water on the brain when she was not quite two years old.

Even Lizzie and Emma came out for the event. While the men were working, the sisters arrived in their carriage. They both got out. Lizzie gave the stone a quick look and returned to the carriage. Emma viewed it for a time and gave the men some instructions before joining her sister. Of course some curious people began to notice. The Borden carriage left immediately.

The large Queen Anne style house that Lizzie and Emma bought soon after the trial (some said 'too soon'), had been built by Charles Allen. He lived in the house from 1890 –

Lizzie Andrew Borden, *Boston Globe*, June 21, 1893

1893. It bore the address of 7 French Street and was renumbered in Lizzie's lifetime to 306.

With 4,500 square feet of living space, the house had fourteen rooms, three full bathrooms, and two half-baths. The home has three stories and though still beautiful, it must have absolutely sparkled in Lizzie's day.

There are six fireplaces. Lizzie had carvings on two of the mantels. Upstairs, the library takes up two rooms, separated by a set of French doors. At one time, Lizzie's floor-to-ceiling bookshelves were filled with her beloved books. On the walnut mantle above the brick fireplace is one of the carvings. It is decorated with thistles and acanthus leaves and reads:

AT-HAME IN-MY-AIN COUNTRIE

It is often mistaken for being lyrics from Allan Cunningham's poem "Hame, Hame, Hame." It actually comes from the poem "My Ain Countrie" by Mary Augusta Lee Demarest.

The other carving has been a mystery to Bordenites. The carving is on a panel above the fireplace in Lizzie's winter bedroom and is further beautified by sprigs of clover. It read:

AND OLD-TIME FRIENDS & TWILIGHT PLAYS,
AND STARRY NIGHTS, AND SUNNY DAYS
COME TROOPING UP THE MISTY WAYS
WHEN MY FIRE BURNS LOW.

On September 18, 2007, Melissa Allen posted on the Lizzie Borden Society Forum: "I think I found the origin of the poem Lizzie had engraved on her mantle."

And she had.

When klingle, klangle, klingle,
Way down the dusky dingle,
The cows are coming home;
How sweet and clear and faint and low,
The airy tinklings come and go,
Like chimings from the far off tower,
Or patterings of an April shower
That makes the daisies grow;
Ko-ling, ko-lang, ko-linglelingle,
Way down the darkening dingle,
The cows come slowly home;
And old time friends and twilight plays,
And starry nights, and sunny days,
Come trooping up the misty ways,
When my cows come home.

The stanza of this poem appeared in *Common School Literature, English and American, with Several Hundred Extracts to be Memorized*, by J. Willis Westlake, copyright 1876, published by C. Sower, page 149. Its author has been debatable. The last line is not the same "when my fire burns low" as was on Lizzie's mantle, and it is not clear exactly where the line came from.

Lizzie had a summer and a winter bedroom. Her winter bedroom had eight big windows that ran the length of the house. Emma occupied a smaller bedroom on the same floor.

The second floor ceilings were all covered in white linen, except the front sun room. That ceiling was done with gold leaf and the walls had a chocolate-colored wallpaper with pink flowers.

The house was heated by coal-burning fireplaces. On the kitchen door, up on top, the letter *B* was gracefully etched. A Tiffany chandelier hung in the dining room. Cherry wood stairways connected the three stories.

The coach house (paneled of course) housed Lizzie's pony cart and carriage. In later years, she kept her automobiles there, as well as the only private gas pump in the city.

Lizzie had a coachman (later a chauffeur), a cook, a housekeeper, and two maids. The third floor held their living quarters.

The house was not always white. Some reporters have described it as "slate colored" or gray. At one time it was said to be a dull bronze-green on the bottom and a buff color on the upper part.

In 1909 both a two-story addition was added and a wrap-around porch. The garage was built in 1911.

She named the house 'Maplecroft,' whether from the maple trees on her property or from her travels to Scotland. It was chiseled into her top step that faces the street. This did not set very well with others. But then, neither did anything Lizzie Borden ever did.

Lizzie loved to read out on the rear piazza in her steamer chair. She fed the birds and squirrels. She had one of the first automobiles in town. She changed her name to Lizbeth A. Borden.

But she stayed. She stayed in the town where her father and stepmother were viciously axed to death, where she was accused, arrested, and jailed. She stayed in the same county where she was imprisoned until her trial the following summer, where she faced death by hanging in New Bedford and, when acquitted and well before the applause had faded away, was still suspected by her townsfolk, her neighbors, her friends. And every year, those horrible anniversary articles in the newspaper on the Borden murders would not let the town forget, even if they wanted to.

Some wonder why she stayed. She could have lived almost anywhere she desired. Instead she chose to remain in Fall River, a mile from the now infamous house on Second Street. The house she bought was almost unassuming, placed on French Street in the Historic Highlands where there were more expensive houses—and less expensive houses. It was a fashionable address, but it was an affordable house. She knew that all eyes were upon her whenever she went into town. She knew of crowds starting to gather, people looking out and hanging out of windows. She knew every move someone saw her make would make the papers. She knew this was home.

In February of 1897, Lizzie Borden made front page news again—in a bad way. The Tilden-Thurber company of Providence, Rhode Island, accused her of the theft of a pair of porcelain paintings called "Love's Dream."

Nance O'Neil

Apparently, Lizzie was visited by a friend at Maplecroft who admired them. Lizzie gave one to her friend (after all, they didn't cost her anything). A newspaper said that her friend was the wife of a cashier in Providence, who wanted the painting framed (or repaired, depending on the paper one reads). Thank goodness Lizzie left the store label still on the back of it. When the friend went to Tilden-Thurber with "her" painting in tow, she was told it was one of two paintings that were stolen by Lizzie Borden.

A warrant was made out, charging Lizzie with larceny. A detective went to Maplecroft to speak to Lizzie in person. Then suddenly nothing. Tilden-Thurber writes in a letter that "the matter was 'adjusted' out of court, and the warrant never served."

It was not until 2008 that Kat Koorey, in her article about Preston Hicks Gardner for *The Hatchet*, revealed that Lizzie had given the painting to Mary Gardner. She was the wife of a cashier in Providence, as stated in the news of 1897. The cashier from Providence referred to was Borden cousin Preston Hicks Gardner, who silently cleared up the matter, ending the newest scandal.

The grandson of Andrew Jennings, the Borden family attorney and Lizzie's during the murder trial, said this in 1992: "Lizzie was a chronic shoplifter. Several years ago after the trial, she was caught shoplifting in Providence. My grandfather got her off, then came home and said, 'I will have nothing to do with that woman.'"

The Nance

Nance O'Neil was born Gertrude Lamson on October 5, 1874, in Oakland, California. Her father, George Lamson, ran a successful auction house. Her father publicly disowned Nance's older sister, Lillian, in front of their church congregation when he found out that Lillian disobeyed his orders of not becoming an actress. Arre Lamson, the mother, promptly left George and took their two daughters to San Francisco, where Nance attended a girls' seminary.

In 1893, weeks after Lizzie Borden's acquittal, Nance went to the Alcazar Theatre in San Francisco with a letter of introduction from Peter Robinson, drama critic from the *San Francisco Chronicle*. It said: "Here is a young friend of mine who wants to go on the stage. Kindly discourage her."

McKee Rankin, a Canadian-born actor and manager, managed Nance's career for years. He changed her name, getting "Nance" from "Nance Oldfield," an English comedienne, and "O'Neil" from "Eliza O'Neil," a famous actress of the period. He first hired her to play small roles at the Alcazar.

By the end of 1897, she had played New York City and received critical acclaim. The papers were full of stories of Nance and the married Rankin's love affair (which may or may not have existed). But whatever the reason, from 1900-1903, Rankin decided that Nance would go on a three-year world tour.

The first stop was Hawaii. Bubonic plague had broken out there, and Nance and company never got off their ship. They traveled to Australia. Their last stop was London, where the three-year tour came to a critical and financial disastrous stop at the Adelphi.

The company was bankrupt. Rankin was always involved in legal battles where he owed people money. He was thought of as a bad influence over Nance in all ways, and she kept sticking with him because he made her what she was.

In November 1904, Rankin booked her to play *Magda* in New York. She got bad reviews, one critic writing of her unlady-likeness. Rankin was bankrupt again.

Rankin borrowed money to have Nance perform in Boston. It was probably during this time that she met Lizzie Borden, most likely at the Colonial Theatre where Nance played in *Macbeth*. Boston audiences loved her. Her reviews glowed.

Legend has always had it that Lizzie went backstage to meet Nance at the theatre in Boston, so entranced was Lizzie with her stage persona.

Edmund Pearson wrote to Hosea Knowlton's son, Frank, in a letter from 1930 about a party held in Tyngsboro for Nance O'Neil that Lizzie paid for. According to his source, Helen Leighton, the party lasted a week.

Lizzie supposedly had also thrown Nance a raucous party at Maplecroft in 1905.

Nance O'Neil purchased a huge home in Tyngsboro, Massachusetts, in 1904. It was called Colonial Hall and was on the Lowell River. The house was originally owned by the Brinley family. The family graveyard is still there. By 1906, she was being sued by the owners. She had not paid the $15,000 price for the place (or the $4,000 down and an $11,000 mortgage) but took up residence there.

Nance lost the house. It was later owned by the Sisters of Notre Dame. According to Carol Bacon of the Tyngsboro Public Library, the house was later "bulldozed into the ground." The property now has an elderly housing complex on it.

Years later, Nance spoke of Lizzie to Minna Littman for the *New Bedford Standard*. She recalled that Miss Borden met her in her dressing room at the Tremont Theatre. Lizzie first sent Nance a bouquet of flowers with a note of admiration, asking if she could call on her. Lizzie came often to Boston to the Bellvue, in the company of a well-known woman writer and her husband and with Mary Rice Livermore.

Nance remembered her as a lonely figure, but distinctly attractive. She was well-read and talked interestingly of her seemingly many travels abroad. She had a general kindness and thoughtfulness to people and a love of animals. She was a life member of the Boston Animal Rescue League.

Nance said she at first only knew her as Lizbeth A. Borden until somewhat later, when someone told her who Lizzie was. This did not make any difference to her, she stated. She did not believe Lizzie could have committed the crimes of which she was accused.

Nance said she had never met Emma Borden, and that talk of Nance spending some time at the Borden home in Fall River was not true. She said that Lizzie did come to her mansion in Tyngsboro for a few days, though.

After their friendship was active no more, for the next nearly twenty-five years, until Lizzie's death, the two exchanged no letters.

At the age of 42 in 1916, Nance married a former co-star, Alfred (Devereux) Hickman who was born on February 25, 1873, in London, England. He first appeared on the stage in 1914. He died in Oakland, California, on April 9, 1931, and is buried at Forest Memorial Park in Glendale, California. He was laid to rest at the Great Mausoleum, Columbarium of the Sanctuaries, Niche 10022.

Nance O'Neil took her acting into motion pictures. Her best-known movies are probably

LIZZIE BORDEN: RESURRECTIONS

Maplecroft, Fall River, Massachusetts.

The Royal Family, *Ladies of Leisure*, and *Cimarron*. She lived for many years at 145 West 55th Street in New York City. In 1964, she moved into the Actors Fund Home in Englewood, New Jersey.

Nance O'Neil died on February 7, 1965, at the Actors Home.

The Actors Fund Home was opened in 1902 on Staten Island, New York. It was moved in 1928 to the former mansion of millionairess Hetty Green on six acres in Englewood, New Jersey. The Green mansion was demolished in 1959, and a modern, one-story building was built in its place in 1961. In 1993, a wing was named in honor of Natalie Schafer (remember Mrs. Thurston Howell III on *Gilligan's Island*?). She left them over $1.5 million when she died.

The Lillian Booth Actors' Home of The Actors Fund of America is located at 155 – 175 West Hudson Avenue, Englewood, New Jersey. Despite several contacts, staff there have been unable to locate any records of Nance O'Neil. She is buried with her husband in Glendale, California.

The Parting of the Ways

In 1905, Emma Borden moved out of Maplecroft and never looked back. It is thought that she and Lizzie never communicated with one another again. No one knows just why. Maybe it was the rumor that Lizzie had a lesbian relationship with Nance O'Neil. Or just that she associated with Nance and her theatre friends. Maybe it was the coachman, Joseph Tetrault, a former barber who was a good looking ladies' man. He was fired from Maplecroft once, and Lizzie had rehired him.

Whatever the case, in 1905, Emma moved to Fairhaven and lived with friend Helen Brownell at 23 Walnut Street.

In August of 1906, Emma vacationed in Scotland. She sent a postcard to Mary Brigham from Glasgow. (Interestingly, Mary Brigham ceased to be Lizzie's friend after 1905 as well.)

In 1909, Emma moved in with Preston and Mary Gardner at 211 Hope Street in Providence, Rhode Island.

In 1913/1914 Emma boarded at the former home of Reverend Augustus Buck, where his daughters Elizabeth, Alice and Mary still lived. The Bucks' address was 114 Prospect Street in Fall River.

In 1919, Emma got her own apartment at the Minden, 121 Waterman Street in Providence, where Preston and Mary Gardner had their own apartment. She kept the apartment until 1926.

In the summer of 1923 Emma boarded at 203 South Main Street in Newmarket, New Hampshire. The house was owned by Annie Connor. It was not long before Emma moved in year-round.

Emma died on June 10, 1927, shortly after 3 a.m. with cousin Orrin Gardner by her side. After Emma's death, Annie Connor told the *Foster's Daily Democrat* "… that she came to board with her about four years ago and her health had been very poor even before that time. About three weeks ago she became worse and her physician ordered her to bed, and from that time she had failed continuously."

Her official causes of death were senility and nephritis (kidney failure).

Emma's body was taken to the funeral home of Brown and Trottier. She was embalmed, then shipped to the funeral rooms of George M. Wilbur in Warren, Massachusetts. She was brought to the Gardner family home in Touisset named 'Riverby.' Services were conducted there by Rev. J. Wynne Jones of Christ Church, Swansea, on June 13. Her funeral was attended by immediate family, friends, and some representatives of the charities she named in her will. She had African-American pallbearers, as was an old custom for prominent persons. Emma Lenora Borden was buried in the Borden family plot at Oak Grove Cemetery in Fall River, Massachusetts.

Goodbye, Lizzie Borden

There is no reason to doubt that Lizzie enjoyed life from the time Emma left Maplecroft in 1905 until her own death.

In 1919 Lizzie wrote her burial instructions. They were handwritten and signed.

> My funeral to be strictly private with a short prayer at the grave. At the house I wish read "The Crossing of the Bar." Also the 14th chapter of St. John and the 23rd Psalm. Also sung the first and fourth verses of "My Ain Countrie." I wish to be laid at my father's feet. A small head stone to match the others of my family. Lizbeth [she underlined her name twice] to be cut on the stone. Lizbeth Andrew [This may read "Andrews". The copy is difficult to read.] with the date July 1860. The minister of the Church of the Ascension is to conduct the services. Grave to be bricked.
>
> /signed/ Lizbeth A. Borden
> March 31, 1919 Fall River

In 1926, Lizzie Borden made a will. She was going into Truesdale Hospital, at the time prestigious and more private, to have her gall bladder removed. She registered under another name (Mary B. Smith). Nurses described her as a woman that was willful and opinionated, more masculine than feminine.

She had been healthy before the operation, but afterwards she never really recovered. She lost weight and people near her could sense her going downhill.

Lizzie Borden died at 8:30 p.m. on June 1, 1927. She passed away in her bedroom of her beloved Maplecroft. Doctor Annie Campbell Macrae had been treating her in her final days. Lizzie died of heart disease. A contributing factor to her demise was the bronchitis she had during her last nine days. She was 66 years old.

The press knew that her body was being prepared for burial when they saw the automobile of the undertaker parked outside of Maplecroft. She was once again a customer of Winward's. The staff inside the home was quiet behind the locked doors. Nothing was said about a funeral or a burial.

Only a few saw the small cortège entering Oak Grove Cemetery for Lizzie Borden's graveside service. The Associated Press ran an article on the event:

Simple Service at Grave.

The Rev. Edmund J. Cleveland, pastor of the Church of the Ascension, officiated at simple services beside the grave and in the house where Miss Borden died last Wednesday. Fred Coggeshall, the coachman, Ernest Terry, her chauffeur, Norman Hall, gardener who served the dead woman in her later years, and Edson Robinson acted as bearers. A little group of former intimates gathered at the grave.

There were many costly floral remembrances, but nothing to indicate from whom they came. The names of those who attended the services were not revealed nor could it be learned if Miss Borden's sister, Emma, from whom she has been separated for many years, was present.
...

The Borden burial lot in Oak Grove cemetery is on a grassy knoll, only a short distance from the Prospect street entrance to the cemetery.
...

Smaller markers on the lot show that Mr. Borden lies between his two wives, with the little child buried beside her mother.

Lizzie Borden's grave is not bricked, to the knowledge of the superintendent of Oak Grove Cemetery in Fall River.

When Emma Borden was buried a week later, she was laid to rest at her mother's feet. Cousins Joseph Luther Morse and Jerome C. Borden had attended her funeral, as well as Mr and Mrs. Everett N. Slade and Mr. and Mrs. William Blaisdell.

The sisters died ten days apart.

Last Will and Testament of Lizzie Andrew Borden

I, Lizzie A. Borden, otherwise known as Lizbeth A. Borden, of Fall River in the County of Bristol and the Commonwealth of Massachusetts, do make this my last will and testament hereby revoking all other wills heretofore made by me.

After the payment of my just debts and funeral charges I give, devise and bequeath as follows;

1. To the City of Fall River the sum of five hundred dollars, the income derived therefrom to be used for the perpetual care of my father's lot in the Oak Grove Cemetery in said Fall River.

2. To my housekeeper and to each one of the servants who shall have been with me five years and shall be in my employ at the time of my death the sum of three thousand dollars.

3. To Charles C. Cook, of said Fall River and Tiverton, for his long and faithful services to me the sum of ten thousand dollars, and my so-called Baker Lot on French Street, across from where I live.

Lizbeth Borden's simple gravestone at Oak Grove Cemetery, Fall River, Massachusetts.

4. To the Animal Rescue League of said Fall River the sum of thirty thousand dollars, also my shares of stock in the Stevens Manufacturing Company. I have been fond of animals and their need is great and there are so few who care for them.

5. To Miss Helen Leighton I give my three diamond rings and diamond and sapphire brooch, my inlaid mahogany desk and chairs in my library, also my library desk with the reading lamp, and I also direct that she shall have the first choice and may take any and all of my rugs, books, china, pictures and furniture that she may choose. I also give and devise to her one-half of my share in the A.J. Borden Building, in said Fall River, if she shall survive me, if not I give and devise my interest therein to Grace H. Howe, to her and to her heirs, executors, administrators and assigns forever.

6. To my cousin, Mrs. Grace H. Howe, my diamond and amethyst ring and I direct that she shall have second choice of my rugs, books, china, pictures and furniture, and I also give to her the privilege, so far as I have the same, to use the Oak Grove Cemetery lot for burial purposes. I also give and devise to her one-half of my share in the A.J. Borden Building in said Fall River, to her, her heirs, executors, administrators and assigns forever.

7. To Mrs. Margaret L. Streeter, of Washington, District of Columbia, the sum of five thousand dollars with my diamond and sapphire ring with five stones which she always liked.

8. To Mrs. Minnie E. A. Lacombe, of Washington D.C. the sum of five thousand dollars.

9. To S. Howard Lacombe, the son of Minnie E. A. Lacombe the sum of two thousand dollars.

10. To Catherine M. McFarland, of said Fall River, the sum of five thousand dollars.

11. To Gertrude M. Baker, of said Fall River, the sum of one thousand dollars.

12. To Mrs. Mary L. Orters of Sharon, Massachusetts, the sum of five thousand dollars; if she shall not be living at my decease I give the same to her husband, Henry L. Orters.

13. To Winnifred F. French, of said Fall River, the sum of five thousand dollars; if she shall not be living at the time of my decease I give the same to her sister, Sara H. French.

14. To Alice I. Soderman, of said Fall River, the sum of two thousand dollars, also my jeweled watch and chain.

15. To Elsie F. Carlisle, formerly of Fall River, now in California, the sum of one thousand dollars.

16. To Dr. Annie C. Macrae, of said Fall River the sum of one thousand dollars.

17. To my old schoolmate, Lucy S. Macomber, of said Fall River, the sum of one thousand dollars.

18. To my old schoolmate, Adelaide B. Whipp, of said Fall River, the sum of one thousand dollars.

19. To my housekeeper, Ellen B. Miller always called Nellie, all the contents of her room if she wants them.

20. To Mrs. Ethel H. Engel, of Los Angeles, California, the sum of one thousand dollars.

21. To my cousin George E. Robinson, of Swansea, Massachusetts, the sum of one thousand dollars.

22. To my cousin Edson M. Robinson, of said Swansea, the sum of two thousand dollars.

23. To my cousin, Percy V. Robinson, of said Swansea, the sum of two thousand dollars.

24. To Grace L. Terry, daughter of my chauffeur, the sum of two thousand dollars.

25. To Ellen B. Terry, wife of my chauffeur, the sum of two thousand dollars.

26. To Ernest Alden Terry, Jr. the sum of two thousand dollars, with the so-called Belmont lot which is west of my home lot.

27. To Animal Rescue League, of Washington D.C., the sum of two thousand dollars.

28. I have not given my sister, Emma L. Borden, anything as she had her share of her father's estate and is supposed to have enough to make her comfortable.

29. The rest and residue of my property of every description or wherever situated I give, devise and bequeath in equal shares to Helen Leighton and my cousin, Grace H. Howe, to her, her heirs, executors, administrators and assigns, forever.

Emma Lenora Borden

I nominate Charles C. Cook to be executor of this my last will and testament and request that he may be exempt from giving sureties on his official bond to any Probate Court.

If said Charles C. Cook shall not be living at my decease I nominate Frederick E. Bemis, cashier of the Fall River National Bank, to be executor of this my last will and testament and request that he may be exempt from giving sureties on his official bond to any Probate Court.

In testimony whereof I hereunto set my hand and in the presence of three witnesses declare this to be my last will and testament this thirtieth – day of January – in the year nineteen hundred and twenty-six.

/signed Lizbeth A. Borden
 Lizzie A. Borden

On this thirtieth-day of January – A.D. 1926, Lizzie A. Borden otherwise known as Lizbeth A. Borden, of Fall River, Massachusetts, signed the foregoing instrument in our presence, declaring it to be her last will and testament and as witnesses thereof we three do now, at her request, in her presence and the presence of each other hereto subscribe our names.

/signed Ellen R. Nottingham
 Carl A. Kerry
 Charles L. Baker

Last Will and Testament of Emma L. Borden

I, Emma L. Borden, of the City of Fall River, in the Commonwealth of Massachusetts, hereby revoking all other wills by me at any time made, do make, publish and declare this as and for my last will and testament, in manner following that is to say:

FIRST: I direct my executors, herein after named, to pay all my just debts, funeral charges and the expenses of settling my estate.

SECOND: I give and bequeath to the Treasurer of the City of Fall River, in the Commonwealth of Massachusetts, the sum of One Thousand Dollars ($1,000), the same to be held by said City of Fall River, IN TRUST, the income thereof to be used and applied for the perpetual care and improvement of the family burial lot, and the monuments and stones thereon, in Oak Grove Cemetery, which was owned by my father, Andrew J. Borden, at the time of his death.

THIRD: I give and bequeath to my friend, Anna C. Holmes, of Rochester, Massachusetts, my gold lorgnette chain.

FOURTH: I give and bequeath to my friend, Josephine Ridlon, of Somerset, Massachusetts, the sum of Two Thousand Dollars ($2,000) and all of my wearing apparel.

FIFTH: I give and bequeath to my cousin, Orrin A. Gardner, of Touisset, Massachusetts, the sum of Ten Thousand Dollars ($10,000), and all of my household furniture and furnishings, including all books, pictures, ornaments and personal effects not otherwise disposed of in this will, if he shall survive me.

SIXTH: If my sister, Lizzie A. Borden, shall survive me and I shall own an interest at the time of my death in that tract of land with the dwelling house theron situated on the northerly side of French Street, in said Fall River, and being the same premises now occupied by my sister and which were purchased by my sister and myself of Charles M. Allen, then I give, devise and bequeath all my right, title and interest in and to said tract of land and the improvements theron, to my said sister, Lizzie A. Borden, and all my interest in and to the household furniture in said house or upon said premises.

If, however, at the time of my death I shall have disposed of my interest in said tract of land located on French Street and in the contents of the house, and my said sister, Lizzie A. Borden, shall survive me, then I give and bequeath to my said sister the sum of One Thousand Dollars ($1,000).

SEVENTH: I give and bequeath to Preston H. Gardner, of said City of Providence, the sum of Fifteen Thousand Dollars ($15,000), if he shall survive me, and if he shall not survive me I give and bequeath the said sum of Fifteen Thousand Dollars ($15,000) to his wife, Mary E. Gardner, and to his daughter, Maude Peterson Gardner, to be shared equally between them, and in the case of the death of either of them then the whole of said sum to the survivor.

EIGHTH: I give and bequeath to Mary E. Gardner and to Maude Peterson Gardner, of said, Providence the sum of Ten Thousand Dollars ($10,000), to be equally divided between them, and if either shall not survive me then said sum of Ten Thousand Dollars ($10,000) to the survivor. I also give and bequeath to said Mary E. Gardner and to Maude Preston

Emma Borden's simple gravestone at Oak Grove Cemetery, Fall River, Massachusetts.

Gardner such jewelry as I may own at the time of my death.

NINTH: I give and bequeath to the following named institutions the sums of money stated, said sums to be held by them, IN TRUST, the income thereof to be applied for the furtherance of the charitable purposes and objects for which they are organized and in which they are engaged; and I declare it to be my intention that in the event that any one of them is not incorporated or is not named correctly herein, such gift is made and shall be held in such manner as to carry out the general purposes of the organization commonly known by the name hereinafter stated: To the Fall River Branch of the Association of Collegiate Alumnae, for the purpose of carrying on the work of the Ninth Street Day Nursery of Fall River, and if it shall cease to exist then for any similar work, the sum of Four Thousand Dollars ($4,000) to the Rescue Mission of Fall River, Massachusetts, the sum of Two Thousand Dollars ($2,000); to the Children's Home of Fall River, the sum of Four Thousand Dollars ($4,000); to the Fall River Women's Union, of Fall River, the sum of Two Thousand Dollars ($2,000); to the Home for the Aged People in Fall River the sum of Ten Thousand Dollars ($10,000); to the Association for Community Welfare in Fall River, the sum of Six Thousand Dollars ($6,000); to the Animal Rescue League of Fall River, the sum of Twenty Thousand Dollars ($20,000); to the Fall River Deaconess Home of Fall River, the sum of Three Thousand Dollars ($3,000); to the Young Men's Christian Association of Fall River, the sum of Ten Thousand Dollars ($10,000); to the Salvation Army of Massachusetts, Incorporated, to be used and applied only in its work in city of Fall River, Massachusetts, and in that vicinity, the sum of Six Thousand Dollars ($6,000); to the Massachusetts Girl Scouts, Incorporated, to be used and applied only to the Local Council of Fall River for work in and about Fall River, the sum of Five Thousand Dollars ($5,000); to the District Nursing Association of Fall River, the sum of Ten Thousand Dollars ($10,000); to The Bishop Stang Day Nursery of Fall River, the sum of Three Thousand Dollars ($3,000); to The Saint Vincent's Home Corporation of Fall River, the sum of Four Thousand Dollars ($4,000); to the Boys' Club of Fall River, the sum of Five Thousand Dollars ($5,000); and to the Massachusetts Society for the Prevention of Cruelty to Children, incorporated in 1878, for the use of its Fall River District, the sum of Five Thousand Dollars ($5,000).

TENTH: I give and bequeath to the Rhode Island Hospital Trust Company, a banking corporation duly incorporated under the laws of Rhode Island and doing business in the City of Providence, the sum of Five Thousand Dollars ($5,000), to be added to the trust heretofore created by me with said Rhode Island Hospital Trust as trustee for the benefit of the Providence Animal Rescue (League) of the City of Providence, to become a part of the principal of said trust fund and to be subject to all the provisions of said trust.

ELEVENTH: I give and bequeath to the B.M.C. Durfee Safe Deposit and Trust Company of Fall River, Massachusetts, and to said Preston H. Gardner of Providence, Rhode Island, the sum of Five Thousand Dollars ($5,000), to be held by them IN TRUST, nevertheless, to invest the same and keep the same invested, and to collect all the income thereof, and after paying from such income all expenses of administering this trust properly chargeable to income, to pay over the remaining or net income for the benefit of the Boy Scout Movement as carried on in the City of Fall River, leaving it to their discretion as to whether the same shall be paid to the local organization carrying on the work of the Boy Scouts, or otherwise expending the same to carry out the objects and purposes of said Movement in behalf of the boys; and I further authorize and empower my said trustee to use any part or all of the principal from time to time as they may in their judgment deem wise and beneficial in furthering the objects of the Movement. Said trustees shall be subject to all the duties and obligations and have all the powers and privileges in the management of said trust set forth in the trust established by the Twelfth clause of this my will.

TWELFTH: I give and bequeath all the rest and residue of the property, real and personal, over which I have any power of testamentary disposition at the time of my decease, to said B.M.C. Durfee Safe Deposit and Trust Company of Fall River, Massachusetts, and to said Preston H. Gardner of Providence, Rhode Island, herinafter called my said trustees, IN TRUST, nevertheless, to invest the same and keep the same invested, and to collect all of the income therof, and after paying from such income all expenses of administering this trust properly chargeable to income, to pay from the net income (in quarterly payments) the annual sum of Two Hundred Dollars ($200) to my cousin, Joseph Luther Morse, if and so long as he shall survive me and divide the remaining or net income (as the same is herinafter defined) into five (5) equal shares, and to pay the same over bi-annually, or oftener as in the discretion of my said trustees they may deem best, in the manner and for the purposes herinafter set forth.

(a) To pay one of such equal shares to the Trustees of the Fall River High School Alumni Scholarships to be used and applied by said last mentioned trustees in the following manner: Such share shall be used to establish and to provide for "The Andrew J. Borden Scholarships" each scholarship to be of such amount not exceeding the sum of Three Hundred Dollars ($300) per annum as said trustees shall determine; and I direct that such scholarships shall be awarded and given annually by said trustees one-half in aggregate amount thereof to such deserving male graduate or graduates and the other one-half thereof to such deserving female graduate or graduates of the High Schools of Fall River as they, in their discretion, shall select, such scholarship to be used to assist such graduates to secure advanced education. In the selection and appointment of such scholarships it is my desire (as printed on will) that preference shall be given to any graduate who may be named by Miss Julia A. Reed of said Fall River, or by said Orrin A. Gardner of said Touisset, during the lifetime of either of them.

(b) To pay one of said equal shares to the Young Men's Christian Association of Fall River, to be used for its general purposes.

(c) To pay one of said equal shares to the Animal Rescue League of Fall River, to be used for its general purposes.

(d) To pay one of said equal shares to the Home for the Aged People of Fall River, to be used for its general purposes.

(e) To pay one of said shares to the Association for Community Welfare of Fall River, Massachusetts, to be used for its general purposes.

And I hereby authorize and empower my said trustees to retain any investments in the form in which they are at my decease, even though of doubtful value or hazardous, and without regard to how large a proportion of my said trust property such securities may constitute, without being responsible for any resulting loss; and to change and vary from time to time any investment or reinvestment of my said trust property, real or personal, and for this purpose or for any other purpose of said trusts to sell from time to time, at either public or private sale or at broker's board any of said investments or reinvestments thereof, real or personal, without the purchaser being under obligation to inquire the necessity or regularity of any such sale or to see to the application of the purchase moneys; and further to lease any real estate at any time constituting part of my trust property for such periods of time, even though by possibility extending beyond the period of these trust, and upon such terms as to said trustees shall seem proper, and to make partition of any such real estate by agreement or otherwise; to pay from the income of my trust estate, including insurance against fire and if my said trustees deem best against casualties, and to remain from my said trust estate and the income thereof their own proper compensation for their services as my trustees.

I hereby authorize and empower the said B.M.C. Durfee Safe Deposit and Trust Company to act in all matters in connection with the trust herein created, including the exercise of discretion on its part, through its officers or committee having the general oversight of trust funds.

THIRTEENTH: In case any person named as a donee, legatee or devisee in this will shall oppose or aid in opposing the probate and allowance of this will, I hereby direct that any gift, legacy or devise given to such person in and by this will shall thereupon become and be null and void, and shall become and be a part of the rest and residue of my estate.

I have intentionally omitted to provide in this will for my relatives and next of kin other than those mentioned herein.

LASTLY. I hereby appoint said B.M.C. Durfee Safe Deposit and Trust Company and said Preston H. Gardner executors of this my will, and direct that they be not required to give any surety upon their bond as such executors, and so far as I have the power so to do that they be not required to file any inventory or to render any public account of my estate; and I further direct that my said executors (or any appointed in their stead) pay all death duties, legacy, transfer or inheritance taxes, or other similar taxes however designated, by whatever jurisdiction imposed, out of my residuary estate, and that the same shall be a charge upon such residuary estate to the exoneration of all legacies and beneficial interests given under this will. IN TESTIMONY WHEREOF, I have hereunto set my hand this 20th day of November, in the year of Our Lord one thousand nine hundred and twenty.

/signed/Emma L. Borden

Signed, published and declared by the said Emma L. Borden as and for her last will and testament, in our presence, who have, at her request, in her presence and in the presence of each other, hereunto subscribed our names as witnesses.

Katherine Noonan	371 Sharon Street, Providence, RI
Alice Noonan	371 Sharon Street, Providence, RI
James Collins	222 Adelaide Avenue, Providence, RI

Codicil to Emma Borden's Will

I, Emma L. Borden, of the City of Fall River, in the Commonwealth of Massachusetts, do make, publish and declare this as and for a Codicil to my last WILL and TESTAMENT made in November, in the year of Our Lord one thousand nine hundred and twenty, that is to say:

FIRST: I give and bequeath to Charles C. Cook, of Tiverton, Rhode Island, the sum of Two Thousand Dollars ($2,000), in appreciation of his faithful services to my father and to myself in connection with the management of the real estate formerly owned by my father.

SECOND: I give and bequeath to my cousin, Frank H. Gardner, of Somerset, Massachusetts, the sum of One Thousand Dollars ($1,000).

THIRD: I give and bequeath to my cousin, William W. Gardner, of Swansea, Massachusetts, the sum of One Thousand Dollars ($1,000).

FOURTH: I give and bequeath to Josephine Ridlon, of Somerset, Massachusetts, the sum of One Thousand Dollars ($1,000), in addition to the sum of Two Thousand Dollars ($2,000) already given to her in the Fourth clause of my said will.

FIFTH: If Andrew J. Jennings, of Fall River, Massachusetts, shall survive me, I give and bequeath to him the sum of One Thousand Dollars ($1,000), as a remembrance of his many acts of kindness and of devotion to my interest and those of my father and mother during a long period of years, and in appreciation of all that he has done for me.

SIXTH: Whereas by the Tenth clause of my said will I gave and bequeathed to the Rhode Island Hospital Trust Company of Providence, Rhode Island, "the sum of Five Thousand Dollars ($5,000), to be added to the trust heretofore created by me with said Rhode Island Hospital Trust Company as trustee for the benefit of the Providence Animal Rescue League of the City of Providence, to become a part of the principal of said trust fund and to be subject to all the provisions of said trust," which trust therein referred to, and which is hereby referred to, was that trust which I established with said Rhode Island Hospital Company as trustee, and declared in that deed of trust given by me to it dated August 14th, 1919, conveying Seven Hundred Dollars ($700) in Third Liberty Loan Bonds, and declaring the trust conditions under which said Rhode Island Hospital Trust Company holds said gift by me then made; I now declare said trust now held by said Rhode Island Hospital Trust Company to be the trust referred to in my said will, and I do give and bequeath a further sum of Fifteen Thousand Dollars ($15,000) to said Rhode Island Hospital Trust Company to be held by it in like manner for the benefit of the Providence Animal Rescue League of the City of Providence under the terms of said trust as declared in said trust instrument made by me to said Rhode Island Hospital Trust Company dated August 14th, 1919, this bequest of Fifteen Thousand Dollars ($15,000) being in addition to the bequest of Five Thousand Dollars ($5,000) mentioned in my will.

SEVENTH: In all other respects I hereby confirm my said will.

IN TESTIMONY WHEREOF, I have hereunto set my hand this twenty-second day of June, in the year of Our Lord one thousand nine hundred and twenty-two.

/signed/ Emma L. Borden

Signed, published and declared by the said Emma L. Borden as and for a codicil to her last WILL AND TESTAMENT in our presence who have, at her request, in her presence and in the presence of each other, hereunto subscribe our names as witnesses.

Alice Noonan	371 Sharon Street, Providence, RI
Katherine Noonan	371 Sharon Street, Providence, RI
James Collins	222/322 Adelaide Ave., Providence, RI

Sources:

Bacon, Carol, Tyngsborough Public Library. Personal correspondence, 21 July 2003.

"Borden House on 'The Hill.'" *Boston Globe* 12 July 1893.

"Borden House Rented at Last." *Boston Globe* 17 October 1893.

Chapman, Sherry. "Lizzie and the Tilden-Thurber Incident." *The Hatchet: A Journal of Lizzie Borden & Victorian Studies* 2.4 (August 2005).

Chapman, Sherry. "Lizzie in Newport." *The Hatchet: A Journal of Lizzie Borden & Victorian Studies* 1.4 (August 2004).

"Cheered by the Crowds." *Boston Globe* 20 June 1893.

"First Hours of Freedom." *Boston Globe* 20 June 1893.

Forest Lawn Memorial Park, Glendale, California. Personal correspondence, 3 February 2004.

Foster's Daily Democrat 10 June 1927.

"Golf All the Go." *Boston Globe* 16 July 1893.

"I am Innocent!" *Evening Standard* (New Bedford) 21 June 1893. Rpt. in *Lizzie Borden, Did She or Didn't She?* NY: Historical Briefs, 1992.

"In Their Own Home." *Boston Globe* 21 June 1893.

Kent, David, ed. *Lizzie Borden Sourcebook*. Boston: Branden Publishing Company, 1992.

Koorey, Kat. "Looking For Emma." *The Hatchet: A Journal of Lizzie Borden & Victorian Studies* 5.1 (February 2006).

Last Will and Testament of Emma L. Borden. LizzieAndrewBorden.com. Web. 16 June 2014.

Last Will and Testament of Lizzie A. Borden. LizzieAndrewBorden.com. Web. 16 June 2014.

Lillian Booth Actors' Home of the Actors' Fund of America. Personal correspondence, 5 December 2003.

"Lizzie Borden Dies; Police May Search Mansion." *Bridgeport Telegram* (Connecticut) 3 June 1927.

Masterton, William. *Lizzie Didn't Do It!* Boston: Branded Publishing Co., 2000.

"Miss Borden at Church." *Boston Globe* 24 July 1893.

"Miss Livermore Rejoices." *Boston Globe* 20 June 1893.

"Miss Lizzie Borden's New Home." *Boston Globe* 2 July 1893.

"Nance O'Neil, 90, Tragedienne of Stage in Early 1900s, Dead." *New York Times* 8 February 1965.

"Not at Church." *Boston Globe* 26 June 1893.

"Not Guilty." *Boston Globe* 21 June 1893.

Rebello, Leonard. *Lizzie Borden, Past & Present*. Fall River, MA: Al-Zach Press, 1999.

"Receiving Hundreds of Letters." *Boston Globe* 24 June 1893.

Schanke, Robert A. and Kim Marra, eds. *Passing Performances: Queer Readings of Leading Players in American Theatre History*. Ann Arbor, MI: University of Michigan Press, 1998.

Schley-Ulrich, William. "The Carvings of Maplecroft." *The Lizzie Borden Quarterly* II.6 (Winter 1995).

Schley-Ulrich, William. Personal correspondence, 1 November 2003.

Silvia, Philip T. Jr. *Victorian Vistas, 1886-1900*. Fall River, MA: R.E. Smith Printing Co., 1988.

"Welcome Back Home." *Boston Globe* 20 June 1893.

Widdows, Harry, Stefani Koorey, Kat Koorey, eds. *The Trial of Lizzie Andrew Borden*. Orlando, FL: PearTree Press, 2005.

Part Nine

P.S.

Edmund Pearson grave at Newburyport, Massachusetts.

Photograph courtesy of Jay S. Williamson, Curator, Historical Society of Old Newbury, Cushing House Museum, Newburyport, Massachusetts.

Edmund Lester Pearson

February 11, 1880 - August 8, 1937

Edmund Pearson was the next major writer of the Borden case after Edwin Porter (*The Fall River Tragedy*, 1893). His first book on the case appeared in *Studies in Murder* (1924), while Lizzie Borden was still alive. Though the book contained four other murder stories, the Borden case was the first in line and the longest. When *Studies in Murder* was published, Pearson was already the author of seven books on other subjects. He also wrote of Lizzie at length in his books *More Studies in Murder* (1936) and *Five Murders* (1928). *The Trial of Lizzie Borden* was his first full-length book devoted to a single murder case. It was the first volume of the series Notable American Trials. It was also his final book. *The Trial of Lizzie Borden* was published in the spring of 1937 and was a best-seller.

Edmund Pearson was born on February 11, 1880, in Newburyport, Massachusetts. His parents were Edmund Carlton and Tamsen Marie (Richardson) Pearson. He graduated from Harvard with his B.A. in 1902. On October 15, 1908, he married Mary S. Sellers of Washington.

After Harvard, Pearson took college courses for librarians in Albany, New York. He was assistant librarian at the Carnegie Library in Washington D.C., and also served on the staff of the Congressional Library there.

His first book was *The Old Librarians Almanac* (1909). In 1910 a collection of mostly essays he wrote to the "librarian department" of the *Boston Evening Transcript* was published as *The Library and the Librarian*. These were the first newspaper columns that were devoted to library copies, which he originated. The column was called "The Librarian" and was published weekly on Wednesdays. He enjoyed writing the column tremendously and continued them from 1906 until 1920.

In 1914, he began many years of work as editor of publications for the New York Public Library.

He almost always wrote either of murder or literary subjects. His *Murder at Smuttynose* was published in 1927. *Instigation of the Devil* came out in 1930. Pearson attended many murder scenes for his research, leaving no stone unturned. He went to murder trials when he could. In his crime writings, it is his first-hand experience that especially set him above later writers tackling the same case. He enjoyed studying the strange, the off-beat, the bizarre. He wrote of nearly all outstanding American murder cases in his many magazine articles and his books.

Some of his literary books were *The Secret Book* (1914); *Books in Black or Red* (1923);

Queer Books (1928); *Dime Novels* (1929), several books for boys, and a biography of Theodore Roosevelt.

In his later life, he was a book review editor for *Outlook*, as well as on the committee of judges for the Detective Story Club (later known as The Crime Club). He was contacted to be an expert consultant in movies. There is a scene of dancing dolls in the film *The Return of Frankenstein* that he originated.

Pearson was a supporter of the death penalty. He did not glamorize or romanticize murder. He believed in swift and absolute punishment. His view on Lizzie Borden? Guilty, of course.

He was only accepted for jury duty once, though he was called several times. He did not try to hide his views and he was usually challenged by the defense.

Pearson enlisted during World War I. He had his training in Plattsburg, New York. He served at Camp Union on Long Island, New York, as a first lieutenant.

Pearson was a member of the Harvard Club and the Coffee House Club.

In early 1937, his health began to fail. On August 8, he died of bronchial pneumonia at Columbia's Presbyterian Hospital in New York. He was survived by his widow; his sister, Mrs. Mabel C. Wheeler of Tuckahoe, New York; and his brother, Philip H.R. Pearson of Newburyport, Massachusetts. He was 57 years old.

Edmund Pearson's funeral took place at the Unitarian Church on Pleasant Street in Newburyport, Massachusetts, at 2 o'clock in the afternoon of August 10, 1937. He is buried in Newburyport, Massachusetts.

Sources:

Gross, Gerald, ed. *Masterpieces of Murder, an Edmund Pearson True Crime Reader*. NY: Bonanza Books, 1963.

Newburyport Daily News 9 August 1937.

> BORN FEBRUARY 11, 1880
> DIED AUGUST 8, 1937
> "E'en as he trod that day to God
> so walked he from his birth,
> in simpleness and gentleness
> and honor and clean mirth."

Close-up of inscription on Edmund Pearson's gravestone at Newburyport, Massachusetts.

Photograph courtesy of Jay S. Williamson, Curator, Historical Society of Old Newbury, Cushing House Museum, Newburyport, Massachusetts.

Porter's *Fall River Tragedy*, both as new reprint on left and original 1893 publication on right.

Photograph courtesy of Michael Brimbau.

Edwin H. Porter

December 29, 1864 – February 28, 1904

Edwin H. Porter was the author of the first and only contemporary book about the Borden murders, *The Fall River Tragedy*, published in 1893. The book was sold by subscription and today is a somewhat valuable collector's item. It continues to be used by researchers of the crime. Porter was also a police reporter for the *Fall River Globe* and a correspondent of the *Boston Herald*.

Edwin Porter was born on December 29, 1864, to parents Margaret (Davis) and Columbus Porter, both of Kentucky. He was born in Glasgow, Kentucky. He first worked as a school teacher in that state then learned the trade of typesetting. He worked for newspapers in Louisville, Memphis, New Orleans, Dakota, Johnstown (Pennsylvania), New York, and Providence, Rhode Island. Porter was hired as the editor of the *Fall River Tribune*. When that paper ceased publication, he began working for the *Fall River Globe*. He remained there, and with his job as correspondent for the *Boston Herald*, until his death.

Porter was married in 1891 to Miss Winnie Leonard. They had two daughters: Florence, who was 12 years old when her father died; and Winnie, aged 5 in 1904. He was an esteemed member of Pocasset Lodge, Knights of Pythias.

It was known only by his closest friends and newspaper associates that he suffered from tuberculosis. He had gone to the sanitarium at Rutland for treatment, but his relief was only temporary. Shortly before his final passing, unconsciousness came, and not once up to that time had he surrendered in his confident belief that he might once more be up and doing the work he loved.

Edwin Porter died on Sunday, February 28, 1904, at the age of 39. He died at home at 704 South Main Street in Fall River, Massachusetts.

"His body was encased in a black casket, which rested in the parlor of the home. Yesterday [February 29] afternoon and evening a large number who knew deceased well in life called there, among them all the men connected with the local papers."

On March 1, he was buried at St. Patrick's Cemetery after a high mass of requiem at St. Mary's Church in Fall River.

Mrs. Porter purchased her husband's grave for eleven dollars. On March 17, 1919, their daughter, Winifred A., died also of tuberculosis at the age of 20. Edwin Porter's grave was opened, and his daughter's casket was placed on top of his.

Edwin Porter lies in an unmarked grave. A fund was started in 2007 to raise money to buy Mr. Porter a gravestone. Donations can be made by contacting Stefani Koorey, the editor and publisher of *The Hatchet* magazine lizzieandrewborden.com.

Sources:

"Death Notice." *Fall River Daily News* 28 February 1904.

"E.H. Porter Buried." *Fall River Globe* 1 March 1904.

"Edwin H. Porter Dead." *Fall River Globe* 29 February 1904.

Furtado, Lisa, Fall River Catholic Cemeteries. Personal letters and phone conversations, 2004 and 2007.

"Obituary: Edwin H. Porter." *Fall River Globe* 28 February 1904.

Edwin Porter's unmarked grave location at St. Patrick's Cemetery, Fall River, Massachusetts.

LIZZIE BORDEN: RESURRECTIONS

Reprinted from *The Hatchet: A Journal of Lizzie Borden & Victorian Studies.*

PORTER LIES IN UNMARKED GRAVE
And what we can do about it!

By Stefani Koorey and Sherry Chapman

Police reporter Edwin H. Porter of the *Fall River Daily Globe* and correspondent of the *Boston Herald*, is probably the most well-known writer on the case of Lizzie Borden at the time it took place in 1892. He was there in the midst of things daily, from the time the double murder was discovered until the "end" of the famous case when Lizzie was acquitted, though the crime was never solved and speculation continues more than 100 years later.

Porter was in the Borden house the day of the murders and talked to several of the key players. He was in the jail house, observing Lizzie and events both in and out of the courtroom. He was named as being one of the persons crowding the stairway in the jailhouse in Fall River the day that Lizzie was supposed to have told Emma, "You have given me away." Then Porter was described as having some defect to one of his eyes. Today scholars and students of the case of Lizzie Borden still use his newspaper articles for research.

Edwin Porter was the first person to write a book on the Borden case, *The Fall River Tragedy -History of the Borden Murders*, soon after the trial in 1893. It is the only contemporary book on the Borden case. Legend has it that Lizzie tried to acquire all copies of the book and have them destroyed. Though still considered finding one available for sale rare, copies are turning up every now and then, enough so that if Lizzie had tried to corner the market she failed.

The book is an important one, not only because it was written first but because of who wrote it. Edwin Porter was a good newspaper police reporter, and he was there. Photos in the book are one of its high points. There are pictures of most of the persons involved and were it not for Porter's book, we may never have known what Eli Bence or Reverend Augustus Buck looked like. They would have likely remained names without faces.

The most interesting photograph is one of the street scene when Lizzie Borden arrived at the Fall River police station, probably for the coroner's inquest not long after the murders. It puts us right there on the sidewalk watching the carriages, striving for a glimpse of Miss Lizzie. Until the transcript of the trial was released in book and CD form, Porter's book could be relied on for much word for word testimony as well.

It is true that Porter thought Lizzie guilty, and it is perhaps this feeling that pressed him to do *The Fall River Tragedy*. As he says in the preface to his book: "...She was tried before the Superior Court of Massachusetts and a jury of her peers and found not guilty of the crimes. This event settled beyond question the probability of her guilt, and yet the case lost none of its absorbing interest. The author of this book therefore, has for a purpose the desire to give the reading public a connected story of the whole case, commencing with the day of the tragedy and ending with the day that Miss Borden was set free…"

Yes, Porter is guilty of taking liberties editing parts to help support his guilty verdict. That was wrong. But to feel strongly enough of her guilt to write a book about the case, publicly taking a stance that went against many a distinguished legal figure, the jurymen, and citizens that knew only bits and pieces of the story, seems a brave act. His book helped preserve the story and, despite his editing, may be the one out of the many Borden books to come out since that may come closest to the real solution.

Porter had his book published by Geo. R. H. Buffinton at the press of J. D. Munroe in Fall River. Then it was sold by subscription.

By 1985 so few copies had appeared, the book was reprinted by Robert Flynn at the King Publishing Company in Portland, Maine. Flynn's book was limited to a thousand copies. The book was selling at the Leary Press in Fall River (once connected to the Borden house on Second Street) for $35 in the 1980's. Now that it has sold its first (only?) run, prices vary, none at $35.

Who Was He?

Edwin H. Porter was born in Thompkinsville, Kentucky on December 29, 1864 to parents Margaret (born September 2, 1847 in Virginia) and Columbus P. Porter (born October 7, 1836 in Patrick County, Virginia), according to Ancestry.com. *The Knowlton Papers* has his birthplace at Glasgow, Kentucky.

Porter taught school before he learned the trade of typesetting. He traveled much and worked for a time for the Providence Telegram in the city of the same name in Rhode Island. He was city editor at the Fall River Tribune until it closed its doors, then worked for the Daily Globe specializing in police reporting. He was also a correspondent to the Boston Herald.

Porter married Miss Winnie Leonard of Fall River in 1891. They had two daughters: Florence and Winifred A. Porter. The Porters lived at 10 Rodman Street in 1892, not far from the Borden house. The house was renumbered to 111 in 1896.

After the Borden trial, Porter continued at the *Fall River Daily Globe* and as correspondent of the *Boston Herald*. Unknown to most, Edwin Porter had tuberculosis and sought treatment more than once at the sanitarium in Rutland.

Porter continued to work until he became too ill on January 1, 1904. He died on February 28 of that year in his home, which was then with his family at 704 South Main in Fall River, according to Leonard Rebello's article in the January, 1994 *Lizzie Borden Quarterly*. His home address according to his burial record was at 740 North Main Street. He was just 39 years of age.

His Unmarked Grave

Visiting his grave at St. Patrick's Cemetery in Fall River and expecting perhaps a monument of some sort, it was surprising to learn that Edwin Porter had no headstone – nothing at all to mark his grave. How could this be? He had been buried there since 1904, a hundred years with nothing to show he was there. Why?

When Edwin Porter died in 1904, his wife, Winifred, purchased his grave for $11.00.

On March 17, 1919 their daughter, Winifred, died also of tuberculosis at the age of 20. Edwin

Porter's grave was noted as a "double single grave". When Winifred died in 1919, the grave was opened and Winifred's casket was laid on top of her father's. But still no marker.

No one had bothered to pay for the perpetual care of his grave. And, without that, no marker could be placed on the site.

Had Mrs. Porter paid for the perpetual care back in 1904 it probably would have cost her ten dollars. But not knowing her circumstances at that time it could have been because of any reason. Most writers we know are not rich and therefore do not leave much of a fortune behind to their bereaved spouse.

It is a barren place where the body of Edwin Porter lays. And nobody knows he's there. He left us such a legacy. He's been gone for more than 100 years, and we're still talking about him, still studying his writings, still selling his book. And it will always be this way until interest in the Borden case should ever cease.

Here's Where We Come In

We researched what it would take to get Edwin Porter – at long last – a headstone. We really can do this!

The first step is to pay the perpetual fee, now known as "the endowment" fee. The cost of that is $320.00. That secures us as owners of the grave. We would basically own the remains of Edwin Porter and his daughter. This gives us the right to put a headstone on the grave.

There is a $10 fee for a permit from the cemetery.

There is an $85 "foundation fee." This is for the monument setter to pour a cement foundation before he sets the marker in place. It is a cemetery rule, but without the foundation grave markers sink – right into the ground and the grass grows right over it.

The cost of the headstone. The cost will not be an astronomical amount. We are only able to put a 2-foot by 1-foot flush marker there.

When can we start? Now! We are now ready to accept donations toward getting Edwin Porter his long-overdue headstone.

The grave will be put in the name of The Lizzie Borden Society. Donors will receive a certificate showing that they contributed to Edwin Porter's headstone as part of the Lizzie Borden Society.

For more information, please contact us at Porter Monument Fund, PearTree Press, PO Box 9585, Fall River, MA, 02720.

Sources:

Furtado, Lisa, Fall River Catholic Cemeteries. Personal letters and phone conversations, 2004 and 2007.

Porter, Edwin H. *The Fall River Tragedy: A History of the Borden Murders*. Fall River, MA: Geo. Buffinton Press, 1893.

Julian Ralph

Julian Ralph

May 27, 1853 – January 20, 1903

Julian Ralph was a well-known journalist and author who wrote prolifically almost all of his life. He covered the trial of Lizzie Borden for the *New York Sun*. Some of these articles can be read today in *The Lizzie Borden Sourcebook* (compiled and edited by David Kent in collaboration with Robert A. Flynn).

From the beginning of his career, he was thought a magnificent writer. He traveled the United States and later much of the world as he wrote about different regions.

Julian Ralph was born on May 27, 1853, at what was then 648 Houston Street, not far from South Fifth Avenue, in New York City. His parents were Dr. Joseph Edward Ralph and Selina Mahoney Ralph.

Ralph began work as a printer's devil at the *Red Bank Standard* (New Jersey) and learned the printer's trade there. At the age of 15, his attempts at reporting were gaining him attention, especially of his gift for description. Ralph and another printer created the *Red Bank Leader* in 1869, however it did not last long.

He then was editor of the *Webster Times* (Massachusetts). Before long he was working as a reporter for the *New York Graphic*. In 1875, he had an assignment to cover the "scenes and incidents in the trial room" at the Beecher trial, where Henry Ward Beecher was accused of adultery. His work at the trial led to a pivotal event in his life. He got the attention of Charles A. Dana, and soon Ralph was on the staff of the *New York Sun*.

His work at the *Sun* is legendary. He covered the funeral of Ulysses S. Grant; Grover Cleveland's first inauguration; international yacht races and for a time the legislature in Albany. He was with the *Sun* in some capacity for twenty years.

Ralph married Isabella Mount of Chapel Hill, New Jersey, in 1876. He started *Chatter* (a literary weekly) in 1889, and, when it failed in 1900, made many important trips for *Harper's Magazine*.

Mr. Ralph was one of the first guidebook authors. He wrote *Harper's Chicago* and the *World's Fair* in 1891, two years before the fair opened. The Columbian Exposition was a much-anticipated event, and things like Julian Ralph's guidebook fueled the public's fervor.

He was sent to England by *Harpers* in 1884. During China's war with Japan ten years later he was in China. From his short time in China, came his publication *Alone in China*. He was sent to Russia, India, and the Black Sea country.

A year after he had left China, he took up residence in England. He became the London correspondent for the *New York Journal*. He covered the coronation of Nicholas II as czar of

Russia (1896) and Queen Victoria's Diamond Jubilee in 1897.

He was with English troops during the Boer War. He endured many hardships during this time, which some say played a part in his early death. A report in the *Oxford Journal* noted: "June 16, 1900 Mr. Julian Ralph, *Daily Mail*, struck by shell fragment at Belmont, and severely injured in accident."

Ralph collaborated with Rudyard Kipling on *The Friend*, the first daily newspaper ever published for the entertainment and information of an army. When the war was over, he returned to London and there worked for Alfred Harmsworth's (*London Daily Mail*) publications. Lester Ralph, his oldest son, often accompanied his father on many of his later assignments, as newspaper artist in the Turkish-Greek war.

In March of 1902, Julian Ralph returned to America. During the summer he wrote a series of letters at Saratoga for the *New York Times*.

He and his wife, Isabella, had three sons and two daughters: Lester (an artist), Willard, Allan, Edith, and Alice.

Ralph's last illness varied in severity and lasted several weeks. At times he was able to go about the city. It began at St. Louis, when he was appointed Eastern representative of the 1904 World's Fair / Louisiana Purchase Exposition. He suffered a series of hemorrhages there and returned to his home in New York.

Julian Ralph died suddenly on Tuesday, January 20, 1903, at 7:45 p.m. at 118 West 76th Street. He suffocated when "an effusion of blood and foreign matter" entered his lungs. He was 49 years old.

His funeral was held on the morning of Friday, January 23, at Christ Church, Broadway and 71st Street. The rector of the church, Rev. George Alexander Strong, officiated. He is buried at Fairview Cemetery near Red Bank, New Jersey.

Sources:

"Death of Julian Ralph." *New York Times* 21 January 1903.

"Funeral of Julian Ralph." *New York Times* 24 January 1903.

ACKNOWLEDGMENTS

Many people played roles behind the scenes during the creation of this book. They all should have their names on the cover but, since there is not enough room, this page will have to suffice.

From the heart, I wish to thank my friend and editor, Stefani Koorey, PhD. She is an amazing woman who has built her publishing company, PearTree Press, and magazine, *The Hatchet: A Journal of Lizzie Borden & Victorian Studies,* from scratch. She has led a new generation to the classic case of Lizzie Borden and the fruits from her endeavors share no equal.

Kat Koorey and Harry Widdows are always there for me with their accuracy of research and as much-loved friends. Also together with Stefani Koorey, they have published the entire trial of Lizzie Borden in three softbound volumes—something that I could only dream of years ago, along with Online resources and documents on CD that they have spent many, many hours assuring all were as exact as possible. What a boon they have been to Bordenites everywhere. My thanks and respect to William Schley-Ulrich, a favorite Lizzie writer of mine and a beloved friend. He has always stepped in with a bit of research whenever he felt I needed it.

Many thanks go to Michael Martins, curator of the Fall River Historical Society, whom I had a celebrity crush on for ten years. I am grateful for his gracious assistance in the archives of the museum and his ever-helpful grants of research requests I have bombarded him with these past five years. Though I worked mostly with Michael, Dennis Binette, co-curator, has been very kind and helpful as well.

Mark Amarantes, a good friend and a good man of Fall River, and his daughter, Hannah, provided several of the photographs in this book. They worked hard, sometimes providing me with 10+ shots to try to give me just the right one. They drove a ways for a photo, too, and did it all smilingly (I think…). I have to thank Mark's wife, Lori, for letting him and Hannah do these, and their youngest, Katrina; well, maybe she didn't take an active role in the photography but her so-cute photo magneted to my filing cabinet always makes me smile.

Jay S. Williamson, curator of the Historical Society of Old Newbury, Cushing House Museum, Newburyport, Massachusetts, was very kind to go to the cemetery that Edmund Pearson is buried at and take photos of his grave for me. And Mr. Joseph F. VonDeck of the Ashburnham Historical Society of the town of the same name in Massachusetts, has my appreciation and thanks for taking photos himself dealing with Melvin O. Adams and furnishing much information on the Adams home.

Tammy Moutinho, Superintendent of Oak Grove Cemetery in Fall River, Massachusetts, has been a huge help to me. The majority of the graves were in Oak Grove Cemetery, and she handled my many requests promptly and so courteously. Anne Schaefer, Head Admin. Clerk for the City of Lowell (Massachusetts) Cemetery Department found a grave that I couldn't and provided me with a photo of it, without me even asking for a photo. Mr. Hay Reid of Evergreen Cemetery in Fairhaven, Massachusetts walked me right to the graves I sought and was delightful. Christopher Richards, Director of Tourism of Fairhaven voluntarily provided me with history of the cemetery.

Stanley J. Walczak, Superintendent of the City of Chicopee (Massachusetts) Parks and Recreation Department, his office clerk, and the cemetery workers at Fairview Cemetery there were more than kind to me. Richard Alexander of Central Cemetery in East Bridgewater, Massachusetts, was very helpful in my locating the grave of Arthur Phillips.

I would not have had one important grave photo included if it were not for the special kindness of Jeffrey Weissman, Chairman, Hebrew Cemetery, Fall River, Massachusetts.

Lisa Furtado of the Catholic Cemeteries of Fall River (St. Patrick's, St. John's, and St. Mary's) was incredibly helpful on many occasions; both in the location of several graves and in her assistance of the missing headstone of Edwin Porter, *Fall River Globe* police reporter who covered the Borden trial and was the first to write a book on the case entitled *The Fall River Tragedy* in 1893.

Many thanks to Pete Smith, curator of the Sippican Historical Society in Marion, Massachusetts. Mr. Smith found for me an original photo of Dr. Handy's cottage in Marion, that played a part in the case of Lizzie Borden. The photo had never been published before, and *The Hatchet* ran my story in its October/November issue (Volume 1, Issue 5), "Dr. Handy's Cottage." Pete took me for a walk down the beautiful street from the Historical Society (on his day off) and, not far from it, showed me the lot it was located at, which now another house stands. I spent two fabulous hours with him.

Special thanks to Anne Ramsey Cuvelier, whose family knew Lizzie Borden. Anne now owns the Sanford-Covell Bed & Breakfast in Newport, Rhode Island. She shared much with me about her ancestors, the family of Charles J. Holmes.

My husband, Steve, and our son, Stevie, pitched in and got me over some rough spots, helping beyond any call of duty, but because they love me, I hope. They know how much I love them. (Yeah, I still would even if you two hadn't have helped at all. But ya did.)

If it weren't for our daughter, Marla, I would never have started writing about Lizzie Borden at all. Thank you, Marla, from one professional to another.

Many thanks to Maynard Bertolet, the past editor of the *Lizzie Borden Quarterly* for laughing at my jokes and encouraging me to keep it up.

Many have given me their love and friendship and encouragement, and I cannot sign off without letting them know how much it has meant to me: Christian and Caroline Peltier, Nanette Degarmo, George Sr., George Jr., and Tim Hubsky; Kristine Lichy; Patricia O'Bar, ever my main cheerleader; and the one that occupied my second office chair through most of my writing days and joyously came on my travels, no questions asked—Dusty, my poodle.

Sherry Chapman
Minnesota, 2014

www.ingramcontent.com/pod-product-compliance
Lightning Source LLC
Chambersburg PA
CBHW080920180426
43192CB00040B/2476